Readings in Mass Communication

Readings in Mass Communication

Media Literacy and Culture

Kimberly B. Massey
San Jose State University

Mayfield Publishing Company
Mountain View, California
London • Toronto

Library of Congress Cataloging-in-Publication Data
Readings in mass communication : media literacy and culture / [edited by]
  Kimberly B. Massey
      p.   cm.
  Includes bibliographical references and index.
  ISBN 1-55934-961-1
  1. Mass media and culture–United States.   2. Popular culture-
United States.   3. Media literacy.   I. Massey, Kimberly B.
P94.65.U6R39   1998
302.23'0973–DC21   98-36731
                                              CIP

Manufactured in the United States of America
10 9   8   7   6   5   4   3   2   1

Mayfield Publishing Company
1280 Villa Street
Mountain View, California 94041

Sponsoring editor, Holly J. Allen; *production editor,* Carla White Kirschenbaum; *manuscript editor,* Darlene Bledsoe; *text designer,* Ellen Pettengell; *cover designer,* Joan Greenfield; *design manager,* Jean Mailander; *manufacturing manager,* Randy Hurst. The text was set in 10/13 New Aster by ColorType and printed on 50# Finch Opaque by Malloy Lithographing.

It is with deep affection and devotion that I dedicate my happiness and this book (my first solo authoring venture) to my parents, Carolyn and Milton Massey. Thanks to their gifts of love, integrity, discipline, and education, I learned to believe that I could accomplish anything.

Contents

Alternate Contents by Topic

Gender Issues in Media

Economics

Preface

We have all heard the statistics: Americans spend more time consuming media than doing virtually anything else, including eating, sleeping, reading, and talking to our children. It only makes sense, then, that we should be educated about how to make this activity more meaningful and productive.

Learning to become a more thoughtful, critical consumer of media requires at least two important steps. First, we must not merely consume, but *study* media by gathering information about them for our review and analysis. Second, we must apply what we learn from our interpretations to our future media-interaction behaviors and processes.

Becoming more media-literate does take some effort. We must be willing to sift through mountains of information coming at us from a variety of sources. We must remind ourselves to consider very basic yet important questions: Where do the media come from? Who creates their content? What is their purpose? Why do they do what they do? What effects do they have on our world? What is our role in the mass communication process? The purpose of this reader is to assist students in their efforts to improve their media literacy. Because this text provides information from a variety of sources as well as political and cultural viewpoints about media it serves as a media-information kiosk of sorts.

Media readers typically rely heavily on academic resources (journals or books) for their content. This text, in contrast, began from the notion that most people learn about the media from media sources. Therefore, in selecting appropriate articles, I have attempted to tap into the wealth and variety of information that exists within a wide array of popular periodicals, including those of the subculture voices, which have been neglected all too often.

Some people might be reluctant to give credence to articles about media that are drawn from the media. The assumption is that the resultant self-evaluation would be positively skewed and/or too forgiving of media producers or the industry in general. As you will see, positive and negative evaluations of media are evident in the articles. And though several of the authors do come from the media industry, many others come from such diverse vocations or backgrounds as the clergy, academia, and political activism.

Faculty and students alike should find that media literacy brings with it an interesting form of enlightenment. It allows people to actively recognize, dismiss, or react to the negative aspects of our media and its effects from a position of knowledge and power. At the same time, media literacy can also lead to gaining more pleasure from and effective use of the more positive contributions the media can make to our society.

Features

The readings are organized similarly to most introductory mass communication textbooks. With this organization, these readings can be easily used as discussion starters to complement the core topics covered throughout the semester in any introductory mass communication course. In addition to the standard table of contents, you will find an alternate contents that organizes the readings by topic. Thoughtful questions have been written for each article to provide an opportunity for students to test their comprehension of the core issues related to each reading.

Acknowledgments

The simplicity of the idea that spawned this reader seemed to suggest that the execution of the project would be just as effortless. In many ways, the scope of the book required special skills and energy in order to locate and then incorporate the many voices represented in the articles. Of course, such a task couldn't be accomplished by one person. It is a pleasure to give credit where credit is due.

Thankfully, Dr. Stanley Baran constantly rips articles from newspapers, magazines, and journals. He also generates copious notes about the remaining information he cannot clip and save. Access to his files provided a great starting point for this collection. As a colleague and mentor, Dr. Stanley Baran is invaluable. Of course, I am most grateful for Stanley's active role as my husband and the father of our daughter, Simmony. His support of my work and his accommodation of my writing and research schedule has helped me to become the scholar, teacher, and mother that I want to be. At the same time, he has kept appropriate distance, allowing me the freedom to make mistakes even when he could see them coming from a mile away. Thank you, Stanley, for your love, loyalty, and respect.

I am also thankful to reviewers whose insights and suggestions were invaluable to the process of selecting and editing the most interesting and useful articles. These reviewers include: David S. Allen, Illinois State University; Tom Grimes, Kansas State University; Kirk Hallahan, Colorado State University; L. Paul Husselbee, Ohio University; Rebecca Ann Lind, University of Illinois at Chicago; Tina Pieraccini, State University of New York at Oswego; and Linda Steiner, Rutgers University.

The rest of the process and the quality of this book can be attributed to Mayfield Publishing Company and its wonderfully warm and professional staff. Mayfield sets an impressive if not unbeatable standard, and it would be a perfect world if all authors had as fulfilling a relationship with their publishers. In particular, I'd like to thank my editor, Holly Allen, who made the process fun and exciting. As a result of her consistent support and charming gratitude, I often forgot how much work I was producing with her (or for her). I truly admire her professionalism, sincerity, and sense of humor. Once the articles were selected, Marty Granahan, Permissions Editor, encouraged me to persevere in my endless search for authors or other holders of copyright. The production process was completed without a glitch under Carla White Kirschenbaum's careful leadership. And the sharp copyediting eye of Darlene Bledsoe improved the quality of the final manuscript immensely. I appreciate the opportunity to publish this collection, and I am very grateful to these people who helped me produce it.

chapter 1

Mass Communication, Culture, and Mass Media

The People's Communication Charter

THE CULTURAL ENVIRONMENT MOVEMENT: AN INTERNATIONAL COVENANT

The Cultural Environment Movement describes itself as,

> *"a coalition of over 150 independent organizations and supporters in every state of the U.S. and 63 other countries on six continents. It represents a wide range of social and cultural concerns, united in working for freedom, fairness, diversity, responsibility, health-promotion, respect for cultural integrity, the protection of children, and democratic decision-making in the media mainstream."*

This charter reflects the coalition's mission.

The originators of this Charter are the Centre for Communication and Human Rights (The Netherlands), the Third World Network (Malaysia), the AMARC-World Association of Community Radio Broadcasters (Peru/Canada), and the Cultural Environment Movement (USA).

The Founding Convention of the Cultural Environment Movement, meeting in St. Louis on March 17, 1996, ratified the Charter and referred it to a committee for refinement. The present draft reflects the comments, interests and concerns of CEM and the other signatories. It has also been informed by the international agreements and publication available from CEM by request.

Article 1. Respect

All people are entitled to be treated with respect, according to the basic human rights and standards of dignity, integrity, identity, and non-discrimination.

Article 2. Freedom

All people have the right of access to communication channels independent of governmental or commercial control.

Article 3. Access

In order to exercise their rights, people should have fair and equitable access to local and global resources and facilities for conventional and ad-

This article first appeared in the *Culture Environment Monitor,* (Fall 1996), Volume 1(1), page 4.

vanced channels of communication; to receive opinions, information and ideas in a language they normally use and understand; to receive a range of cultural products designed for a wide variety of tastes and interests; and to have easy access to facts about ownership of media and sources of information. Restrictions on access to information should be permissible only for good and compelling reason, as when prescribed by international human rights standards or necessary for the protection of a democratic society or the basic rights of others.

Article 4. Independence

The realization of people's right to participate in, contribute to, and benefit from the development of self-reliant communication structures requires national and international assistance. This includes support of development communication and of independent media; training programs for professional media workers; the establishment of independent, representative media associations, syndicates or trade unions; and the international adoption of standards.

Article 5. Literacy

All people have the right to acquire information and skills necessary to participate fully in public deliberation and communication. This requires facility in reading, writing, and storytelling; critical media awareness; computer literacy, and education about the role of communication in society.

Article 6. Protection of Journalists

Journalists must be accorded full protection of the law, including international humanitarian law, especially in areas of conflict. They must have safe, unrestricted access to sources of information, and must be able to seek remedy, when required, through an international body.

Article 7. Right of Reply and Redress

All people have the right of reply and to demand penalties for damage from media misinformation. Individuals concerned should have an opportunity to correct, without undue delay, statements relating to them which they deem to be false and which they have a justified interest in having corrected. Such corrections should be given the same prominence as the original expression. States should impose penalties for proven damage, or require corrections, where a court of law has determined that an information provider has willfully disseminated inaccurate or misleading and damaging information, or has facilitated the dissemination of such information.

Article 8. Cultural Identity

All people have the right to protect their cultural identity. This includes respect for people's pursuit of cultural development and the right to free expression in languages they understand. People's right to the protection of their cultural space and heritage should not violate other human rights or provisions of this Charter.

Article 9. Diversity of Languages

All people have the right to a diversity of languages. This includes the right to express themselves and have access to information in their own language, the right to use their languages in educational institutions funded by the state, and the right to have adequate provisions created for the use of minority languages where needed.

Article 10. Participation in Policymaking

All people have the right to participate in public decision-making about the provision of information; the development and utilization of knowledge; the preservation, protection and development of culture; the choice and application of communication technologies; and the structure and policies of media industries.

Article 11. Children's Rights

Children have the right to mass media products that are designed to meet their needs and interests and foster their healthy physical, mental and emotional development. They should be protected from harmful media products and from commercial and other exploration at home, in school, and at places of play, work or business. Nations should take steps to produce and distribute widely high quality cultural and entertainment materials created for children in their own languages.

Article 12. Cyberspace

All people have a right to universal access to and equitable use of cyberspace. Their rights to free and open communities in cyberspace, their freedom of electronic expression, and their freedom from electronic surveillance and intrusion, should be protected.

Article 13. Privacy

All people have the right to be protected from the publication of allegations irrelevant to the public interest, or of private photographs or other private communication without authorization, or of personal information given or received in confidence. Databases derived from personal or workplace communications and transactions should not be used for unauthorized commercial or general surveillance purposes. However, nations should take care that the protection of privacy does not unduly interfere with the freedom of expression or the administration of justice.

Article 14. Harm

People have the right to demand that media actively counter incitement to hate, prejudice, violence, and war. Violence should not be presented as normal, "manly," or entertaining, and true consequences of and alternatives to violence should be shown. Other violations of human dignity and integrity to be avoided include stereotypic images that distort the realities and complexities of people's lives. Media should not ridicule, stigmatize or demonize people on the basis of gender, race, class, ethnicity, language, sexual orientation, and physical or mental condition.

Article 15. Justice

People have the right to demand that media respect standards of due process in the coverage of trials. This implies that media should not presume guilt before a verdict of guilt, invade the privacy of defendents or others, and should not televise criminal trials in real time while the trial is in progress.

Article 16. Consumption

People have the right to useful and factual consumer information, including information about wasteful, unnecessary, harmful or ecologically and otherwise damaging qualities of all advertised products and services. Advertising directed at children should receive special scrutiny.

Article 17. Accountability

People have the right to hold media accountable to the general public for their adherence to the standards established in this charter. For that purpose, media should establish mechanisms, including self-regulatory bodies, that monitor and account for measures taken to achieve compliance.

Article 18. Implementation

In consultation with signatories, national and international mechanisms will be organized to publicize this charter; implement it in as many countries as possible and in international law; monitor and assess the performance of countries and media in light of these standards; receive complaints about violations; advise on adequate remedial measures; and to establish procedures for the periodic review, development and modification of this charter.

Agenda for Action*

1. Organize a day of "Action for the Cultural Environment," including a Parents' March, teach-ins on college campuses and town meetings in selected cities, in collaboration with affiliated and supporting groups.

2. Convene a Second International Broadcast Standards Summit of CEM affiliates and supporting organizations, media executives, and representatives of producers and creative workers in participating countries, to develop a mechanism for regular consultation and broad participation in the development of media policy standards and international trade.

3. Set up a Global Marketing Awareness Task Force to expose the "dumping" of cultural products worldwide that drive out home-produced and quality materials.

4. Initiate a formal complaint procedure to investigate and publicize violations of the People's Communication Charter. A People's Media Inquiry, in collaboration with local and regional affiliated and supporting organizations, would hold open hearings and publish a report at the end of the year.

5. Support a Women's Roundtable committed to strengthening women's voices in male-dominated media.

6. Arrange a Media Literacy and Critical Awareness Program Development and Coordination project, culminating in an international assembly of leaders of the movement.

7. Advocate that schools, churches, youth organizations in the community include media literacy in their programs. Attend school board meetings, promote candidates, support teachers and students active in the media literacy movement. Oppose the use of media literacy as a public relations tool to rationalize the existing media system.

8. Hold forums with community leaders and media professionals devoted to creating alternatives for the cult of violence and brutality that hurt our youth, cultivate meanness, glorify domination, deform masculinity and sexuality, and polarize our society.

9. Promote the development of and access to successful resource-generating and organizing models for independent productions and

*Based on recommendations by 15 working groups at the founding convention.

We, the Signatories of this Charter, recognize that:

- Communication is basic to the life of all individuals and their communities.
- All people are entitled to participate in communication, and in making decisions about communication within and between societies.
- The majority of the world's peoples lack minimal technological resources for survival and communication. Over half of them have not yet made a single telephone call.
- Commercialization of media and concentration of media ownership erode the public sphere and fail to provide for cultural and information needs, including the plurality of opinions and the diversity of cultural expressions and languages necessary for democracy.
- Massive and pervasive media violence polarizes societies, exacerbates conflict, and cultivates fear and mistrust, making people vulnerable and dependent.
- Stereotypical portrayals misrepresent all of us and stigmatize those who are the most vulnerable.

Therefore, we ratify this Charter defining communication rights and responsibilities to be observed in democratic countries and in international law.

journalism. Explore what mechanisms (e.g. media laws, direct and indirect subsidies) democratic societies around the world use to support independent voices.

10. Enhance regular monitoring of media ownership, employment, and content, and release annual reports of the health and diversity of the cultural mainstream. These reports should include assessments of and guidelines for: (1) diverse and equitable media ownership and employment practices; (2) fair and realistic gender, racial, ethnic, aging, disability and mental illness portrayal; (3) health-related presentations, including depiction of addictive substances without consequences, promotion of prescription drugs to the public, the aggressive marketing of pharmaceuticals as "miracle drugs," and other inducements for "pill popping" that, together, make for a drug culture; (4) fast and reckless driving both as a dramatic and sales feature; (5) violence with invidious patterns of victimization and without realistic consequences or suggesting alternative approaches to conflict; and (6) impossible standards of beauty, especially for high fashion, diet programs, cosmetics, cosmetic surgeries, and other products that imply that normal women are defective.

11. Conduct cross-national comparative studies to document trends in global homogenization vs. diversification.

12. Publish major CEM documents widely, including full-page advertisements with lists of affiliated and supporting organizations and donors, soliciting other affiliations, and announcing forthcoming action.

13. Develop a center to serve as an information service, clearinghouse, speakers bureau, and newsletter editorial office to coordinate action on the national and international levels. Publish a calendar of events to link independent producers and publications to local communities. Include notification of teach-ins, town meetings, open hearings, policy briefings, and activities of affiliates.

14. Use CEMNET and Internet as organizing tools and forums for independent voices, while also noting that powerful technologies are used most effectively by powerful institutions; there is no technological fix to social and cultural problems.

15. Propose ad-free zones for schools; oppose the use of school time and space for commercial messages.

16. Design a cultural environment education course showing how media-driven consumer lifestyles impact the environment.

17. Devise a pilot program to promote communication skills through storytelling and to counteract media-driven expectations. Propose at least one storyteller's presence in every school or school district.

18. Launch a campaign for the establishment of a National Endowment for Telecommunications to support alternatives to cultural dependence on private corporate advertising.

19. Explore the feasibility of a Constitutional challenge of the giveaway of the public airways for private profit.

20. Join legal action to (1) reverse media monopoly; (2) force strict compliance with EEOC diversity and FDA food and drug testing and disclosure rules; (3) limit surveillance of consumers in the market place and employees in the work place, and (4) encourage and protect Micro-Radio projects of low power broadcasting; (5) ensure that all individuals have equitable access to new communication technologies at affordable rates, and (6) reinstate the Fairness Doctrine and strengthen the Equal Time provisions of the FCC; and (7) restore the family viewing hour and require substantial quality children's programming per week, some of it in primetime, as a licensing requirement.

21. Create a CEM Awards and CEM Censure program that (1) honors outstanding media challenges to media stereotyping and other harmful or wasteful practices, and (2) exposes the most flagrant examples of media "pollution."

22. Establish an Award category for productions, including children's programs, that promote portrayals of older adults, especially women, as vital productive persons in realistic, believable situations with the full range of human emotions, hopes and desires.

23. Start a network for mentoring young, alternative-oriented media professionals through internships with affiliated and supporting organizations and media.

24. Work with communities of faith and spirituality to help express their views and concerns about diversity and freedom in the cultural environment.

25. Collaborate with the AFL-CIO and the media workers unions (1) to develop labor participation in CEM and union leadership in communications and cultural policy-making, and (2) to create public support for diversity efforts and avoid policies that result in loss of jobs in the cultural industries.

Questions for Critical Thinking and Discussion

1. Do you think there is a need for a People's Communication Charter? Why or why not?

2. The articles in the People's Communication Charter lay out some basic rights. Are there any rights that you think should be added to the charter? Are there any that you think should be removed?

2

The Stories We Tell

GEORGE GERBNER

George Gerbner, Professor Emeritus of the Annenberg School of Communications of the University of Pennsylvania, is internationally known for his work over the past four decades on mass media and culture.

Media Development provided an excellent introduction to this article, which focuses on media violence effects: "Most of what we know, or think we know, we have never personally experienced. We live in a world erected by the stories we hear and see and tell. . . . Today that age-old process faces enormous and insidious changes in the form of entertainment violence that wrecks attempts to promote a culture of peace. The following article explores what might be done to diversify, pacify, democratize and humanize the mainstream story-telling process that shapes the cultural environment in which we live."

Through the magic of stories we live in a world much wider than the threats and gratifications of the immediate physical environment, which is the world of other species. Stories socialize us into roles of gender, age, class, vocation and lifestyle, and offer models of conformity or targets for rebellion. They weave the seamless web of the cultural environment that cultivates most of what we think, what we do, and how we conduct our affairs.

The story-telling process used to be hand-crafted, homemade, community-inspired. Now it is mostly mass-produced and policy-driven. It is the end result of a complex manufacturing and marketing process. The situation calls for a new diagnosis and a new prescription.

Revelation, Description and Advice

The stories that animate our cultural environment have three distinct but related functions. These functions are (1) to reveal how things work; (2) to describe what things are; and (3) to tell us what to do about them.

Stories of the first kind, revealing how things work, illuminate the all-important but invisible relationships and hidden dynamics of life. Fairy

This article originally appeared in *Media Development* (April 1996), pages 13–17. Earlier versions of parts of this essay are published in *Culturelink* (August 1996) and *Nieman Reports* (Fall 1996).

tales, novels, plays, comics, cartoons, and other forms of creative imagination and imagery are the basic building blocks of human understanding. They show complex causality by presenting imaginary action in total situations, coming to some conclusion that has a moral purpose and a social function. You don't have to believe the "facts" of Little Red Riding Hood to grasp the notion that big bad 'wolves' victimize old women and trick little girls—a lesson in gender roles, fear, and power.

Stories of the first kind build, from infancy on, the fantasy we call reality. I do not suggest that the revelations are false, which they may or may not be, but that they are synthetic, selective, often mythical, and always socially constructed.

Stories of the second kind depict what things are. These are descriptions, depictions, expositions, reports abstracted from total situations and filling in with "facts" the fantasies conjured up by stories of the first kind. They are the presumably factual accounts, the chronicles of the past and the news of today.

Stories of what things are may confirm or deny some conception of how things work. Their high 'facticity' (i.e. correspondence to actual events presumed to exist independently of the story) gives them special status in political theory and often in law. They give emphasis and credibility to selected parts of each society's fantasies of reality. They convey information about finance, weddings, crime, lotteries, terrorists, etc. They alert us to certain interests, threats, opportunities and challenges.

Stories of the third kind tell us what to do. These are stories of value and choice. They present things, behaviours or styles of life as desirable (or undesirable), propose ways to obtain (or avoid) them, and the price to be paid for attainment (or failure). They are the instructions, laws, regulations, cautionary tales, commands, slogans, sermons, and exhortations. Today most of them are called commercials and other advertising messages and images we see and hear every day.

Stories of the third kind clinch the lessons of the first two and turn them into action. They typically present an objective to be sought or to be avoided, and offer a product, service, candidate, institution or action purported to help attain or avoid it. The lessons of fictitious Little Red Riding Hoods and their more realistic sequels prominent in everyday news and entertainment not only teach lessons of vulnerability, mistrust and dependence but also help sell burglar alarms, more jails and executions promised to enhance security (which they rarely do), and other ways to adjust to a structure of power.

Ideally, the three kinds of stories check and balance each other. But in a commercially driven culture, stories of the third kind pay for most of the first two. That creates a coherent cultural environment whose overall function is to provide a hospitable and effective context for stories that sell. With the coming of the electronic age, that cultural environment is increasingly monopolized, homogenized, and globalized. We must then look at the historic course of our journey to see what this new age means for us and our children.

Defining Communities

For the longest time in human history, stories were told only face to face. A community was defined by the rituals, mythologies and imageries held in common. All useful knowledge was encapsulated in aphorisms and legends, proverbs and tales, incantations and ceremonies. Writing was rare and holy, forbidden for slaves. Laboriously inscribed manuscripts conferred sacred power to their interpreters, the priests and ministers. . . .

State and church ruled in a symbiotic relationship of mutual dependence and tension. State, composed of feudal nobles, was the economic, military and political order; church its cultural arm. The industrial revolution changed all that. One of the first machines stamping out standardized artifacts was the printing press. Its product, the book, was a prerequisite for all the other upheavals to come. Printing begins the industrialization of story-telling, arguably the most profound transformation in the humanization process.

The book could be given to all who could read, requiring education and creating a new literate class of people. Readers could now interpret the book (at first the Bible) for themselves, breaking the monopoly of priestly interpreters and ushering in the Reformation.

When the printing press was hooked up to the steam engine the industrialization of story-telling shifted into high gear. Rapid publication and mass transport created a new form of consciousness: modern mass publics. Publics are loose aggregations of people who share some common consciousness of how things work, what things are, and what ought to be done—but never meet face-to-face. That was never before possible.

Stories could now be sent—often smuggled—across hitherto impenetrable or closely guarded boundaries of time, space and status. The book lifts people from their traditional moorings as the industrial revolution uproots them from their local communities and cultures. They can now get off the land and go to work in far-away ports, factories and continents, and have with them a packet of common consciousness—the book or journal, and later the motion picture (silent at first)—wherever they go.

Publics, created by such publication, are necessary for the formation of individual and group identities in the new urban environment, as the different classes and regional, religious and ethnic groups try to maintain some sense of distinct integrity and also to live together with some degree of cooperation with other groups.

Publics are the basic units of self-government. They make it possible to elect or select representatives to an assembly trying to reconcile diverse interests. The maintenance and integrity of multiple publics makes self-government feasible for large, complex, and diverse national communities. People engage in long and costly struggles to be free to create and share stories that fit the reality of competing and often conflicting values and interests. Most of our assumptions about human development and political plurality and choice are rooted in the print era.

One of the most vital provisions of the print era was the creation of the only large-scale folk-institution of industrial society, public education. Public education is the community institution where face-to-face learning and interpreting could, ideally, liberate the individual from both tribal and medieval dependencies and all cultural monopolies.

The second great transformation, the electronic revolution, ushers in the telecommunications era. Its mainstream, television, is superimposed upon and reorganizes print-based culture. Unlike the industrial revolution, the new upheaval does not uproot people from their homes but transports them in their homes. It re-tribalizes modern society. It challenges and changes the role of both church and education in the new culture.

For the first time in human history, children are born into homes where mass-produced stories can reach them on the average more than seven hours a day. Most waking hours, and often dreams, are filled with these stories. The stories do not come from their families, schools, churches, neighbourhoods, and often not even from their native countries, or, in fact, from anyone with anything relevant to tell. They come from a small group of distant conglomerates with something to sell.

The cultural environment in which we live becomes the by-product of marketing. The historic nexus of state and church is replaced by the new symbiotic relationship of state and television. The 'state' itself is the twin institution of elected public government and selected private corporate government, ruling in the legal, military and economic domains. Media, its cultural arm, is dominated by the private establishment, despite its use of the public airways.

Giant industries discharge their messages into the mainstream of common consciousness. Channels proliferate and new technologies pervade home and office while mergers and bottomline pressures shrink creative alternatives and reduce diversity of content.

These changes may appear to be broadening local, parochial horizons, but they also mean a homogenization of outlooks and limitation of alternatives. For media professionals, the changes mean fewer opportunities and greater compulsions to present life in saleable packages. Creative artists, scientists, humanists can still explore and enlighten and occasionally even challenge, but, increasingly, their stories must fit marketing strategies and priorities.

Viewing commercials is 'work' performed by audiences in exchange for 'free' news and entertainment. But, in fact, we pay dearly through a surcharge added to the price of every advertised product that goes to subsidize commercial media, and through allowing advertising expenditures to be a tax-deductible business expense. These give-aways of public monies for private purposes further erode the diversity of the cultural mainstream.

Broadcasting is the most concentrated, homogenized, and globalized medium. The top US 100 advertisers pay for two-thirds of all network television. Four networks, allied to giant transnational corporations, our private 'Ministry of Culture' control the bulk of production and distribution, and shape the cultural mainstream. Other interests, religious or educational, minority views, and the potential of any challenge to dominant perspectives, lose ground with every merger.

Formula-driven assembly-line produced programmes increasingly dominate the airways. The formulas themselves reflect the structure of power that produces them and function to preserve and enhance that structure of power. Perhaps the leading example of such story functions is violence. It is a good example of how the system works; it is also an indication of the magnitude and nature of the challenge before us.

Violence as a Power Structure

Humankind may have had more bloodthirsty eras, but none as filled with images of crime and violence as the present. While violent crime rates remain essentially flat or decline, news of crime surges to new highs.

US television networks doubled the time given to crime coverage between 1992 and 1993. *TV Guide*'s August 13, 1994 survey also showed a steep increase in stories of violence, especially in local television news.

Monitoring by the Des Moines (Iowa) *Register* (March 27, 1994) illustrated how crime and violence skew news priorities. Of the six top stories on Des Moines evening newscasts during February, 1994, one out of four (118 stories) dealt with crime and violence. By comparison, 27 featured business, 17 dealt with government, 15 reported about racial relations, and 2 were stories about the schools.

A University of Miami study of local television news found that time devoted to crime ranged from 23 to 50 percent (averaging 32 percent) while violent crime in the city remained constant, involving less than one tenth of one percent of the population.[1]

A study by Robert Entman for the Chicago Council on Urban Affairs[2] found not only that local news shows are dominated by vivid images of violence, but that 'a high percentage of African Americans and Latinos are shown as victimizers of society, and few as social helpers,' contributing to a sense of fear and distrust (that our own research diagnosed as the 'mean world syndrome')[3] and to the notion that 'the inner city is dominated by dangerous and irresponsible minorities.'

Another study of homicide news reporting[4] found that only one of three actual homicides was reported, and that the most likely to be selected were those in which the victims were white rather than black or Latino, contrary to the actual crime statistics. University of Pennsylvania Sociologist Elijah Anderson also noted in the November 1994 issue of *Philadelphia Magazine* that media portrayals of crime and violence involving blacks and the resulting demonization of black males, becomes a major reason for 'white flight.' In fact, however, African American men, not whites, are the most likely to be the victims of violence.

Our Cultural Indicators[5] study of local news on Philadelphia television found that crime and/or violence items usually lead the newscast and preempt any balanced coverage of the city. Furthermore, 80 percent of crime and violence reported on Philadelphia local news was not even local to the city. It is as if a quota were imposed on the editorial staff to fill from wherever they can. It is also the cheapest way to fill the time. We also found that whites are more likely to be reported when they are the victims and African Americans are more likely to be reported when they are the perpetrators. Black-on-white crime is less frequent but more newsworthy than any other combination.

The percent of prime time television dramatic programmes with overt physical violence was 58 in 1974, 73 in 1984, and 75 in 1994. The saturation of violent scenes was 5 per hour in 1974, 5 per hour in 1984, and 5 per hour in 1994 — unchanged. In Saturday morning children's programmes, scenes of violence occur between 20 and 25 per hour. They are sugar-coated with humour, to be sure; that makes the pill of power easier to swallow.

Violence is, of course, a legitimate and even necessary news and dramatic feature to show the tragic costs of deadly compulsions. However, such tragic sense of violence has been swamped by 'happy violence' produced on the television dramatic assembly-line. 'Happy violence' is cool, swift, and painless, and always leads to a happy ending. Far from Shakespeare or the Bible, it occurs five times per hour, designed to deliver the audience to the next commercial in a receptive mood.

Action movies cash in on the trend. *Robocop*'s first rampage for law and order killed 32 people. *Robocop 2* slaughtered 81. The sick movie *Death Wish* claimed 9 victims. In the sequel, the 'bleeding heart liberal' turned vigilante disposed of 52. *Rambo: First Blood* rambled through Southeast Asia leaving 62 corpses. *Rambo III* visited Afghanistan, killing 106. *Godfather I* produced 12 corpses, *Godfather II* put away 18 and *Godfather III* killed no less than 53. The daredevil cop in the original *Die Hard* saved the day with a modest 18 dead. *Die Hard 2* achieved a phenomenal body count of 264.[6]

Violence is a demonstration of power. Its principle lesson is to show quickly and dramatically who can get away with what against whom. That exercise defines majority might and minority risk. It shows one's place in the societal pecking order.

The role of violence in the media mainstream of television emerges from our analysis of prime time network programmes monitored since 1967. Women play one out of three characters in drama, one out of six in the news. Young people comprise one-third and old persons one-fifth of their actual proportions of the population. Most other minorities are even more underrepresented. Most of the groups that are underrepresented are also those who suffer the worst fate.

The typical viewer of prime time television drama sees, every week, an average of 21 criminals arrayed against an army of 41 public and private law enforcers. Crime and violence engage or employ more characters than all other occupations combined. About one out of three speaking parts, and more than half of all major characters, are involved in violence either as victims or as victimizers, or both.

We calculated the violence 'pecking order' by counting the number of victims for every ten perpetrators of violence. That 'risk ratio' expresses the 'price' groups of characters pay for committing violence. We found that overall average risk ratio (the number of victims per 10 perpetrators) is 12. But the ratio for women is 17, for lower class characters is 19, for elderly characters is 20, and for women of colour is 22. In other words, minority groups tend to pay a higher price for their show of force than do the majorities.

Our surveys show that heavy viewers express a greater sense of apprehension and vulnerability than do light viewers in the same groups. Heavy viewers are more likely than comparable groups of light viewers to overestimate their chances of involvement in violence; to believe that their neighbourhoods are unsafe; to state that fear of crime is a very serious personal problem; and to assume that crime is rising, regardless of the facts of the case. Heavy viewers are also more likely to buy new locks, watchdogs, and guns 'for protection' (thus becoming the major cause of handgun violence).

Moreover, viewers who see members of their own group underrepresented but overvictimized develop an even greater sense of apprehension and mistrust. Insecure, angry, mistrustful people may be prone to violence but are even more likely to be dependent on authority and susceptible to deceptively simple, strong, hard-line postures and appeals.

What Drives Media Violence?

The usual rationalization that media violence 'gives the public what it wants' is disingenuous. The public rarely gets a fair choice in which all elements but violence, including placement, headline, promotion, airtime, celebrity-value, treatment, etc., are equal. There is no evidence that, cost and other factors being equal, violence per se gives audiences 'what they want.' As the trade paper *Broadcasting & Cable* editorialized on September 20, 1993 (p. 66), 'the most popular programming is hardly violent as anyone with a passing knowledge of Nielsen ratings will tell you.'

We compared the ratings of over 100 violent and the same number of non-violent shows aired at the same time on network television. The average Nielsen rating of the violent sample was 11.1; the rating for the non-violent sample was 13.8. The share of viewing households in the violent and non-violent samples, respectively, was 18.9 and 22.5. The non-violent sample was more highly rated than the violent sample for each of the five seasons studied. The amount and consistency of violence further increased the unpopularity gap.

Concentration of ownership denies access to new entries and to alternative perspectives. Having fewer buyers for their products forces the remaining 'content providers' deeper into deficit financing. As a consequence, most television and movie producers cannot break even on the US domestic market. They are forced into video and foreign sales to make a profit. Therefore, they need a dramatic ingredient that requires no translation, 'speaks action' in any language, and fits any culture. That ingredient is violence.

Syndicators demand 'action' (the code word for violence) because it 'travels well around the world,' said the producer of *Die Hard 2*. 'Everyone understands an action movie. If I tell you a joke, you may not get it but if a bullet goes through the window, we all know how to hit the floor, no matter the language.'[7]

Our analysis shows that violence dominates US exports. We compared 250 US programmes exported to 10 countries with 111 programmes shown in the US during the same year. Violence was the main theme of 40 percent of home-shown and 49 percent of exported programmes. Crime/action series comprised 17 percent of home-shown and 46 percent of exported programmes. NAFTA and GATT will dump even more mayhem on the world in the name of 'free trade.'

What can we do? People suffer the media violence inflicted on them with diminishing tolerance. A March 1985 Harris survey showed that 78 percent disapprove of violence they see on television. In a *Times-Mirror* national poll in 1993, 80 percent said entertainment violence was 'harmful' to society, compared with 64 percent in 1983.

Local broadcasters, legally responsible for what goes on the air, also oppose the overkill and complain about loss of control. *Electronic Media* reported on August 2, 1993 that in its own survey of 100 general managers, three out of four said there is too much needless violence on television and 57 percent would like to have 'more input on programme content decisions.' A *US News & World Report* survey published on April 30, 1994 found that 59 percent of media workers saw entertainment violence as a serious problem.

Formula-driven media violence is not an expression of freedom, popularity, or crime statistics. It is a *de facto* censorship that chills originality and extends the dynamics of domination, intimidation, and repression domestically and globally. The media violence overkill is an ingredient in a global marketing formula imposed on media professionals and foisted on the children of the world.

There is a liberating alternative. It exists in various forms in all democratic countries. It is an independent citizen voice in cultural policy-making. More freedom from inequitable and intimidating marketing formulas, and a greater diversity of sources of support, are the effective and acceptable ways to increase diversity of content. That is also the democratic way to reduce media violence to its valid role and reasonable proportions.

Changing the Media Environment

The Cultural Environment Movement was launched in response to that challenge. Its Founding Convention was held in St. Louis, Missouri, March 15–17, 1996. It was the most diverse international assembly of leaders and activists in the field of culture and communication that has ever met.

The concepts that motivated us developed after 30 years of media research. It became clear that research is not enough; we must reclaim the rights gained through centuries of struggle. Working separately on individual issues, rallying to meet each individual crisis, was not sufficient. Treating symptoms instead of starting to prevent the wholesale manufacturing of all the conditions that led to those symptoms was self-defeating. The new approach of the CEM involves:

- Building a new coalition involving media councils worldwide; teachers, students and parents; groups concerned with children, youth and ageing; women's groups; religious and minority organizations; educational, health, environmental, legal, and other professional associations; consumer groups and agencies; associations of creative workers in the media and in the arts and sciences; independent computer network organizers and other organizations and individuals committed to broadening the freedom and diversity of communication.

- Opposing domination and working to abolish existing concentration of ownership and censorship (both of and by media), public or private. It involves extending rights, facilities, and influence to interests and perspectives other than the most powerful and profitable. It means involving in cultural decision-making the less affluent and more vulnerable groups, including the marginalized, neglected, abused, exploited, physically or mentally disabled, young and old, women, minorities, poor people, recent immigrants—all those most in need of a decent role and a voice in a freer cultural environment.

- Seeking out and co-operating with cultural liberation forces of all countries working for the integrity and independence of their own decision-making and against cultural domination and invasion. Learning from countries that have already opened their media to the democratic process. Helping local movements, including [those] in the most dependent and vulnerable countries of Latin America, Asia, and Africa (and also in Eastern Europe and the former Soviet Republics), to invest in their own cultural development; opposing aggressive foreign ownership and coercive trade policies that make such development more difficult.

- Supporting journalists, artists, writers, actors, directors, and other creative workers struggling for more freedom from having to present life as a commodity designed for a market of consumers. Working with guilds, caucuses, labour and other groups for diversity in employment and in media content. Supporting media and cultural organizations addressing significant but neglected needs, sensibilities, and interests.

- Promoting media literacy, media awareness, critical viewing and reading, and other media education efforts as a fresh approach to the liberal arts and an essential educational objective on every level. Collecting, publicizing and disseminating information, research and evaluation about relevant programs, services, curricula, and teaching materials. Helping to organize educational and parents' groups demanding pre-service and in service teacher training in media analysis, already required in the schools of Australia, Canada, and Great Britain.

- Placing cultural policy issues on the social-political agenda. Supporting and, if necessary, organizing local and national media councils, study groups, citizen groups, minority and professional groups and other forums of public discussion, policy development, representation, and action. Not waiting for a blueprint but creating and experimenting with ways of community and citizen participation in local, national and international media policy-making. Sharing experiences, lessons, and recommendations and gradually moving toward a realistic democratic agenda.

The condition of the physical environment may determine how long our species survives. But it is the cultural environment that affects the quality of any survival. We need to begin the long process of diversifying, pacifying, democratizing and humanizing the mainstream story-telling process that shapes the cultural environment in which we live and into which our children are born.

Notes

1. University of Miami Office of Media relations, August 18, 1994.
2. Entman, Robert M., 'Violence on Television News: News and "reality" Programming in Chicago.' A Report Commissioned and Released by the Chicago Council on Urban Affairs, 1994.
3. Gerbner, George. 'Television Violence: The Power and the Peril.' In Gail Dines and Jean M. Humez (eds.) *Gender, Race, and Class in Media: A Critical Text-Reader.* Sage Publications, Inc.: 1995.
4. Johnstone, John W. C., Darnell F. Hawkins, and Arthur Michener. 'Homicide Reporting in Chicago Dailies.' *Journalism Quarterly,* Vol. 71, No. 4, Winter 1994, pp. 860–872.
5. Cultural Indicators is a database and a research project that monitors selected media content and relates recurrent features to public conceptions of social reality. For more information, write to the author at University City Science Center, 3624 Market Street, One East, Philadelphia, PA 19104, USA. E-mail: FGG@ASC.UPENN.EDU
6. Count by Vincent Canby (*The New York Times*, July 16, 1990, p. CII). Canby observed that William Wellman's 1931 'Public Enemy' shocked viewers and critics (The *Times* reviewer noted its 'general slaughter') despite the fact that each of its eight deaths takes place offscreen. But, Canby observes, 'death and mortal injury were treated with discretion then, at least in part because the then new Production Code took a dim view of mayhem for its own sake.'
7. Cited by Ken Auletta in 'What Won't They Do,' *The New Yorker,* May 17, 1993, pp. 45–46.

Questions for Critical Thinking and Discussion

1. Consider the stories of your life and how they have constructed your cultural environment. Identify specific stories that demonstrate each of the three functions discussed in the Gerbner article: (a) a story that reveals how things work; (b) a story that describes what things are; (c) a story that tells you what to do.

2. Think about violence that you have seen recently (either on television or at the movies) and "rewrite" the script to describe how the conflict could have been resolved *without* the use of violence.

chapter 2

Media Literacy and Culture

3

Folklore in a Box

LANCE MORROW

Lance Morrow is a senior writer for Time *magazine. He joined the editorial staff of* Time *in 1965 and, since that time, has written over 130 cover stories. For more than a decade, he has specialized in writing* Time *essays on a wide variety of subjects.*

In this article, Morrow argues that each era has its own way of storytelling and that television "truths" sometimes seep into the pool of cultural "truth." He explains how history is represented by media content through images, events, and stereotypes from the past—and why that may not be a good thing.

It is very strange, and metaphysically untidy: television has eaten a hole through the membrane separating America's right brain and left brain.

Fantasies seep into facts. Entertainment and journalism drift back and forth across the borders. The bicameral arrangement of culture and politics dissolves. The baby of the (nonexistent) Murphy Brown flies out of its cradle and hovers like an illicit pink cherub over the American presidential succession.

About these spectacles—the Sister Souljah nonsense a few months ago, the Vice President of the U.S. wagging his finger at hallucinations of the popular culture, denouncing Murphy Brown, or telling the *MacNeil-Lehrer NewsHour,* "I will continue to speak out against Ice-T," as if he were preparing for the Lincoln-Douglas debates—there is something both confused and vaguely degrading. Something unworthy and a little stupid. Here is American history deteriorated to *Roger Rabbit,* to interactive slapstick, to 'toons. What will America do at the end of history? Francis Fukuyama asked. Well, maybe watch a little TV.

But the new electronic metaphysics is not always trivial. It harbors wild disproportions. A homemade videotape could burn down a large section of Los Angeles. The videotape told a story: Los Angeles cops hit Rodney King on the head and, doing so, split the social atom.

The movie director Spike Lee set off a small tabloid uproar not long ago when he suggested that young blacks should skip school if necessary to see his movie biography of Malcolm X when it opens this fall. A hideously wrong message, people said, undermining discipline and education. But

---

This article first appeared in *Time* (September 21, 1992), pages 50–51.

Spike Lee understands a central truth: what is occurring today is a war of American myths, a struggle of contending stories. And pop culture, often television, is the arena in which it is being fought.

Stories are precious, indispensable. Everyone must have his history, her narrative. You do not know who you are until you possess the imaginative version of yourself. You almost do not exist without it. Blacks were mostly excluded or held in the margins of the national story. As Spike Lee knows, blacks more than other Americans need their stories now, the recovered histories of what they have been and fantasies of what they might be. The American family, as well, desperately needs a new folklore, a new driving myth. The old version, which in caricature is a 1950s suburban setting out of *Ozzie and Harriet*, does not entirely work anymore, except in nostalgia, in Kennebunkport, Maine, or in Ronald Reagan's afternoon naps.

America needs to restock its repertoire of folklore and self-images and archetypes. The 1992 presidential campaign has made its noisy way across a nation that has lost many of its defining ideas about itself. The cold war's end gave Americans only a kind of abstract triumph—and left a void. The collapse of communism and the Soviet empire suddenly removed the dark moral counterweight by which Americans measured their own virtue. Chronic recession, the rise of Japanese and European economic competitors, the vast inflow of immigrants from non-European sources (strangers to the older American tradition), the shrinking of the buffering Atlantic and Pacific oceans (jet travel, satellites, global distribution of goods), all these have eaten away at the long American smugness, the postwar sense of superiority, of grace.

The oldest version of the narrative glowed with a confidence of divine sponsorship: America was lit from within. Later, Americans adopted the more aggressive myth of Manifest Destiny. Curiously, the members of the baby-boom generation came to believe that the ideas of divine sponsorship and Manifest Destiny were intended to apply to them. Now the boomers, who transform every moment that they encounter and every twig that they step upon into unprecedented trauma or revelation, have arrived at midlife crisis. Noises of the generation's falling hair and its disillusionments—*is that all there is?*—are muzzling in the American background. A certain unease with grownups maybe: in *JFK*, Oliver Stone took apart a representative American myth with a chain saw and reassembled it in strange shapes. During the '60s, the boomers watched in some wonder as American authority (the university system, for example, and the presidency of Lyndon Johnson) seemed to fall before them. But they have been slow to install their own authority in its place.

America is littered with the unorganized and unassimilated marvels and griefs of recent years. Enormous questions about the relations between men and women, for example. The country is changed. It has taken a lot of curves very fast, on two wheels. Many old habits are useless and even destructive now.

Much of folklore and myth is embedded in oddments of visual memory (stereotypes, propagandas, stray entertainments) and in a few national epics like the story of the Kennedys, with its bright, shining moments and its darker subplots and disgraces. The narratives that Americans need may be somewhat more advertent, and morally organized. People invent stories to explore their own behavior and to imagine their own possibilities. Few moments in America's moral life have surpassed the soliloquy, product of Mark Twain's imagination, in which Huck Finn agonizes over what to do about turning over the runaway slave Jim to the white authorities. Huck ends by accepting the consequences of his decision not to do so: "All right, then, I'll *go* to hell."

Especially when venturing into new territory where mere habit will no longer suffice, people require the stabilizing, consoling, instructing influence of other human tales. People without a surrounding atmosphere of myth and example are prone to the stupidity that arises from being isolated and incurious about the nuances of others' experience.

It misses the point to say that Murphy Brown is not a real character. Fiction is real enough in its powers. When Abraham Lincoln met Harriet Beecher Stowe, the author of *Uncle Tom's Cabin*, he said, "So this is the little lady who made this big war." That, at least, is the legend. Little Eva perhaps belongs to a higher order of symbolism than Murphy Brown's baby, but the simple principle, the power of stories, remains the same.

Poets and playwrights and novelists have always processed political events into entertainments and legends. Television now hastens reality into art with a sort of Irish efficiency: when an Irish Republican Army terrorist-hero blows up a British army truck in midafternoon, the deed will probably be a song in the pubs that night. Such ready glorification is one reason that no peaceful settlement has been found. Sitcom writers have developed similar reflexes. Topicality, however, ages a script rapidly. It strands an episode in time, and makes reruns seem alienated, quaint.

Fictions that get mixed up in politics—or religion—can become dangerous. Salman Rushdie has reason to know this: sitting alone with his imagination, he conjured up a story, *The Satanic Verses*, that has had him in hiding, under an ayatullah's *fatwa*, a sentence of death, for the past 3½ years. But as Rushdie has said, "The idea that writers should not argue about the world and simply write their little stories is a defeat."

Television is almost always unsettling and amazing when one thinks about it. It imposes upon America a strange simultaneity, if not a unity. It makes for a coast-to-coast viewers' version of what Kurt Vonnegut Jr. called a granfalloon, a wholly artificial brotherhood. TV characters themselves, whatever good lines their writers give them, almost inevitably have the flat soulless quality of people dropped on earth and hatched from a pod. Maybe it's the electron dust on the screen.

Still, surely it is preferable to have television dramas and sitcoms addressing important dilemmas now and then—single motherhood, for example, or drug addiction or wife battering. Better that than to revert entirely to *Gomer Pyle* and *Gilligan's Island* and *My Little Margie*.

On certain levels, the U.S. is a dangerously splintered and tribal country. America's historically indiscriminate embrace has depended on economic opportunity to make the whole enterprise (The Dream) function. Obviously, angers and abrasions deepen when many are competing for fewer jobs. In such an atmosphere, television acts often as a universalizing, mediating influence. It becomes a kind of third eye, however myopic on occasion, or however silly. By telling stories as it does (however skewed its critics, like Quayle, may think the stories are), television may militate against fanaticism and fantasies of revenge. The medium's demographic gyroscopes almost inevitably discourage bigotry. It is sometimes a shaming agent: a drama about the dilemmas of homosexuals, for example, may shame many Americans into being more tolerant on that score. The medium has a ceremonial and sacramental role when it covers tragedies, *Challenger* explosions, state funerals and the like. It even performs some of the functions of an American conscience. Its priestly influences reach into areas of everyday attitude and morals.

Ross Perot proposed an instantaneous participatory television democracy—a national electronic town meeting in which Americans could directly register their opinions on issues. Television has already swallowed the political parties, and Perot's hookup would override the Constitution's framework of representative democracy and deliberation.

But in a bizarre way, television's storytelling has become a form of representational democracy—or symbolic democracy, anyway. Perhaps, as Quayle says, the mythmaking roles are in the hands of a cultural élite that is alien to much of America. Still, being sensitive to the market economy of ideas and entertainment preferences, television naturally represents various American points of view and dilemmas. It churns out a visual rhetoric, an electronic folklore. It is the griot of American transience.

In the struggle of the stories, whose is the authentic American voice? Murphy Brown (played by the daughter of the long-ago-famous puppeteer-ventriloquist Edgar Bergen, and manipulated by activist fortysomething Hillary Democrats) represents a certain constituency. Dan Quayle, having no television surrogate to manipulate, has passed through the looking glass, playing himself, representing another America. He has become a moral symbol and performer himself: statesman and 'toon.

American storytelling is too important to be left so much to television. In American TV, a spirit only modestly gifted—and sometimes flat stupid—sits at the wheel of a trillion-dollar vehicle. The machine, being commercial, has that tendency to veer toward the ditch, seeking the least common denominator. The medium's technological prowess—and its relentless, pervasive presence in the society—imposes a responsibility that its writers and producers and directors probably should not have to bear. National Bard . . . and banality. Television does its work. But there are better ways to tell a story.

Questions for Critical Thinking and Discussion

1. In your opinion, what is it to be an American? What positive stories accompany the idea of being an American? What are some of the negative stereotypes or propaganda about the United States? Do you think the social stories about Americanism are true? Where did you learn these stories?

2. Television may be the biggest (and some might say the best) storyteller of our culture. But consider the motive behind the stories that are told on television. Why does television tell specific stories (targeting) to specific demographic groups? How does this skew the stories that are told?

4

The Big Sellout: Is Creative Independence a Luxury We Can No Longer Afford?

JOHN SEABROOK

John Seabrook is the technology correspondent for the New Yorker.

In this article, Seabrook explains how marketing and economics have changed the number (less) and type (mostly mainstream as opposed to independent) of voices available in contemporary culture. In order to understand our culture and ourselves, it is important to consider where and from whom our life knowledge is derived.

I—The New Suits

Back in the dawn of the age of content, six or seven years ago, the future of the content creator looked bright. The proliferation of channels for creativity, from up-band cable-TV stations to the Internet to CD-ROMS to zines, would give writers, artists, filmmakers, and musicians new leverage in the struggle with their old adversaries the suits. In his 1990 book *Life After Television* the futurist George Gilder forecast a golden age of artistic expression, to be ushered in by the telecommunications explosion: "The medium will change from a mass-produced and mass-consumed commodity to an endless feast of niches and specialties. . . . A new age of individualism is coming, and it will bring an eruption of culture unprecedented in human history. Every film will be able to reach cheaply a potential audience of hundreds of millions."

But is the age of content a good time to be a content provider after all? Or is Gilder's scenario one of those gotchas that the future likes to pull on futurists? Yes, the old culture monopolies have toppled. As the channels of distribution have multiplied, what economists call "the barriers to entry" have fallen in the culture industry. Steven Bochco, the creator of *Hill Street Blues* and *NYPD Blue*, thinks that the artist-suit balance of power in his business has definitely shifted toward the artist. "Twenty-five years ago the networks were incredibly powerful, because there were just three of them," he said recently. "Boy, you couldn't afford to run afoul of too many of these

---

This article first appeared in the *New Yorker* (October 20, 1997), pages 182, 184–185, 186, 188, 190–192.

characters, or you'd be out of the business. There just weren't enough places to go. Today, there's always someone who's hurting badly enough to take more of a risk—Fox, Warner Brothers, UPN, HBO, Lifetime. . . . There are tremendous opportunities out there for a kind of creative adventurism."

Yes, technology has made publishing and recording much cheaper. Undiscovered pop stars no longer need labels to front them the money to make records. You can literally make a CD in your bedroom with a computer and software to create a soundscape, a remixer to clean up the sound, and a wax machine to press the disk. Danny Goldberg, the chairman of Mercury Records Group, told me, "Twenty years ago, Stevie Wonder, to make *Songs in the Key of Life,* spent months in the studio getting all the sounds he wanted, and only Stevie Wonder could do that. Now anyone can. Ninety-nine per cent of the sounds you can imagine are available to you digitally. It used to be you'd say, 'Can I have a violin player?' and the label would say, 'No, you can't have a violin player—it's too expensive.' 'Can I do another vocal?' 'No, there's no time to do another vocal.' Those constraints don't exist anymore."

But, because more people *can* make content, more do. The market is flooded with content. There are too many film festivals, too many books, too many new bands, too many "new voices" and "stunning débuts." As a result, the old culture mediators, the people who owned the means of production, have been replaced by new mediators—the marketers, whose role is to make scrumptious little idea packages to wrap around the content ("It's Jonathan Swift on acid") and to tweak each package to make it fit a particular demographic niche. Where there once was a producer with a "golden gut," there is now a guy from market research—"some weird cross between a psychiatrist and a cheerleader," as the science-fiction writer William Gibson put it to me after seeing his film *Johnny Mnemonic* go through test-marketing—who gets up in front of a focus group and asks, "How did that character make you *feel?*"

It's not just in Hollywood that marketing and the bottom line are bullying the content providers. In the publishing world, editors act much more like marketers than they used to. Cathleen Black, the president of Hearst Magazines, said in a speech last spring, "Time was when it was enough for an editor to have a Rolodex full of writers' names . . . but today it's also necessary for them to steward their brands into other media, and outside the realm of media." And advertisers have become more a part of the editorial process than they used to be. I.B.M. recently pulled all its advertising—six million dollars a year—from *Fortune* and placed all its employees off limits to *Fortune* reporters, as a result of a piece that the company thought was unfavorable to Louis V. Gerstner, Jr., its C.E.O. *Esquire's* literary editor, Will Blythe, resigned when a David Leavitt short story involving homosexuality was pulled on the eve of its scheduled publication; the magazine's editors maintained that the story was pulled for "editorial reasons," but Blythe believed otherwise, having learned that the magazine was expected to notify Chrysler, an advertising client, of any "provocative" content that the conservative car manufacturer might not want appearing alongside its ads. He wrote in his resignation letter, "The balance is out of whack now. . . . We're taking marching orders (albeit, indirectly) from advertisers." Magazines are fighting the erosion of their editorial independence, but the age of content is working against them as well. There are too many magazines—hundreds of startups in 1997 alone—chasing too few ad dollars, and as a result advertisers can demand concessions that they never got before.

Paul LeClerc, the president of the New York Public Library, asked rhetorically if it would be possible for a single work of any kind to have the cultural impact today that Goethe's *Faust* had in Europe in the early nineteenth century. "If not, then what we've seen is a huge shift in the relationship between consumption and cultural output," he reflected. "In our day, with so much information coming through the line, and with the constant necessity to shift between the trivial and the important, it's hard to imagine a single text having that kind of impact. In the late twentieth century, we are a society that values output, speed, and productivity, whereas art requires time, reflection, tranquillity, and space—all commodities that are in limited supply these days."

In short, content creators have gained ample means to produce the product, but in the resulting cultural deluge they've lost the means of getting people to notice it. And while the marketers are always getting better— gathering more research, refining the demographic niches—the old methods of creative inspiration remain unimproved. The Information Highway is an immensely useful research tool: every home with a computer becomes a potential focus group. Market research seems to be creating a kind of neo-Darwinian sociology, a hybrid of science and business, that is on its way to replacing class, race, gender, and cultural identity with patterns of consumption behavior. If things keep going this way, there will soon be no difference between what the market wants to hear and what the individual is allowed to say. The only morality will be the morality of the demo, the first commandment of which is *The market is always right*.

II—The New Artists

For most of history, artists have worked for the suits, usually those worn by the Crown or the Church. Michelangelo did what the Pope told him to do. Mozart composed his music for the Holy Roman Emperor Joseph II. Only since Byron has the artist as rock star, as pure individualist, been a popular icon. Oscar Wilde updated the Byronic ideal for the modernists, in his 1891 essay "The Soul of Man Under Socialism":

> A work of art is the unique result of a unique temperament. Its beauty comes from the fact that the author is what he is. It has nothing to do with the fact that other people want what they want. Indeed, the moment that an artist takes notice of what other people want, and tries to supply the demand, he ceases to be an artist, and becomes a dull or an amusing craftsman, an honest or dishonest tradesman.

Out of this statement flows the concept of artistic integrity—of remaining true to your vision regardless of the market—and of "selling out," which is still very much with us. In the technical arts, the notion that the best inventions come from independent inventors has been exploded in the twentieth century, but the romantic doctrine of individualism is still the rule in the culture industry. Individuals are supposed to be better at creating "heart" and "vision" than groups are; groups take on the values of the group, which are less pure. As the saying in show business goes, "A building can't make a movie." But in fact buildings help make movies all the time. Penny Marshall was insistent on casting Robert De Niro in the lead role of *Big*, even though marketing said they couldn't sell that; in the end Tom Hanks got the part and was brilliant. Executives at Paramount worried that the prolonged kiss between Kevin Kline and Tom Selleck in *In & Out* would turn off some viewers, but when preview audiences howled with delight at the kiss, the scene stayed. . . .

Sometimes limits imposed by the suits can sharpen and focus an artist's vision: . . . [T]ake Ani DiFranco, a twenty-seven-year-old singer-songwriter with a devoted cult following, who has put out nine albums in seven years, all on her own label, Righteous Babe Records. For DiFranco, independence has been artistically and commercially rewarding: she gets four dollars and twenty-five cents per record, as opposed to the two dollars that a major label pays its artists. But for the consumer is it such a good deal? You go to the record store to get an Ani DiFranco record, and there are nine of them! Which one should you choose? A major label would have forced her to limit her output to one album every two years, in order not to flood her own market. You have to spend twice as much money, and devote twice as much time plowing through the less than great stuff, to hear her best songs.

Thomas Schatz, the author of *The Genius of the System*, a study of the Hollywood studio system, argues that movies made in the thirties and forties, when the artists were controlled by the suits, were just as good as the movies made in the later auteur period. "The quality and artistry of all these films were the product not simply of individual human expression, but of a melding of institutional forces," he writes. "In each case the 'style' of a writer, director, star—or even a cinematographer, art director, or costume designer—fused with the studio's production operations and management structure, its resources and talent pool, its narrative traditions and market strategy." Schatz says of Hitchcock, who was the model for later auteurs, "[When] Hitchcock could write his own ticket in an industry that seemed to be patterning itself after his career, both the quality and the quantity of Hitchcock's work fell sharply." Many have said that George Lucas made his best movies, *American Graffiti* and *Star Wars*, while he was under the control of the hated studios.

Some would argue that the culture industry as a whole is entering a period like the days of the studio system—a period when art and commerce will be more rationally integrated, and the church-state divide between the artist and the suit will gradually become obsolete. The rise of modern marketing seems to be dismantling that old dualism. Though marketing emerged out of the black lagoon of advertising—it was always about selling content—as time goes on it has an ever greater role in the *creation* of content. In an increasingly cluttered marketplace, the content, which the creator supplies, and the idea about the content, which the marketer confects, become harder to distinguish from each other.

At the same time, technology is changing traditional notions of authorship. The ability we have to rapidly access many different ideas on a subject with ever more refined searches increases the chance that an author is using someone else's ideas, or rather blending original and borrowed thoughts. On the Web, where hypertext links to many other authors may be embedded in a single text, the decline of the physical separateness of texts is challenging traditional notions of authorship. In the music world, "sampling," the mingling of one person's sounds with appropriated or "quoted" bits of other people's music, has become as legitimate a way of composing pop tunes as the old method of making them up yourself. James Schamus, a screenwriter and independent-film producer, thinks that what's happening is not so much the rise of corporate control over artistic freedom but a rethinking of who the artist is. There seems to be a new kind of creator emerging, whose job is to execute the wishes of the marketers and the executives in a creative way—to synthesize various ribbons of creative input—rather than to be a solitary auteur. "Notions of authorship have been blown wide open," Schamus says. "The author is really the person who owns the activity, who is paying the artists for their time while they are doing that work—that's the author."

III—The Two Grids

George W. S. Trow, who saw the future so long before it happened that he wrote about it in the past tense, perceived the fate of artistic independence in his "Within the Context of No Context," published in this magazine in

1980. According to Trow, there are two grids of pop culture: the big grid, the America of two hundred and sixty million, and the small grid, the grid of you and your intimate feelings. The age of content has progressed along Trovian lines. The big grid has become far more massive, while the intimate grid has grown smaller, tighter, augering in on itself. Occasionally, the grid of two hundred and sixty million and the grid of one lurch into alignment. The death of a princess or the terrible last hours of an Everest victim suddenly makes intimacy and massiveness feel like the same thing.

On the big grid are the stadium concerts, the latest Tom Clancy novel, the huge Broadway spectacular, and the "event movies." One of the basic truths of the big grid is that a culture project that relies on artistic execution is riskier than a market-tested project that will make money even if it's bad, because it's aimed at the all-important under-twenty-five-year-old-male demographic quadrant and because Stallone is huge in India. The content of the big-grid events is as shape-changeable as the cyborg in *Terminator 2*, and it keeps coming back, in the form of books, videos, computer games, merchandise, and Happy Meals, so that even if, say, a movie bombs at the box office the studio has a shot at making money. And the global marketplace is so new, so vast, the money involved in these ventures so big, that no one—not even people who work at the studios—really knows if these movies are making money or not. Profits are less important than the attention the events generate in the culture; the perception of profitability is the main thing. Here, too, marketing is all.

The big grid has been a disaster for the arts: the homogenization that plagued mass culture is worse than ever now that culture is global. In the case of the worst movies, in fact—the blockbuster sequels to blockbusters that have reached their endlife as content—the American public can smell death and stays away. Kids seem to have an especially acute nose for carrion. "How do they know?" Tom Sherak, a longtime executive at Twentieth Century Fox, asked me recently. "How do they know they want to see *The Fifth Element* and they don't want to see *Father's Day*? They know something we don't know. All our research, and we don't know. We think it's the look. They perceive *Fifth Element* to be about something that's hip, fresh, and different, while *Father's Day* looks old and tired."

The intimate grid, lying at the opposite end of the mediascape, is the repository of all that's hip and different. It's the world of the Off-Off-Broadway one-act, the cutting-edge zine, the genre-busting band, and the "tweener"— the small film that falls between genres and cuts across demographic quadrants (male, female, under twenty-five, over twenty-five). The intimate grid is Jarvis Cocker, of the glamrock Brit band Pulp, in song No. 4 on the CD *Different Class*, telling the big grid to "take your year in Provence and shove it up your ass." The more alienated people feel by the merchandising-driven, corporately compromised state of the big grid, the more comfort they take in the small one, where the artists are "independent" and the art is "real." On the small grid, the message "It's cool to be different" has replaced the big-grid message "It's cool to be the same."

An optimistic view of the mediascape is that the small grid acts as a dialectical force on the big grid and, over time, improves the general level of culture. Because the public now has a choice, the good art will triumph, the bad art will be driven out, and the market will be right in the moral sense as well as the economic. This is the view currently held by the filmmaker Lawrence Kasdan. "What we saw this summer," he explained, "was certain executives' misunderstanding the lessons of their elders, who always, finally, trusted the filmmakers in the end, because they knew suits could not create an actual movie. The younger guys came in and thought, Oh well, we're supposed to be the boss of all bosses, we'll make this movie. So we saw some actual movies made by executives, and they were utterly soulless and chaotic, without any connection to storytelling or any of the values people used to go to movies for—they were suit movies. But the wheel always turns. Things will always come around. There will always be this enormous need for the fresh idea. That's what all success and money is generated from."

The small grid *is* a lot better than it was ten years ago. Look at all the styles of hip-hop music available from D.J. Lenny M., who sells his tapes on the corner of St. Marks Place and Third Avenue: everything from trance to jungle to underground house to smooth reggae. The moviegoer who likes "art house" films no longer has to go to art houses (which by and large don't exist anymore) to see them. *Sling Blade* and *Shine* and *Cinema Paradiso* play next to *Air Force One* at the multiplex. Independent films received four of the five Oscar nominations for best picture last year. But in the process the word "independent" has undergone an Orwellian inversion and now means almost the opposite of what it used to mean. Words like "independent," "alternative," and "extreme" have become slick and empty containers into which marketers can pack tons of content. That's why Geffen, Time Warner, and Microsoft were so eager to buy into Sub Pop Records, the Seattle-based indie label (Time Warner won), and why big beer brands have started adorable homey microbreweries (which in turn have inspired Miller Genuine Draft's recent ad campaign, "It's Time for a Good Old Macrobrew"), and why all the major studios have acquired stakes in "independents" like Miramax and Fine Line and October Films. Now the eighties' corporate raider Carl Icahn is getting into the independent-film business, too. "Independent film was an oxymoron to begin with, and is probably a misnomer to finish with," James Schamus says. "Who cares if you're independent? You want to be independent, sharpen your pencil and write a poem. You want to spend twenty million—well, you know, get real."

As true independence becomes a nostalgic memory, the idea of independence becomes more marketable still. Nicholas Barker, a young British filmmaker who took his first film to Telluride this year, says, "A festival like Sundance has become an institution in which the studios use a dubious title like 'independent' to confer sexy status on films which are in fact not independent at all. I met a whole load of guys who were simply donning the independent cap because it was the fastest route to Hollywood." (When I said, "O.K., thanks, I won't quote you," Barker said, "Oh, by all means, quote me.") Oliver Stone told me, "Real independence is independent thinking, and we don't see much of that. Yeah, these films are raw, and sometimes they're not finished. The thought process isn't completed. They can often be an interesting little slice of life, but whether they can have any interest to anyone outside a sectarian portion of the population is debatable. And look at the second pictures—too many people are selling out the moment they have success."

The second-picture virus has attacked all the art forms. Many artists who are great as small independents can't survive the leap to the big grid, but because the big-grid marketers are always on the lookout for independent talent they can introduce, the young talents get pushed along too fast. "We're in a period where the new artist is expected to be the new messiah," says George C. Wolfe, the producer of New York's Public Theatre. "The whole concept of the journeyman artist has disappeared. You are not allowed to go on a journey. There is no journey. You're either extraordinarily brilliant or you're dead." Lindsay Law, the president of Fox Searchlight, recalls a small-grid project he snapped up: "The provocative new film by nineteen-year-old Matty Rich. That was the selling point. He was nineteen. And he was this young black kid—I was like the third or fourth white person he had ever met. He finally got a second movie, and it was dreadful."

This strip-mining of talent is producing an age of one-hit wonders, an age more favorable to art than to artists; but the system is addicted to the hype generated by the changes in scale. Instead of the small grid exerting salutary force on the big grid, the big grid is sucking the life out of the small. In the theatre world, Wolfe says, "a corporate thought process is beginning to dictate what has always been a small, individual- or community-driven art form." The reason, he explained, is that in response to rising costs Broadway producers have made alliances with corporations, and this has brought about a relentlessly box-office-driven approach to Broadway theatre. "As the commercial landscape gets more and more bland in an attempt to appeal to everyone," he said, "the pressure's put on the not-for-profits to be what Broadway used to be once upon a time—to provide exciting and challenging theatre for the commercial landscape. As opposed to being what the not-for-profit originally was, which was a breeding ground for maturing talent, and an alternative to the commercial landscape. We're instead expected to pick up the slack. So in the nonprofit world you have to be smarter about every single thing that you do. There are plays that I did two or three years ago at the Public which I would be very cautious about doing now, because I now understand that I'm not just letting a new artist be discovered, I'm introducing a new 'product,' which is a daunting task."

The midspace between the grids has become an apocalyptic heath, which the mid-list authors, the good but not brilliant filmmakers, and the solid but not spectacular bands, who once were the de-facto standard-bearers of the culture, haunt like ghosts. It's like Las Vegas at night: a tantalizing, amoral world, lit by the sparks of artists, actors, musicians, and writers who are in transit between success and failure—the prodigies arcing upward from the small grid and feeling that wallop as their identities are zapped by money and fame; the thirty-year-old instant has-beens spinning back into the small grid, spent and forgotten. There's Jean-Pierre Jeunet, the talented co-director of *Delicatessen,* who has just finished making *Alien Resurrection* for Twentieth Century Fox. There's James Mangold, whose first film was the low-budget *Heavy,* and whose second film was *Cop Land.* Have a most excellent adventure, dudes! There's Fiona Apple, the fresh-faced, too skinny new pop star, whose video for "Criminal" borrows from heroin chic. There's Charles Frazier, the author of *Cold Mountain,* one of the best-selling first novels in history; he recently sold it to U.A./M.G.M. for one and a quarter million dollars, to be directed by Anthony Minghella of *The English Patient.* Hey, Charles, are you still the same old guy you used to be? Do you still clean the bugs off the windshield of that junky old ride?

IV—The Marketer Within

The proliferation of new media may or may not bring more artistic freedom to the next generation of content creators, but it seems certain to inculcate in them a better sense of the awesome reality of the market. There is no sign that advertising, the traditional source of support for popular art, on which our church-state system of art and commerce has been erected, will work on the Web, where the audience has the technological advantage of being able to choose what it wants to see. The music video, a seamless synthesis of content and advertising, is a model for the content creators of the future. Some of the most original morsels on network television these days are the brief avant-garde stories that form the "content" of the Levi's ads, or the Nike series featuring the picaresque adventures of Li'l Penny.

The writer and director Michael Tolkin told me a story about a lecture he gave recently to aspiring filmmakers. He mentioned Jimmy Cagney, and was shocked to discover that virtually none of them knew who Cagney was.

"People in their twenties have for the most part no memory of history or art or anything else that's older than fifteen years," he said. "This generation, which grew up on cable TV, and on more recent movies, has been spoon-fed culture that was much more market-oriented than the culture of an earlier generation. Today the marketer is within." In other words, the artists of the next generation will make their art with an internal marketing barometer already in place. The auteur as marketer, the artist in a suit of his own: the ultimate in vertical integration.

So what's the future of selling out? Of what value are artistic principles in an age when the moral logic of remaining true to your vision or your heart has been overrun by the economic logic of the market? The starving artist, the visionary who can't make money from his art, has lost his resonance as a cultural archetype. He has been replaced by the charismatic grifter—the nineteen-year-old kid who makes a movie on his parents' credit card. He won't starve if the movie flops. He'll roll his debt over onto a new credit card that offers a six-month, six-per-cent grace period and try again.

Questions for Critical Thinking and Discussion

1. Capitalists typically forward the idea that a fair and open market-place leads to competition that leads to a better quality product that ultimately advantages the consumer. The problem is that culture has become the product and people are treated as consumers instead of cultural participants. What effect has technology had on your life? Is technology making it easier or more difficult for you to participate in your culture? Is it creating a false culture that you must now understand in order to belong and/or relate in social groups?

2. Seabrook quotes Oliver Stone as saying, "Real independence is independent thinking, and we don't see much of that." When is the last time you saw something in the media that was truly new and original? If something is "too different," will people understand it? Will folks be too uncomfortable to interact with something that is completely different from anything they've seen before?

5

History? Education? Zap! Pow! Cut!

PICO IYER

Pico Iyer's first novel was entitled Cuba and the Night *(Knopf, 1995). Iyer also works as an essayist for* Time *magazine.*

    In this article, Iyer discusses the effects that television and new technology have on our minds, our society, and our literacy.

In his new novel, *Vineland,* Thomas Pynchon, that disembodied know-it-all hiding out somewhere inside our nervous system, performs an eerie kind of magic realism on the McLuhanite world around us. His is an America, in 1984, in which reflexes, values, even feelings have been programmed by that All-Seeing Deity known as the Tube. Remaking us in its own image (every seven days), TV consumes us much more than we do it. Lovers woo one another on screens, interface with friends, cite TV sets as correspondents in divorce trials. And the children who have grown up goggle-eyed around the electric altar cannot believe that anything is real unless it comes with a laugh track: they organize their emotions around commercial breaks and hope to heal their sorrows with a PAUSE button. Watching their parents fight, they sit back and wait in silence for the credits. History for them means syndication; ancient history, the original version of *The Brady Bunch.*

    All this would sound crazy to anyone who didn't know that it was largely true. As the world has accelerated to the fax and satellite speed of light, attention spans have shortened, and dimension has given way to speed. A whole new aesthetic—the catchy, rapid-fire flash of images—is being born. Advertising, the language of the quick cut and the zap, has quite literally set the pace, but Presidents, preachers, even teachers have not been slow to get the message. Thus ideas become slogans, and issues sound bites. Op-ed turns into photo op. Politics becomes telegenics. And all of us find that we are creatures of the screen. The average American, by age 40, has seen more than a million television commercials; small wonder that the very rhythm and texture of his mind are radically different from his grandfather's.

    Increasingly, in fact, televisionaries are telling us to read the writing on the screen and accept that ours is a postliterate world. A new generation of

---

This article first appeared in *Time* (May 14, 1990), page 98.

children is growing up, they say, with a new, highly visual kind of imagination, and it is our obligation to speak to them in terms they understand.
MTV, *USA Today*, the PC and VCR — why, the acronym itself! — are making
the slow motion of words as obsolete as pictographs. The PLAY button's the
thing. Writing in the New York *Times* not long ago, Robert W. Pittman,
the developer of MTV, pointed out just how much the media have already
adjusted to the music-video aesthetic he helped create. In newspapers,
"graphs, charts and larger-than-ever pictures tell the big story at a glance.
Today's movie scripts are some 25% shorter than those of the 1940s for the
same length movies." Even TV is cutting back, providing more news stories
on every broadcast and less material in each one.

There is, of course, some value to this. New ages need new forms, and
addressing today's young in sentences of Jamesian complexity would be
about as helpful as talking to them in Middle English. Rhetoric, in any case,
is no less manipulative than technology, and no less formulaic. Though TV
is a drug, it can be stimulant as well as sedative. And the culture that seems
to be taking over the future is a culture so advanced in imagemaking that it
advertises its new sports cars with two-page photographs of rocks (though
the Japanese, perhaps, enjoy an advantage over us insofar as their partly
ideogrammatic language encourages them to think in terms of images:
haiku are the music videos of the printed word). Nor would this be the first
time that technology has changed the very way we speak: the invention of
typography alone, as Neil Postman writes, "created prose but made poetry
into an exotic and élitist form of expression." No less a media figure than
Karl Marx once pointed out that the *Iliad* would not have been composed
the way it was after the invention of the printing press.

Yet none of this is enough to suggest that we should simply burn our
books and flood the classroom with TV monitors. Just because an infant
cannot speak, we do not talk to him entirely in "goos" and "aahs"; rather, we
coax him, gradually into speech, and then into higher and more complex
speech. That, in fact, is the definition of education: to draw out, to teach
children not what they know but what they do not know; to rescue them,
as Cicero had it, from the tyranny of the present. The problem with visuals
is not just that they bombard us with images and information only of the
user-friendly kind but also that they give us no help in telling image from illusion, information from real wisdom. Reducing everything to one dimen-
sion, they prepare us for everything except our daily lives. Nintendo, unlike
stickball, leaves one unschooled in surprise: TV, unlike books, tells us when
to stop and think. "The flow of messages from the instant everywhere," as
Daniel Boorstin points out, "fills every niche in our consciousness, crowding
out knowledge and understanding. For while knowledge is steady and cu-
mulative, information is random and miscellaneous." A consciousness born

primarily of visuals can come terrifyingly close to that of the tape-recorder novels of the vid kids' most successful voice, Bret Easton Ellis, in which everyone's a speed freak and relationships last about as long as videos. Life, you might say, by remote control.

If today's computer-literate young truly do have the capacity to process images faster than their parents, they enjoy an unparalleled opportunity—so long as they learn to process words as well. They could become the first generation in history to be bilingual, in this sense, fluent onscreen as well as off. We need not, when we learn to talk, forget to communicate in other ways. But only words can teach the use of words, and ideas beget ideas. So just as certain tribes must be taught how to read a TV set, we must be taught how to read the world outside the TV set. Much better, then, to speak up than down, especially when speech itself is threatened. Nobody ever said that thinking need be binary. Nobody, that is, except, perhaps, a computer.

Questions for Critical Thinking and Discussion

1. Identify three specific visual literacy components or skills. Now identify three reading and writing literacy components. How can these literacies be useful in everyday life?

2. The author paints a very threatening scenario about the dangers of too much visual literacy in terms of its "robbing" time previously spent on reading and speech literacy. How have your literacies (reading, writing, visual, computer) changed over the past five years? How have you prioritized your literacies—that is, which do you spend the *most* time developing (computer literacy, reading, writing, visual literacy)? Which do you spend the *least* time developing? What do you think the results of such prioritizing might be in the long term?

chapter 3
Books

6

The Crushing Power of Big Publishing

MARK CRISPIN MILLER

Mark Crispin Miller is the chairman of the writing seminars at Johns Hopkins University.

In this article, Miller takes a look at what happens when conglomerates take over an industry. He argues that this runs against the idea of fair competition. American capitalism is based on the idea that a fair and open marketplace leads to competition, which leads to a better quality product, which ultimately advantages the consumer. In fact, our democracy is based on equal opportunity for participation and on a multiplicity of voices.

Gentle reader, here is what the world of letters looks like toward the end of the millennium: It's a small world after all. It might look vast inside a Borders or a Barnes & Noble, and the big numbers do seem to reinforce the sense of matchless cultural bounty: more than $20 billion in U.S. book sales (the most ever!) for 1996, with trade books at an unprecedented $5.7 billion!

And yet that world is small. . . . Aside from Norton and Houghton Mifflin (the last two major independents), some university presses and a good number of embattled minors, America's trade publishers today belong to eight huge media conglomerates. In only one of them—Holtzbrinck—does management seem to care (for now) what people read. As to the rest, books are, literally, the least of their concerns. For Hearst, Time Warner, Rupert Murdoch's News Corporation, the British giant Pearson, the German giant Bertelsmann, Sumner Redstone's Viacom and S.I. Newhouse's Advance, books count much less than the traffic of the newsstands, TV, the multiplex: industries that were always dominated by a few, whereas book publishing was, once upon a time, a different story.

The trade has also shrunk in other ways. Yes, it's easy to idealize the past, but it's even easier to shrug it off entirely: "There were bad books then, and we have good books now, so what's the difference?" The difference is immense. Where once the trade was based on love of books, today it's based on something else—as these brief histories may remind us.

§ Little, Brown (est. 1837) was one of two great Boston houses that survived the trade's gradual removal to New York. (Houghton Mifflin was the

This article first appeared in *The Nation* (March 17, 1997), pages 11, 12, 14–18.

other.) After a staid half-century of local sure things (John Quincy Adams, Francis Parkman) and solid reference works, L.B. flowered—with Emily Dickinson and Louisa May Alcott, Balzac and Dumas (and Fannie Farmer's cookbook). Later came Marquand, Evelyn Waugh, James Hilton and C.S. Forester, all of whom Alfred McIntyre, L.B.'s beloved director, supported well before the market justified it.

As part of Time Warner (Time Inc. bought it in 1968), L.B. now mainly sells Time Warner and its peers. In L.B.'s latest list, we find *Joan Lunden's Healthy Cooking* (ABC/Disney), a bio of La Streisand (Sony), a "tribute" to Kurt Cobain (Universal), *McCall's Best One-Dish Meals* (Bertelsmann), *Star Wars: The Death Star* (Fox) and Alan Grant's *Batman and Robin*, timed for the next T.W. bat-boom in the multiplexes.

In these turbid shallows are some books that aren't just marketing: John Fowles's essays, Martin Lee on neo-Nazism. But they get pennies for promotion, whereas say, for *Dr. Bob Arnot's Program for Perfect Weight Control*, T.W. will shoot the works (eleven-city tour, big ads, TV), since Dr. Bob is famous for his health-bites on the *CBS Evening News*. Celebrity is all at Little, Brown, which—despite the quaint old logo—*is* Time Warner. Thus could the house whose credo after 1930 was "Fewer and Better Books" now be the house that does *I Want to Tell You* "by" O.J. Simpson, for whose warm musings ("I'm a loving guy") Time Warner paid enough—$1.4 million—to cover his defense.

§ Random House (est. 1927) soon led the upstart New York houses that awoke the business after World War I. Into what had always been a WASP profession, such ardent Jewish book lovers as Alfred Knopf, Ben Huebsch and the Boni brothers introduced a spirit of cultural adventure. Thus did the trade take on the glamour of a bold and elegant modernity, as those innovators broke ideological taboos and otherwise took risks—and none took more or better ones than Horace Liveright, Random's accidental father.

As head of Boni and Liveright ("Good Books"), then briefly on his own, that charming and tormented gambler brought American readers every sort of modern classic, lavishly. It was Liveright who first published Faulkner, Hemingway, Hart Crane, cummings, Dorothy Parker, Djuna Barnes and Lewis Mumford; who published Dreiser, Anderson, O'Neill and Pound, *The Waste Land* and Anita Loos, Freud's first U.S. title and several books by Bertrand Russell. (Liveright often braved the censors, twice in court.)

His cash cow was The Modern Library, which he sold to Bennett Cerf in 1925. On that rich basis Cerf and Donald Klopfer started Random House, so named because, while fussing over Liveright's baby, they wanted just "to publish a few books on the side at random." A far sharper businessman than Liveright, Cerf nonetheless did share with him a lifelong passion for the objects of their trade. Random did *Ulysses* in 1934 (having fought for it in court), and Proust in Scott Moncrieff's translation; soon added over 300 titles to The Modern Library and created the Modern Library Giants; and ended up as home to an unprecedented range of authors—hard Modernists like Auden, Faulkner and Gertrude Stein, traditional craftsmen like John Cheever and Robert Penn Warren, sure winners like John O'Hara and James Michener, as well as Ayn Rand (and *Masters of Deceit* "by" J. Edgar Hoover).

Cerf wanted to get big. In 1960, with Random taken public, he and his associates kicked off the Age of Mergers by acquiring Knopf (and Vintage Paperbacks), Beginner Books and textbook firm I.W. Singer, then Pantheon. RCA bought it all in 1966, and in 1980 sold it to S.I. and Donald Newhouse, who by now also own *The New Yorker, Vanity Fair, Parade, GQ, Gourmet* and *Vogue* (among other glossies), the nation's fourth-largest newspaper chain and a cable operation—and Times Books, Fawcett, Crown, Villard, Ballantine et al.

This "Random House" is something else. Where Liveright courted T.S. Eliot to get *The Waste Land* (because Pound had recommended it), and where Cerf went to Paris to ask James Joyce for *Ulysses* (because Morris Ernst had pledged to fight the ban in court), Newhouse made his bones as publisher by getting Donald Trump to do *The Art of the Deal* (because Trump's puss had sent sales of *GQ* through the roof).

§ Bantam Books (est. 1946) was the second U.S. house to offer paperbacks—a momentous trend begun by Pocket Books in 1939. Ian Ballantine's first list included (at 25¢ apiece!) *Life on the Mississippi, The Great Gatsby, The Grapes of Wrath, What Makes Sammy Run?*, Booth Tarkington's *Seventeen*, Sally Benson's *Meet Me in St. Louis* and Saint-Exupéry's *Wind, Sand and Stars*, as well as several mysteries, Rafael Sabatini and Zane Grey.

Today, as part of Bertelsmann (since 1980), Bantam Books does *Acupressure for Lovers, Diet 911, David Letterman's Second Book of Top Ten Lists* and *Strong Women Stay Young*, among many others, some hardbound (*The Rocky and Bullwinkle Book*, $50), most in paper (*The Corporate Mystic*, $13.95). Bantam also has a cool new series out for (male) preteens: "Barf-O-Rama" offers them *The Great Puke-Off, The Legend of Bigfart* and *Dog Doo Afternoon*. These tales of "buttwurst" and "scab pie" are quite a stretch from Bantam's *Flavors of the Riviera*—a range that shows how broad the vision is at Bertelsmann.

Critiques like this one tend to jar, because they threaten the big myth that we have more and better "choices" today than our poor parents did with their three channels and two colas. Surely any hard look back at what folks really used to read will show that most of it was lousy—just like now. "'Twas ever thus: anyone who imagines that a hundred years ago Americans were rushing out to buy the new Henry James is kidding himself," writes Anthony Lane in *The New Yorker*.

Of course, the common run of literature has always been just that. Revisit any seeming "golden age" and read it all, and you'll find mostly dreck. Here, it was mostly dreck in Liveright's day—as in England, even back when Dickens and George Eliot were writing. And earlier, throughout the first great "golden age" of English fiction—Richardson, Fielding, Sterne—dreck ruled.

So there's been no golden age—yet books are worse, despite the gems. Today's worst, first of all, is much worse than the trash of yesteryear. Low intellectually—and morally, as William Bennett might care to observe (although his publisher is also Butt-head's)—books are even poor materially, because of editorial neglect. Where the houses prized the subtle labor of their editors, the giants want their staff not pouring over prose but signing big names over lunch. Hence countless books are incoherent and obese—as reviewers often note, decrying flaws that ought to have been caught already by an editor. . . .

The text today is often slighted too by proofreaders: not out of indolence but because they've been replaced by less-experienced freelancers; and the giants often further "save" by skipping galleys, so that manuscripts go straight to page proofs. Typos abound. . . .

Such goofs would not have been permitted by the houses' prior owners—for whom the product *was* the payoff. This is the all-important difference between then and now: As book lovers and businessmen, they did the high-yield trash so as to subsidize the books they loved (although those books might also sell). No longer meant to help some finer things to grow, the crap today is not a means but (as it were) the end.

That shift started in the sixties, and grew out of several factors. The ruinous overvaluation of best sellers was first an economic consequence of the great boom in subsidiary rights: book-club and, especially, paperback rights. As the paperback houses were, throughout the go-go years, paying hardcover publishers ever-higher prices to reprint the hottest titles, the value of sub-rights exploded—until the publishers were making more on those once-secondary deals than on their own hardcover sales. Soon dependent on such income (in 1979, $3 million to reprint *Princess Daisy*), the publishers became less interested in "good books" than in this or that potential monster. (Now that the giants also do paperbacks, such competition has waned.)

Meanwhile, the sway of hype had been expanded hugely by TV, in whose national sales-arena modest readerships seemed ever less worthwhile. It started early: In 1957 Prentice-Hall did Art Linkletter's *Kids Say the Darndest Things*, and the book—flogged weekly by the author on his show—was a best seller for more than a year. . . . TV was soon a grim necessity, with the houses jockeying to get their authors on *Today, Tomorrow*, Johnny, Merv and Donahue. Now that TV's grip is tighter still, the giants are that much deeper into it, staying close to shows like *60 Minutes, 20/20* and—above all— *Oprah* (whose "Book Club" can increase sales by more than 1,000 percent). The books thus plugged are few, and will rarely blow your mind, since TV likes friendly monosyllables and authors with great hair, thereby abetting the survival of the cutest.

Lite books have been encouraged also by the overconcentration at the sales end of the business: a field long shadowed by bookstore chains but whose seizure by a few has reached the crisis point. By 1980, the two leading chains—B. Dalton and Waldenbooks—had reduced the independents' market share to less than 40 percent. Today that scrap looks ample, now that countless independents have been broken by those two hip predators, Borders (which owns Waldenbooks) and Barnes & Noble. Whereas prior chains stayed mainly in suburbia, the Big Two take over city blocks, often near each other, going head to head to wipe each other out.

While it offers benefits to local shoppers—kids' programs, folk music, good espresso—that corporate feud is, in the long run, only further narrowing the culture. The gross demand of those commercial fortresses requires the giants to provide them with the dumbest titles in fantastic quantities: enough to fill each fortress with proud towers of, say, *Airframe*— an in-store boost for which the giants pay the superstores (who also sell window placement). The independent stores get no such subsidy; and that collusion also hurts the smaller houses, who lack the cash to have their books heaped up so awesomely.

Then there's the practice of returns. The superstores have generally ordered tons more books than they could ever sell—and then paid for those they've sold by sending back the ones they haven't. This titanic ripoff has distorted the whole trade. While the Big Two do, in fact, stock more small-press titles than the independent bookstores can, they also "pay" the smaller houses with returns; and those houses can't afford it, while the giants— with their bad dailies, cable TV, talk-radio, etc.—have sufficient capital to take the hit. But the giants too are losing; and so they spend still more to push their crudest items, and that much less (if anything) to find the smaller market for their mid-list titles. (Those items sit not only in the superstores but in airports, supermarkets, Wal-Marts—venues that now sell more books than bookstores do.)

While the Big Two get lots of press, the trade is lessened also by another— and invisible—duopoly. Book distribution is now dominated by two national companies: Ingram and Baker & Taylor. Those two, in fact, have gone beyond mere distribution to active marketing of books to B&N and Borders, a service only the giants can afford. The distributors can also hurt the little guy in other ways, their size enabling them to pay their bills when they feel like it—a casualness inimical to modest houses. "Small publishers are not being paid [quickly] enough to keep them in business," Lyle Stuart, owner of Barricade Books, said of his tiff with Ingram. "They feel you can't do business without them. But we can't stay in business if we keep dealing *with* them."

Finally, the giants' drift toward dreck has been accelerated also by the mad increase, since the sixties, in the sums they pay up front to V.I.P.s. Now that all the imprints are unstable, with editors forever leaving, writers go from house to house searching not for a home but for the sweetest deal. As elsewhere in the culture of TV, epidemic self-promotion has made stars of some agents, who have lately jacked advances up to drug-lord levels: $2.5 million for Dick Morris (Newhouse), more than $5 million for Gen. Norman Schwarzkopf (Bertelsmann), $6.5 million for Gen. Colin Powell (Newhouse), $3.5 million for former O.J. pal Paula Barbieri (Time Warner), etc. The editors seem heedless as to whether this or that big book will ever make the money back. Nor do they mind the gross inequity of those advances—because of which so many other authors just scrape by, or simply don't get published.

Although the giants did not create this system, they are themselves the biggest problem with it, for it is they—and not the TV-addled masses, or the bursting superstores or greedy agents—who have done the most to wreck the trade. From their book units, they expect profits way too steep for publishing, which never yielded high returns. For decades, notes New Press publisher André Schiffrin, the trade thrived on an after-tax profit rate of roughly 4 percent, most of it re-invested. By contrast, the giants want their houses to show profits of from 12 to 15 percent—comparable to what they make from movies, dailies and TV, but absurd for publishing.

Before the giants came, publishing was, for book lovers, a great way to make a living, albeit low-paying (and at the top, of course, all-white and mostly male). Today, fiduciary pressure is incessant and direct. With the houses now absorbed into the media trust, its top dogs tend to relegate the trade to others like themselves—not readers, or even lucid speakers of the language. This is true not only of the Hollywood imprints like Disney's Hyperion and Viacom's MTV Books. Avon has a three-year, thirty-title deal with Brandon Tartikoff, onetime programming whiz at NBC. "I think when you hear a star is interested in a film project, it could lend itself to a book property," Tartikoff told *Publishers Weekly*. "Some things can be baked into the literary work."

Likewise, Michael Lynton, C.E.O. and chairman of Pearson's Penguin Group, was formerly a suit at Disney, where he ran Hollywood Pictures—helping to produce, among other winners, Demi Moore's *The Scarlet Letter*, with its happy ending and her excellent jugs. HarperCollins C.E.O. Anthea Disney's previous work for Rupert Murdoch included running Fox TV's

A Current Affair, then overseeing *TV Guide*—and goosing up its numbers with a *People*-style "INSIDER" and, on every other cover, hunks flexing or babes pouting. Disney had no background in book publishing when Murdoch (who also has none) appointed her.

Under those who cut their teeth in TV, or at *TV Guide,* books themselves become TV—and not only in content. While B&N is jammed with weightless items "by" such telestars as Seinfeld, Leno, Oprah and Ellen, books are also getting televisual in *form.* Thus, while the text may be a mess, the cover cost some money—since, in this universe, that's what counts most. And nonfiction is being stripped of its least viewer-friendly features. Notes, for instance, are in trouble even at the academic presses. "Our marketing department tells us that footnotes scare off people," says an editor at Harvard—so perhaps it shouldn't be surprising that there are no notes in, say, John Keegan's *Fields of Battle* (Knopf) or Richard Meryman's life of Andrew Wyeth (HarperCollins) or Edvard Radzinsky's *Stalin* (Doubleday). On the other hand, it's strange to see nonfiction books with no index, as if that elementary guide might also "scare off" readers: Walter Cronkite's and David Brinkley's memoirs (Knopf) are index-free, as is Jane Kramer's book on modern Germany, *The Politics of Memory* (Random House).

When book publishing was still a cottage industry, it was "the freest form of expression we have," Curtice Hitchcock wrote in 1937. "The large circulation magazine, the newspaper, the motion picture, or the radio program, since they are intended for a mass audience, must perforce avoid taboos held sacred by any substantial portion of that audience, or they fail. A book can, and to a considerable extent does, find its own level of taste, appreciation and intelligence." Gradually, it might make people think and see. "If the book is important, however unpalatable it may be to large groups of people, the author can feel with some measure of truth that despite a small sale his ideas have been started in circulation and may seep (as ideas have a way of doing) beyond the range of the actual cash customers."

A long shot at the best of times, such dissemination is less likely than ever. The slow course of an idea or vision through some subculture of thoughtful readers (as opposed to the endless wildfire on the Internet) is hardly possible when those who own the trade want only the big returns right now. Thus have the giants shrunk the culture automatically, through that objective "market censorship" . . . by dumping, or red-lighting, any book that offers revelations irksome to themselves. Such titles quickly end up on the same unspoken *index librorum prohibitorum* that lists important books on U.S. foreign policy by authors like Christopher Simpson, Burton Hersh, Noam Chomsky, Gerard Colby, Frank Kofsky. Although solid and eye-opening, such works usually induce an eerie quiet in the mainstream press—and not always by accident, as John Loftus learned from someone at the C.I.A. A former assistant to the Attorney General (in the Nazi War Crimes unit), Loftus must let Langley vet his work, and did so with *The Secret War Against the Jews* (St. Martin's), his and Mark Aarons's dark history of the C.I.A.'s relations with big oil. The manuscript would be O.K.'d, he heard from an agency source—"but you'll never get a review in America."

This being the national entertainment state, books are also whacked in New York or Hollywood without a word from Langley. Full of creepy news about its subject (F.B.I. fink, anti-Semite), Marc Eliot's *Walt Disney: Hollywood's Dark Prince* was aborted suddenly by Bantam in 1991, because, his editor said, it was "not of publishable quality" (although he'd only sent some notes). Eliot then learned of Bantam's "Disney Library" series for sale in supermarkets—a deal worth far more than his book would have been. (It later came out from Birch Lane Press.) . . .

While killing books distasteful to its bosses, the media trust can also flood the world with its own sunny counterstory. Starting in December 1979, all copies of *Katharine the Great*, Deborah Davis's life of *The Washington Post's* Katharine Graham, were pulped by Harcourt Brace Jovanovich, despite the house's late enthusiasm for the work. H.B.J. had been spooked (so to speak) by a threatening letter from Ben Bradlee alleging factual errors. Davis believes that Bradlee was angered mainly by her claims that he and Graham had C.I.A. connections. Whereas Davis's bio vanished (it came out from National Press Books), Graham's own big *Personal History* has gotten quite a push from her machine: cover story in the *Post's* Sunday mag, a rave in that day's *Book World*, then excerpts in the *Post's* style section and in *Newsweek*, etc.

The bigger the mogul, the deader any book that might offend him—a truth confirmed by the Orwellian experience of Thomas Maier, author of a 1994 book on our pre-eminent Stealth Mogul. *Newhouse* tells the whole absorbing story of S.I.'s rise to dominance: the newspaper monopolies set up in city after city; the commercialist aesthetic of the magazines, whose articles are meant to look like ads; one of the biggest tax-evasion trials in U.S. history—a contest fumbled by the I.R.S.; Newhouse's lifelong friendship with Roy Cohn, through whom the family helped Joe McCarthy, Jackie Presser and the Chicago mob; and all those brusque beheadings at Random, Condé Nast and *The New Yorker*. Thorough and low-key, *Newhouse* is a sobering "parable on American media power," as Maier puts it—but what befell it is, on that subject, almost as edifying as the book itself.

At the start, no one would touch it—not even in London, where the Bloomsbury Press responded typically: "'We love it, but we're sorry, we do business with S.I. Newhouse,'" as Meier recalls it.* St. Martin's finally took the book—and had a hard time selling it: *Vanity Fair* refused an ad, and Liz Smith's item was, that day, oddly missing from her column in the Newhouse newspapers. The book was not reviewed or even mentioned in New York— where Maier also found *himself* blacklisted. Although Dr. Benjamin Spock had granted him permission—and full access—for a first-ever biography, Maier found he had "become persona non grata with about 40 percent of the book-publishing world." *Newhouse* would have sunk without a trace had not Johnson Books (in Boulder, Colorado) brought it out in paperback.

And so B&N's offering is not as comprehensive as it looks; for all the books that do shine there, important others can't. A title's initial shelf life, furthermore, is often now its whole life—and that span grows ever less. While we lack hard numbers on it, those who know say that most new books have—at most—as long to live as most new TV shows. First of all, the giants keep tiny backlists, since the I.R.S. decreed, in 1979, that publishers may not write off the costs of warehouse inventory. With shelf-space tight inside the superstores, moreover, a book often has a mere few months—or less—before it gets returned. And so the giants' mid-list books, deprived from birth, now have the life expectancy of houseflies.

And what of the alternative—the independents and the university presses? Many independents are worrying that they may not make it through the year, as libraries cut back on orders and returns keep pouring in. Meanwhile, the academic houses are now pressed by cost-conscious university administrators to make it on their own, without institutional subsidies. Thus those houses too are giving in to market pressure, dumping recondite monographs in favor of trendier academic fare or, better yet, whatever sells at Borders— which, presumably, means few footnotes. Those publishers are so hard pressed there's talk in the academy of changing tenure rules, because it's next to impossible to get an arcane study published—a dark development indeed.

Defenders of the system like to charge its critics with elitism. That pseudo-populist stance is quite belied by the history of publishing, which at its best had always sought mass readership. "He was a genius at devising ways to put books into the hands of the unbookish," Edna Ferber said of Nelson Doubleday. "A publisher who can do that is as important—or nearly—as Gutenberg." If today's giants are so good at selling to the people, why is the trade in trouble? Like the culture trust's big movies and CDs, its

---

*In Britain, Newhouse owns Chatto & Windus, Jonathan Cape, the Bodley Head, Century, Hutchinson, Arrow Books, Ebury Press, etc., and will soon buy Heinemann, Secker & Warburg, Methuen, Sinclair Stevenson, Mandarin and Minerva.

books are mostly duds: Last summer was the worst season in five years, with returns as high as, or exceeding, 40 percent of gross sales.

Inside a B&N or Borders, such failure is not obvious—nor is the actual sameness underlying all that seeming multiplicity. Look closer, and you'll see how many of those new books from Hyperion are merely ads for Disney—including Oprah's aptly titled *Make the Connection* (she and Disney have a multi-picture deal). You'll see that Pantheon has done four volumes of *The Flavors of Bon Appetit* (and *Bon Appetit 30-Minute Main Courses*) because Newhouse also owns *Bon Appetit*. Find *The New Yorker* on the magazine rack, and chances are that the issue's fiction, or nonfiction, came from one of S.I. Newhouse's houses. (Last year more than half the magazine's twenty-six excerpts came from Random titles.) Look too at Random's books on *other* giants, and note how uncritical they are—Kay Graham's memoir (Knopf) and Steven Cuozzo's *It's Alive* (Times Books), a paean to Rupert Murdoch.

Then think ahead, imagining the day when either B&N or Borders wins their war—and try to picture what that seeming multiplicity will look like. When there's just one chain left, its superstores will not be ordering those offbeat books from the remaining small houses, which will then fold. For those who like to read, the prospect is a frightening one, but not as frightening as the fact that people won't know what they're missing. Before that happens, we should ask some serious questions about culture and democracy—and antitrust—before there's nothing left to help us answer them.

Questions for Critical Thinking and Discussion

1. Mark Miller's arguments are compelling. On the other hand, as a result of conglomerates and fair competition, a large number of books are now available at lower prices to the consumer. What is your role as the individual consumer in the book industry business? How can you support democracy through your participation in the process?

2. Miller poses the argument that today's worst books are much worse than the trash of yesteryear, but he addresses this problem of selective hindsight by acknowledging that there hasn't been a true golden age for books. Consider some contemporary books you've read. Which ones do you think will stand the test of time and become classics? Who or what system will decide this? Will it be the best-seller lists? Will the critics decide?

3. With the advent of new technology, books are developing into new forms (books on tape, CD-ROMs, etc.). How is technology changing the book experience?

7

The Oprah Effect: How TV's Premier Talk Show Host Puts Books over the Top

BRIDGET KINSELLA

Bridget Kinsella is a writer and interviewer for Publishers Weekly *magazine.*

This analysis provides a look at Oprah Winfrey's "Book Segment" and the effects it has had on society in terms of book industry economics, community literacy, and general interest in reading.

It's turned out to be the most fun she's had in years, Oprah says, but believe it or not, the Book Club wasn't her idea.

"I thought we would die in the ratings," Oprah tells *PW*, about her reaction when her producers first introduced the idea last summer. "I thought they had lost their minds."

Not that Oprah is anti-fiction, of course. It's just that whenever this rabid reader tried to promote it on *The Oprah Winfrey Show* the way she has successfully promoted nonfiction, the effort, she says, "just bombed." In 1993, for example, she hosted a show of writers she'd like to have dinner with, and although book sales leaped for those authors, ratings sunk.

"The problem with fiction is that most people haven't read the book and so they can't follow the story," says Winfrey. "It's the same problem when I have soap opera stars on the show; if you haven't been watching *Guiding Light*, I have to explain to everyone who the character is and what's the storyline."

Then, just before the fall season, thanks to a new segmented program format that allows her to spend as little or as much time on a topic as she feels both the subject and the audience can take, Oprah rethought the viability of a televised Book Club.

"I started thinking about it again one morning in the shower," she recalls. "It would be great if we could do this club and do what I've always wanted to do: sit down with authors I really love."

The rest, of course, is history. Starting with a new first novel, Jacquelyn Mitchard's *The Deep End of the Ocean*, followed by backlist titles *Song of Solomon* and *The Book of Ruth*, Oprah's Book Club has put literature in the limelight, earned steady ratings and provoked unprecedented, bestseller sales. And as news reports proliferated regarding this "Oprah Effect," Oprah

This article first appeared in *Publishers Weekly* (January 20, 1997), pages 276–278.

Is Oprah Bringing in New Readers?

Beyond selling many copies of her Book Club selections, booksellers have recognized another Oprah Effect — new customers coming into the stores.

"She really does seem to be bringing in new people, and they're people who specifically said they wouldn't otherwise have bought a book at all," notes Isabella Reitzel, frontlist buyer for Barbara's Bookstores, which has six Chicago locations and one in Boston.

While there is no scientific way to measure this effect, Bob Weitrack, director of merchandise for Barnes & Noble, says the store managers feel that a good percentage of shoppers coming in for Book Club titles are "new readers." B&N has also noticed that the Book Club sales often include multiple copies or other ISBN numbers. "Seventy-five percent of the people who buy the Book Club title are buying something else, too," he says. "They shop, they browse, they engage in conversations with our booksellers, and then they come back."

Lisa Johnson, vice-president and director of publicity at Plume, publisher of the trade paperback edition of *Song of Solomon*, thinks Winfrey is broadening the market for literary fiction. Since October, Plume has gone back to press 10 times, for an additional 830,000 copies, and Johnson notes that the books are selling in places, such as warehouse clubs, that are generally not considered good trade paperback venues.

As an independent bookseller, Reitzel says this is one instance where she has " 'no problem' with the warehouse clubs of the world." She adds, "Maybe they will bring a certain number of people to the habit of reading for pleasure and for their emotional health, and the more people that get into that habit, we can't lose."

Weitrack observes that Winfrey has been encouraging her audience to come into the bookstore for years, although with the Book Club the customers want the books *now*. "Even before the Book Club, people would come in and say Oprah had this author or that author on her show. It is as if they mean, 'My friend Oprah recommended this,'" he explains. "People are frequenting the stores more, and the more often they go, the more comfortable they feel."

Particularly with *Song of Solomon*, booksellers credit Winfrey with bringing literary fiction to a wider readership. "If you approach great literature with your heart and your mind instead of as an academic assignment, then it really can be accessible," Reitzel says. "Oprah seems to be very capable of eliciting that response from a broad audience, and that's terrific."

Like everyone else in the industry, booksellers are hoping that the Oprah Effect lingers.

herself realized she had taken on a new mission: to get America — indeed, the world — reading.

I feel strongly that, no matter who you are, reading opens doors and provides, in your own personal sanctuary, an opportunity to explore and feel things, the way other forms of media cannot," she tells *PW*. "I want books to become part of my audience's lifestyle, for reading to become a natural phenomenon with them, so that it is no longer a big deal." And *what* an audience she has: at last count, *The Oprah Winfrey Show*, the country's consistently top-ranked talk show and winner of 25 Emmy Awards, had an estimated 15–21 million viewers worldwide, the majority in the key reader demographic of women age 18–54.

Remaining 'Pure' — and Personal

As always on her show, it's Oprah's personal approach — in this case her interest in particular books — that drives Oprah's Book Club. Oprah insists selections will remain her own and thus be "absolutely pure." Even though publishers have deluged her with suggestions (there are rumors of extra warehouses having to be rented to handle the overflow), Oprah doesn't pick from them, and will not consider a children's book, for example, because she feels unqualified to recommend one. To take the Book Club in a "male direction," she is currently rereading male authors she has liked over the years. Besides, she thinks the Book Club could be lightened up with something "wicky-wacky-doodle," as she describes Wally Lamb's *She's Come Undone* (Pocket Books). . . .

As Book Club momentum grows, Oprah is beginning to realize the huge repercussions her selections have on her audience and on the publishing industry. For example, there has been some sniping that Oprah chose Toni Morrison's *Song of Solomon* because her production company, Harpo Entertainment, owns the rights to the author's Pulitzer Prize–winning novel, *Beloved*, but that's a suggested vested interest that Oprah dismisses. "It would be unthinkable to do a book club without Toni Morrison," she says emphatically. "If I am only doing books that I love, does that eliminate this as a good book to read, just because I might do a movie?" She is still considering Connie May Fowler's *Before Women Had Wings* as a choice, despite Harpo's current development of it as a TV movie.

Another complaint from publishers has been the lack of advance warning about her selection, thus running the risk of drastic out-of-stock conditions. Although Oprah enjoys the dramatic element of surprise, she is now trying to provide early warning to publishers, as well as asking them to donate 10,000 copies of the chosen book to libraries in order to keep waiting lists down. . . .

Ever mindful of her audience, Oprah is also trying to choose books that are available in paperback, particularly after receiving complaints from viewers that they couldn't afford the hardcover price for *The Deep End of the Ocean*. . . .

The sensual pleasure the book world can bring also informs the author-dinner part of her show, in which the feast is set forth accompanied by the finest linen and china. These dinners, which appear only in part on Oprah's Book Club, are being enhanced in a variety of ways, partly in response to audience demand. In addition to the dinners, the authors participate in on-line auditorium chats on Oprah's site on America Online (keyword: Oprah), which also features additional live book chat and discussion. Starting February 24, an edited hour-long version of the dinners will be aired on the Lifetime cable channel.

Oprah will also start providing a brief advance description about a Book Club selection to viewers, but won't go beyond that before the author dinner. "I know the way to sell a book is to have people who are just like you, excited, interested and stimulated by the book," she says, echoing the strategy of every bookstore handseller.

And although she'll space them out, she won't shy from offering challenging works like *Song of Solomon*. "That, my dear, is called reading," she says, playfully echoing Morrison's own retort on the subject. "One of the things that has been most rewarding for me is the thought that has been provoked by people who never read before," she says. "It's one thing to win an Emmy, but it's another thing to influence somebody who hasn't picked up a book since they were forced to in high school to read *Song of Solomon* and start thinking differently about their own life as a result of that."

Questions for Critical Thinking and Discussion

1. Oprah Winfrey's book segment is made up of several dimensions. Consider the following "Oprah effects" and discuss whether you think they are positive or negative contributions to the book reading experience: author dinners, book club membership, live book chats and discussions, added advertising for books and reading in general, higher book sales.

2. Winfrey hopes that her book segment will promote literacy and spread her love of books. Her segment has definitely affected the sales and best-seller listings, but do you think these measurable economics are actually associated with the support of reading literacy? If so, how? If not, why?

8

The Dumb-Down

TODD GITLIN

Todd Gitlin is a professor of culture, journalism, and sociology at New York University. He is also a well-known columnist and the author of many books and articles on media and culture.

Gitlin analyzes sentence length and the number of punctuation marks in order to reveal cultural change associated with the "advent and consolidation of television at the center of national culture."

As publishers have become farm teams where "product" is worked up for the "synergistic" use of the parent entertainment conglomerates, one frequently hears the charge that books have been dumbed down. The assumption is that, once upon a time, in a galaxy far far away, popular taste was higher. To which the industry clucks that there's no proof—and anyway, they give the people what they want.

Now, it is true that, in the politics of culture, to mutter about decline is the first refuge of a scoundrel. There's something, well, predictably *fin de siècle* about this sort of lamentation. It reeks of snobbery and unearned nostalgia, because the past is always tinted with afterglow, and because homesickness for the golden haze age is a cheap substitute for hard thinking about the complexities of cultural change. It's true that no one writing today is Melville, but it is also true that, a century and a half ago, hardly anyone was Melville. Only one writer was Melville, in fact, and while he had some early successes, *Moby-Dick* sold fewer than 5,000 copies during the forty years between its publication and Melville's death.

But what might be learned if we compare present-day popular reading taste not with high moments of literature but with the popular reading taste of the past? Let's compare books that get on today's best-seller list with books that used to get on best-seller lists, and for a moment, forget about relative quality, about which reasonable people may disagree. Instead, let's crunch some numbers—the sort of hard goods social science can best deliver—and look to (you'll pardon the expression) objective evidence.

In this spirit, my research assistant, Marco Calavita, and I studied the top ten novels on *The New York Times* best-seller list during the first week of

---

This article first appeared in *The Nation* (March 17, 1997), page 28.

October in 1996, 1976, 1956 and 1936. (After omitting two children's books, and titles from the 1936 list that could not be unearthed despite searches of the New York Public Library and other repositories, we were left with thirty-six titles in our sample.) The question is, Has popular writing become, on average, more simplified?

It is, on the face of it, breathtaking that in 1956, Simone de Beauvoir's *The Mandarins* ranked number 4 (and had done so for four weeks in a row) and Yukio Mishima's *The Sound of Waves* showed up at number 13. But those could be flukes. How to determine complexity in a way that could be easily, unambiguously counted?

We settled on the following methodology: We took the first sentence beginning on pages 1, 50, 100 and 150 (page 120 in two books that did not get up to page 150) and counted three things about the sentence:

1. The number of words in it.

2. The number of punctuation marks of all kinds before the period (admittedly a crude measure of sentence complexity but quantifiable).

3. Whether the sentence was dialogue or in the authorial voice.

As the chart on the following page shows, the use of dialogue has grown steadily, by a total of 40 percent between 1936 and 1996. Between those same years, sentence length declined by 27 percent and the number of punctuation marks by 55 percent. With respect to all three variables, the biggest changes took place between 1956 and 1976, with 1996 representing a considerable bounce-back in the case of punctuation and length.

The brevity record for all thirty-six books goes to Tom Clancy for his 1996 *Executive Orders,* with a total of twenty-three words spread out over the four first sentences. ("It had to be the shock of the moment, Ryan thought." "Its symbolism was clear." "Mark Durling was whimpering now." "Not everyone did.") Two 1976 titles are close runners-up. In the first, Harold Robbins's *The Lonely Lady,* the four sentences add up to twenty-nine words. ("She sat at the top of the stairs and cried." "There was something wrong with her." "She looked thoughtful for a moment." "I'm afraid I'll never understand you, Jerilee.") In the other, Jacqueline Susann's *Dolores,* they total thirty-three. ("There was a mean chill in the air as Air Force One began its slow approach toward Washington." "The family stays together." "Oh God . . ." "That will take some of the pressure off me.")

If you skipped the numbers, here's the conclusion: Between 1936 and 1976, best-seller sentences got shorter and simpler, though there were upticks in 1996. The eighth-ranked best seller in October 1936 was Francis Brett Young's *Far Forest,* which begins with what is by far the longest opening line of all thirty-six books: "Jenny Hadley was born and reared—or

Here Are the Findings

In 1936, the average sentence length was 22.8 words; in 1956, 17.75 words; in 1976, 13.55 words; in 1996, 16.55 words.

In 1936, the average number of punctuation marks was 2.2; in 1956, 1.5; in 1976, 0.85; in 1996, 0.98.

In 1936, 25 percent of the sentences were dialogue; in 1956, 27.5 percent; in 1976, 32.5 percent; in 1996, 35 percent.

	Length	Punctuation	Dialogue
1936	22.80	2.2	25.0%
1956	17.75	1.5	27.5
1976	13.55	0.85	32.5
1996	16.55	0.98	35.0

dragged up, as they say in those parts—at Mawne Heath on the Staffordshire side of the River Stour which at this point divides it from Worcestershire: a heath only by courtesy, and a blasted heath at that if ever there was one." The first sentence beginning on page 100 numbers 103 words, which I shall spare the reader. Whether *Far Forest* is anomalous or not, the point is that in 1936 it was possible for a book to be a best-seller while including a sentence of 103 words.

Skeptics may object that shorter and simpler does not necessarily mean shallower. "In the beginning God created the heaven and the earth" clocks in at a mere ten words, and a more rounded and sonorous ten words are hard to imagine. Still, the sentences in our sample lack the compensating virtue of poetry. Tom Clancy is no Author of Genesis. (He's no Hemingway, either.)

The span between 1936 and 1976, of course, coincides with the advent and consolidation of television at the center of national culture. So it comes as no surprise that popular novels read more like scripts. There is likely both a supply and a demand side to this shift. Authors aspiring to write popular fiction are writing more simply, with an eye on the camera angle; readers are looking for uncomplicated prose and more dialogue. The upshot is that popular fiction is stripped down to resemble TV scripts—to go down easier, make fewer demands.

As for the significant bounce-back of sentence length and number of punctuation marks in 1996, what may we surmise? Is some law of literary compensation at work, with oversimplification generating a countertrend, the way fat-free pasta produces a yen for zabaglione at the end of the meal? As social scientists like to conclude, further research needs to be done.

Questions for Critical Thinking and Discussion

1. What did Gitlin mean when he wrote: "Now, it is true that, in the politics of culture, to mutter about decline is the first refuge of a scoundrel. There's something, well, predictably *fin de siècle* about this sort of lamentation."

2. In an attempt to address selective hindsight of quality assessment of books, Gitlin analyzes length, punctuation, and dialogue to demonstrate the difference between books printed over the past few decades. What do these categories tell us about books? What other comparisons could be made beyond these three categories?

chapter 4

Newspapers

A Tour of Our Uncertain Future

KATHERINE FULTON

Katherine Fulton is the founding editor of the North Carolina Independent, *an alternative weekly. She currently works for the Global Business Network, a consulting firm that specializes in helping businesses and organizations prepare for the future.*

What will be the future of journalism and journalists in a digital age? Fulton's essay considers the questions, issues, and possibilities surrounding future economics, credibility, and access of new media journalism.

Two and a half years ago, I assigned myself the story of my professional lifetime. I wanted to explore the fate of journalism in the digital age.

Like most challenging beats, this one was hopelessly large, so I approached it in an unusual way. I didn't want to cover the breaking news — the corporate mergers, the cuts in news budgets, the declining audiences for daily newspapers and broadcast networks, the initial reluctance to confront the new on-line medium followed by the panicked rush to embrace all things Internet.

Instead, I got a job teaching at Duke University and looked under the surface, at the technological, economic, and social forces that rarely make headlines. For five semesters I read, I wandered on-line, I conversed with original thinkers and with twenty-year-old students eagerly exploring their free high-speed network connections. The payoff came when I was forced to examine assumptions I didn't even realize I had.

I had hoped to trace this journey in the usual linear narrative style. . . . But this time I found myself facing a vast puzzle in which new technological pieces are constantly introduced, in which the old borders keep changing, in which some new and even some old pieces may not fit at all. The puzzle can't be put together yet. Indeed, there's every sign that the pieces will stay in the air for a long time. Out there in cyberspace, a massive research and development project is under way, and mutating daily. Anyone can pull up a ringside seat.

This article first appeared in *Columbia Journalism Review* (March/April 1996), Vol. 35, pages 19–26.

With this in mind, I've created a guided tour of interesting on-line experiments. . . . Every boldfaced word or phrase in the piece indicates an Internet site you can experience yourself by linking to it. Just click.

This tour, however, is not about the bells and whistles, as enticing as those can be. It's about who will shape the future of journalism. So I've adapted that useful on-line staple, "frequently asked questions," as a way of organizing the tour and thinking out loud about how some of journalism's longstanding moral, practical, and economic certainties are eroding.

Shall we begin?

I'm Not Interested in Technology and I'm Sick of the Hype, So Why Should I Care?

We live in a world in which original journalism is a smaller and smaller component of a larger and larger media and communications system. When *Vanity Fair* named its fifty "leaders of the information age" in its annual look at "The New Establishment" last fall, only one leader—Norman Pearlstine, editor in chief, Time Warner—was a journalist working for a mainstream news organization.

Journalism companies used to control the megaphone—and therefore had a monopoly on who got heard. New technologies such as satellites, cable, fiber optics, and, of course, computers have destroyed that world forever.

Some of what we hear about the future *is* hype. Two years ago everyone was busy touting the future of interactive television. Soon everyone would be ordering up movies on demand and enjoying the 500-channel universe. Then a new graphical browsing software called Mosaic suddenly made it fun to navigate the Internet. Now interactive TV trials have disappeared into technical and balance-sheet quagmires while hundreds of new "channels" are added to the World Wide Web every single day. Next up for a publicity blitz: the Internet through your cable television connection.

The point is that while specific, short-term predictions may be wrong, it's a mistake to ignore the overall longer-term trends. "Take it as given that within five years, networked computers in the workplace and the home will compete on an equal footing with the existing news media as a routine source of news for over half the public in the industrialized world," writes Professor W. Russell Neuman of Tufts University, who is known for his careful scholarship. "Skeptical? OK, then make it ten years. We're not discussing the end point anymore, just the shape of the diffusion curve."

Journalism faces a historic challenge to adapt to a new medium, whether people relate to it through a television screen, a computer monitor, or some new hybrid. All journalists—even the most technophobic—need to understand how digital communication systems are challenging both the business models and journalistic conventions we've inherited from other eras of technological innovation.

Take, for example, our first journalistic stop on this tour—*The Boston Globe*, which has rethought old notions of proprietary products. Instead of just taking their newspaper on-line, as so many have done, the *Globe* people have opened a gateway—**boston.com**—to their whole region. They convinced all the major television stations and museums in the city to join them as content partners, creating in the process an impressive new media genre. Citizens can play, too, by voicing an opinion, or using the site's resources to help address community problems, or linking their home pages, or their organizations', to the site.

The task facing any thoughtful journalist today, says Arthur Sulzberger, Jr., publisher of *The New York Times*, "is to take the brand we have today and to translate it for this new medium. Some of the parts will be shockingly familiar to all of us. Twenty and twenty-five years from now, other parts none of us can even imagine."

Won't There Always Be a Market for Journalism?

To answer this question, you have to decide what you mean by the word "journalism." The term refers to many things, from the most honored traditions of reporting to live cable coverage of events to all the varied activities that happen under the banners of journalistic institutions.

Most reporters and editors think journalism means covering and uncovering news and telling people what they've learned. Their calling is to test hunches and hypotheses, gossip and conflicting accounts against the evidence, to organize and analyze and sometimes synthesize information into compelling stories.

What inspires journalists, however, is neither what pays the bills nor necessarily what draws audiences. The reporters' and editors' definition doesn't describe the business of most commercial American journalism, which is selling advertising. And it doesn't incorporate all the things the average American newspaper and some of its broadcast counterparts provide—commodity information (weather reports, sports statistics, stock tables, television listings), community bulletin boards (calendars, obituaries), community forums (letters to the editor, op-ed pages, call-in shows), entertainment (features, comics, trivia, crossword puzzles, people gossip).

Strip away some of the more profitable or popular items under this current umbrella, and you could strip away the means of paying for serious reporting aimed at mass audiences. One very important thing to understand about the new media world is just how easy such unbundling becomes.

Classified ads, that huge profit center for every newspaper, are particularly vulnerable. **Job listings services** have been among the first types of ads on-line, and newspapers have finally formed a **CareerPath** consortium to compete. It doesn't take much imagination to see how phone companies, already in the yellow-pages business, could move on-line and take away just enough newspaper classifieds business to seriously threaten the newsroom budget. (The major phone companies are already moving aggressively to sell mass Internet access.)

The on-line environment provides retail advertising, too, with a new possibility—speaking directly with potential clients. . . .

On the editorial side, private and public-sector entrepreneurs are nibbling away as well. **ESPNET SportsZone**—widely considered one of the best on-line publications—provides in-depth, multimedia features and interactive games as well as up-to-the-minute scores. **Intellicast** offers extensive current weather satellite maps and forecasts for every major city in the world. If you want to see what the president said last week, or last year, you can go directly to the **White House.** If you want to check out the tour schedule for your favorite band, you can turn to **Ticketmaster**—which one day could be the dominant events-listing service on the Internet.

The point is that journalists and journalistic institutions are not necessarily better qualified or better positioned to provide these and other basic services than a host of potential competitors. . . .

The electronic environment flattens everything—making a talented college sophomore's home page, say, seem equivalent to **CNN**'s—and this raises obvious questions about credibility of information. Still, people will have many more choices. There will surely be a strong market for much of what now falls under journalism's umbrella. But the playing field is wide open for new competitors.

Isn't Technology Just One of Many Pressing Problems for Journalism?

Yes, of course. "The journalist's challenge isn't the medium but the message," argues Ellen Hume in her Annenberg Washington Program report, **Tabloids, Talk Radio, and the Future of News.** "The problem is not the strength of the competition but the weakness of today's journalism, hobbled as it is by formulas, attitudes, and habits that alienate many customers."

Hume is certainly right that winning new audiences and holding onto old ones will require more than simply using a new medium to do the same old things. But she also knows it's a mistake to focus on changing journalistic conventions without understanding the way the technological and economic environment shapes them.

The fast-food part of the modern media diet—conflict, celebrities, and catastrophe—exists in part because of burgeoning technology. To be heard above the din of growing competition, much of journalism today finds itself in tabloid mode, shouting and trivializing to attract attention.

On the positive side, changing technologies force journalists to reexamine what they do and why. What exactly is news, and who has the right to report it? How do you make it useful? Do people select and absorb information differently in the on-line environment? Every new media service has to ask questions like these. The answers will create a new generation of journalistic conventions that could well affect old media as well. New technologies, therefore, give journalistic reformers an ideal opening to try new ideas.

What's Really New About This New Medium?

. . . Indeed, anyone who spends any significant time on the Web experiences how the old limitations of time, space, medium, and place seem to collapse magically. . . .

Now weekly magazines, such as *Time,* can have daily on-line editions, and daily newspapers, such as *USA Today,* can compete with TV and radio twenty-four hours a day. Indeed, immediacy is one of the new medium's advantages.

Newsholes and newscasts no longer have bounds. A local television station such as **WDIV** in Detroit can go on-line with a virtual tour of its studios, while **PBS's** *Frontline* can provide a schedule, a library detailing past broadcasts, and additional information about documentary topics.

Journalists used to work in one medium, and spent their lives mastering its nuances. In the future, when print, sound, and pictures are all simply digital bits, they may find themselves asking which tools are right for what stories, since their news organization may provide the same news in different media. Already, when, say, the poet Seamus Heaney wins the Nobel Prize for literature, a newspaper can turn a reader into a listener by connecting on-line to the **Internet Poetry archive,** where Heaney reads his poems in a resonate brogue.

These things seem rather straightforward. Less obvious are the somewhat contradictory ways new technologies change the journalists' relationship to geography.

Historically, American journalism was locally based. Slowly, technologies made it easier for many newspapers and local broadcasts to fill increasing amounts of space and time with commodity national and international news. Profit pressures, fueled by large absentee ownership, have also driven this trend.

Now, however, audiences can get news headlines from many sources. So in coming years the smart money in local journalism will give people more of a reason to need their product. That means investment in local news, rather than the editorial cutbacks now so prevalent.

At the same time, new media can nurture specialized interests, creating new interactive communities not based on geography. *The Indianapolis Star/News* **auto racing site** and the Cleveland *Plain Dealer*'s site featuring **The Rock and Roll Hall of Fame** illustrate how journalists may be able to create potential new markets that extend beyond their local base.

You have to look beyond journalists' efforts, however, to see how this trend could create a whole new media genre. Rich on-line environments such as **Netnoir** ("the cybergateway to Afrocentric culture," from politics to religion to sports) and **Rocktropolis** (a graphically sophisticated site devoted to rock music) could draw just the sorts of people advertisers most crave. Will on-line "places" such as these become the familiar, reliable "hometown papers" of the twenty-first century for young people no longer very attached to where they live?

What's new about new media is not limited to these examples. But let's catch our breath a moment.

Can Technology Help Solve Some of Journalism's Problems?

Yes, although it's easier to see how things fall apart than how they might reassemble. The problem is defining the problems.

Professor Neil Postman of New York University turns the question around in a way I find helpful: What is the problem to which the profession of journalism is the solution? (And what will you need to be like in twenty years to solve whatever problem you think journalism solves?)

The power of this formulation is that it forces journalists to think about the needs of their customers rather than the needs of journalists or the limits of current news manufacturing and distribution processes. Why, after all, do people need journalists?

Postman argues that journalists haven't adapted to the world they've helped create. In the nineteenth century, he says, the problem journalism solved was the scarcity of information; in the late twentieth century the problem has become information glut. The problem isn't getting more diverse forms of information quicker. "The problem," says Postman, "is how to decide what is significant, relevant information, how to get rid of unwanted information."

Too much of what journalists do adds to the clutter. Much of the new media does the same. The information glut, meanwhile, masks a corresponding scarcity—high-quality reporting and interpretation that helps people make sense of their world. "I think the scoop of the future will be the best interpretation, the best written account, the most descriptive account, but most of all the one that explains to you why you need to know it and what it means," said the veteran broadcaster Daniel Schorr as he watched the on-line world unfold before him at the Annenberg Washington Program last winter.

This, of course, is what much great journalism has always done. The difference is that journalists now have powerful new tools for dealing with the bias against understanding so prevalent in modern media.

Hypertext—which allows you to move easily among files and computers by pointing and clicking—really does connect people easily with information, ideas, and other people. Consider reading the latest story on Bosnia and linking to a timeline and a map to remind yourself what it means. Or imagine reading a book review, linking to the first chapter of the book, and ordering it on-line if you like. You can already do those things as part of *The Washington Post*'s Digital Ink service (which as we went to press was not yet accessible from the Internet).

Nora Paul of the **Poynter Institute** envisions a whole new genre, which she calls **annotative journalism.** Here, if, say, the president gave a speech, you might link to what he said before on the subject and to the counter-arguments of the critics. The innovative on-line magazine *Feed,* the Net's answer to *Harper's,* illustrates a version of this: somebody writes an **opinion** and then several people offer counter-arguments to specific points, via links that the reader can hit or not. Experiments in creating information webs challenge the often well-guarded borders of today's journalistic products. Sometimes, another journalist, or a university, or a nonprofit organization, will provide the best link—or a viewpoint that doesn't make it through today's mainstream media filter.

What's happened so far is probably quite tame compared to what's coming. And again, you have to look beyond pure journalistic efforts to see the potential. . . .

These experiments begin to hint at the really radical thing about new technologies: they enable people to have more control over what they want to know and when they want to know it. Already on the Internet, very different sorts of information providers are scrambling to create services to help you **choose a city to live in, buy a house,** or **purchase a car.** . . .

As people get used to asking for what they need, whole new businesses will be created to serve them. "The future belongs to neither the conduit or content players, but to those who control the filtering, searching, and sense-making tools we will rely on to navigate through the expanses of cyberspace," writes Paul Saffo, of the Institute for the Future, a non-profit think tank based in Menlo Park, California. Some of these tools may include software "agents" that explore on-line networks for us, alerting us that our favorite band will be playing nearby next month or that the airlines have just announced a sale. Other new businesses are already competing to become the next generation's Internet version of *TV Guide,* as capital flows into on-line indexing and searching systems such as **Yahoo** and **Magellan.**

Eventually money may also flow to information brokers who will charge to find the information you need. If I'm diagnosed with breast cancer, I'd be willing to pay a fee to receive the best recent news reports, the Web-site references, and the addresses of mailing lists and newsgroups where patients offer each other support and information.

The great on-line opportunity is finding ways to inform people more deeply—*and* save them time. The question is whether people will turn to journalists or to someone else in ten or twenty years, when they need a better information filter. Journalists, who have already lost so much authority and standing in the culture, are going to have to re-earn their right to both.

If This Is a New Medium No One Yet Understands, Shouldn't Journalists Focus on Preserving Traditions and Values?

"Do I really think we need to change what it is we are? On the contrary, I think the only thing we know for sure is that we can't afford to change what we are," *The New York Times's* Arthur Sulzberger, Jr., told a gathering sponsored by the Nieman Foundation last spring. "We've got to keep our center. We've got to know what it is that we do, what are our core competencies, and other fancy terms being used these days in business, and build on those cores. That leaves lots and lots and lots of room for lots of other people to do very interesting and exciting things, and they're going to do them, and *mazel tov.*"

I want to believe the journey is going to be that simple and clear for journalists, but I can't.

The reason is that journalism institutions have long played a role that transcended providing information. Facts are the tangible product, but other things—such as a favorite writer, commentator, or host, connection to a community, or access to experiences outside our own—are often what bring people back time and again to a hometown newspaper, a favorite broadcast show, or a niche magazine.

Content is *people,* as well as information, and new media change the equation. For all the talk of interactivity, I find very few journalists who really understand its import.

Last year, by one count, 95 billion e-mail messages were sent in the United States—a number that exceeded the number of ordinary messages sent through the U.S. mail. Digital technologies really do make it easy to contact friends and strangers alike. That means they make things happen that were not possible before.

For instance, last spring, a moving exchange took place on-line as Tom Mandel died. He had spent eighteen months trying to build community at

Time magazine's America Online experiment, and for many years he'd been an active participant in the WELL, the prototypical cyberspace community. As cancer ate his insides up, Mandel shared his feelings—and received an outpouring of support from people he had met and others who had known him only on-line. Time Inc.'s **Pathfinder** Internet site has edited and preserved **the exchanges that took place between Mandel and his friends.** Reading Mandel in memorial, watching that kind of intimacy and community form on-line, changed how I thought about the role of journalism.

"A journalist with little on-line experience tends to think in terms of stories, news value, public service, and things that are good to read," writes Melinda McAdams, in her **account of helping start *The Washington Post's* on-line service.** "But a person with a lot of on-line experience thinks more about connections, organization, movement within and among sets of information, and communication among different people."

Journalists are often so wrapped up in the quite legitimate worry that responding to e-mail will drain time from reporting that they miss the larger point: the most successful on-line sites, such as America Online's The Motley Fool, create a dynamic community that makes you want to return again and again. The journalistic stars of the future may well include those who delight in a new kind of media theater, who enjoy facilitating discussions or figuring out how to involve audiences meaningfully in gathering information. . . .

Where can people listen to each other? Where can they be heard? Where can they meet new people? The answer to these questions could turn out to be as important a factor in the long-term survival of some journalism institutions as the quality of their information.

Who Will Win and Who Will Lose?

At last fall's American Magazine Conference, the president and chief executive of Time, Inc., Don Logan, was asked whether electronic publishing would be an important moneymaker in the next five years. "To be perfectly honest," he said, "I don't have a clue."

Neither do I, obviously. It's a whole lot easier to dream up editorial models for new media than to create the business models to pay for them. . . . And it's probably a whole lot cheaper and easier to create something interesting than it is to market it in the growing cacophony. Still, we all need some way to grasp what's happening. It helps me to make some key distinctions: between journalists and the institutions that currently employ them; between old journalism brand names and new media innovators; and between different sorts of markets.

Let's begin with journalists. It's hard to imagine a world in which reporting, writing, visual, design, and editing skills won't continue to be needed. The question is who will employ journalists? And to do exactly what?

Michael Kinsley became one of the first well-known journalists to jump on the new-media wagon when he announced last fall he was moving to Washington—state, that is—to start a new on-line magazine for **Microsoft.** Reporters laid off by old media companies may be snapped up by local Internet providers or commercial on-line services, such as America Online, which in September launched a news and information network, Digital City, so far available only in Washington, D.C.

And in an economy increasingly dominated by independent contractor relationships, more journalists could find themselves in business for themselves. Famous names—say, Barbara Walters or Russell Baker—might be able to sell themselves to audiences directly. Others may find themselves specializing in a particular skill or a particular subject matter, and collaborating with other specialists on a project-by-project basis (the way Hollywood operates now). Another model might be ***The American Reporter,*** an early on-line cooperative effort, "owned by the writers whose work it features."

Many journalists, of course, will continue to work for the big newspapers and networks. Those institutions have formidable marketing advantages, but, on the other hand, they have to fight large bureaucracies and decades of institutional habits to try new things. Their new competitors can simply start from scratch, as Apple Computer, Adobe Corporation, and the Borders books and music chain did when they combined forces and launched a new on-line magazine, ***Salon,*** edited by an experienced journalist. (Borders is distributing millions of bookmarks promoting the effort.) Indeed it's far more likely that the next ten years will produce another Ted Turner or Michael Bloomberg than a wildly innovative *New York Times*.

New and old ventures alike have to face challenges posed by different types of markets (national, international, and local; mass audience and special interest). Surely only a few major mass media organizations—Reuters, Microsoft/NBC, News Corp./MCI, Disney/ABC, Time Warner/CNN—will fight it out for widespread international reach as headline services. And all of these may one day find themselves facing unexpected new competition (Netscape? AT&T?). At the same time, the few excellent national-news brand names, such as ***The New York Times*** and ***The Wall Street Journal*** (both of whom are moving onto the World Wide Web), face quite unique problems and opportunities in serving their increasingly elite audiences.

While most media attention will be focused on these big players, much of the most interesting and innovative activity will take place in narrower niche markets often aimed at smaller audiences. And the most important question will be whether general-interest local and regional news operations (new or old) can generate enough profits to pay for excellent reporting, which a multimedia world will make both more expensive and even more essential. New local business models are likely to evolve hybrids that were previously unimaginable. In addition to *The Boston Globe* experiment already mentioned, innovations include The New Century Network, a major new joint venture by some of the nation's largest newspaper companies to support local newspapers in providing and sharing on-line content; **Infinet,** a joint Knight-Ridder/Landmark Communications project to offer Internet access in local communities across the country; and new journalistic umbrellas such as the Raleigh *News & Observer*'s **Nando.net,** which provides new bundles of specialized content and services. . . . One longed-for innovation so far remains elusive — that secure transactions on-line will yield whole new profit lines (calendar listings tied to ticket sales, for instance).

And what about citizens and consumers? Will they win? Those who can afford it are likely to be better informed, in less time, than ever. But the quality gap is likely to continue to grow, with mass-audience products under ever-intensifying pressure to succumb to entertainment values. The issue, as ever, is who will be left behind.

What Can Journalists Do to Avoid Being Left Behind?

Certainly one can paint a scenario in which consumers really don't want interactivity, no one can figure out how to make the new medium profitable, huge technical problems cannot be solved, and legal and ethical issues such as censorship, liability, privacy, and copyright slow on-line growth to a crawl.

But I wouldn't bet on it. The wisest strategy, I believe, is to remain committed to high-quality reporting and storytelling — and to invest seriously in understanding new media. That doesn't mean you have to take on the near-impossible task of mastering all the changing currents and cross-currents. As I was polishing this piece at the turn of the year, for instance, there was no way to know that the big telecommunications reform bill would be passed a few weeks later, or whether the new Java programming language would live up to the predictions that it will transform the World Wide Web. But we still have to keep our eye on the big picture.

Everything I've learned argues that digital technologies will continue to grow, eventually creating a new medium that will force all previous communications media to redefine themselves, just as radio had to do when television came along. The microprocessor has been marching slowly and steadily into every corner of our lives for a half-century already — the average new automobile today has more computer power than the spaceship that went to the moon just a generation ago—and it shows no signs of slow-ing down.

Of my many fears about the future of journalism, this is the one that scares me the most: that journalists and their companies will keep their eyes on the horizon of the next deadline, the next paycheck, or the next quarterly shareholder report and fail to understand the horizon of history, which could yet yield a journalistic renaissance.

I worry that now-profitable journalism companies will join the on-line fray, then pull out or cut back too soon, when they don't get immediate re-sults or definitive answers. I worry that the profits that now support the great journalism a democracy needs will disappear into niche businesses run by people with little interest in journalism but more imagination or staying power. I worry that too many of the best journalists will cling to the past, which will work about as well as it did for the guilds in the Industrial Revolution. And I worry that the most successful innovators—the ones who will write the rules for the new medium—will be technophiles who don't give a damn about the difference between a news story and an ad and who think the First Amendment is a license to print money.

The horizon may be long, but, actually, time is short. The choice is simple: follow, or lead.

Questions for Critical Thinking and Discussion

1. Fulton makes several predictions about what journalism will look like in light of new technological innovations. Based upon your experience and ideas, how accurate do you think her predictions are?

2. The author proposes that in order to affect the future of journalism, journalists must be players in the game. She emphasizes that news reporters must become new-technology savvy as quickly as possible or else technophiles will be the innovators. The fact is, technophiles were the innovators of radio and television in their early days. What lessons can we learn from the histories of previous technologies?

3. How can consumers (users) of news media contribute to the mainte-nance of credible sources and truth in journalism?

10

Shop Talk at Thirty: A Look at Asians as Portrayed in the News

JOANN LEE

Joann Lee is co-director of journalism at Queens College in New York.

Lee examines media portrayals of Asians because, as she writes, "Media images are so important to our construction of opinions and attitudes; they play a key role in not only how society sees Asians as a minority but how Asians see themselves in the context of larger society."

During the past four years, the number of hate crimes against Asian-Americans as reported by newspapers has increased dramatically.

From San Francisco to New York, the story is similar: Asians are attacked or made the target of racial slurs.

Newspapers attribute this in part to the tough economic times. When jobs are hard to come by and the economy is in a recession, Asians, regardless of their ethnicity, economic class, educational background or immigration status, are seen as one, a group of people most identifiable in terms of skin color.

Race is a uniform that cannot be hidden by economic achievement, the neighborhood where one lives or the kind of car one drives. Asians by virtue of their race are increasingly targets of bias.

A U.S. Civil Rights Commission study released Feb. 28, 1992, finds that violence aimed at the 7.3 million Asian-Americans in the United States (the fastest-growing ethnic group in the country) is "a serious national problem."

Two days before the commission's report was released, a Japanese-American was stabbed to death in front of his home by a disgruntled unemployed Caucasian, who indicated that he blamed Asians for his economic problems.

Media images are so important to our construction of opinions and attitudes; they play a key role in not only how society sees Asians as a minority but how Asians see themselves in the context of the larger society.

A look at the types of stories that are being reported yields a pattern of repetitive themes and stereotypes. The stereotypes are well known: Asians as

This article first appeared in *Editor and Publisher* (April 30, 1994), Volume 127(18), pages 56–46.

the hard-working minority, as a docile, meek people. The themes are also familiar: Chinatowns as exotic ghettos where crime is rampant; gangs that kill indiscriminately; and a flood of new immigrants who are straining our resources and taking away jobs.

The era of on-line data searches has ushered in a new way to look for these patterns. Going through such data systems as Nexis, which has a collection of more than 350 full-text information sources from U.S. and overseas newspapers, magazines, journals, newsletters, and wire service and broadcast transcripts, it is possible to get a bird's-eye view of the media landscape.

One can look at not only what types of stories are being printed about Asians by the various mainstream publications nationwide; it is possible to get a solid sense of how various minority communities are covered.

For instance, the on-line system at the City University of New York provides news clippings published by 27 major newspapers nationwide. In it, I found 2,007 entries on Asian-Americans filed since 1989. Out of curiosity, I searched the system for the word "African-Americans" and found that more than twice that number—5,282 entries—were listed. A search of "Hispanic Americans" yielded 4,710 stories.

In short, it is possible to find out what key media news organizations, among them the *New York Times, Los Angeles Times, Washington Post, Wall Street Journal, San Francisco Chronicle, Boston Globe, Chicago Tribune* and *Christian Science Monitor,* are printing when it comes to Asian-Americans. It is a telling look, indeed.

It is important to note that the majority of Asian-Americans live in California, Hawaii and New York; there are also sizable Chinatowns in Boston, Seattle and Chicago.

It is possible therefore to access through on-line data retrieval most of the newspapers located in cities where there is a large Asian population.

As such, the articles and information available and gathered reflect a relatively comprehensive record of what is (and is not) being written in mainstream newspapers about Asian-Americans in just about all corners of the country today.

By far, the largest number of stories on Asian-Americans was reported in connection to aspects of immigration, crime and gang violence.

The interesting point, though, is that Asians are more likely to be mentioned in "the news" when the context is of majority social interest. The news angle or event oftentimes must have social significance for the social majority.

For instance, the 50th anniversary of the bombing of Pearl Harbor triggered general interest in certain kinds of Asian-American stories. As part of the event, there was a noticeable increase in coverage about Japanese-Americans as well as stories on Japan-bashing.

Along the same vein, news about Asian-Americans coming from a federal or government source seems to have a greater likelihood of getting nationwide play.

For instance, the Civil Rights Commission's 1992 report about discrimination against Asian-Americans generated coverage in papers from coast to coast.

The angles that various newspapers chose ranged from the boycott of Korean stores by blacks to Asian-bashing, anti-Asian prejudice and discrimination.

But the news event that triggered the coverage clearly came from outside the Asian-American community.

What this says is that news about Asian-Americans often comes from outside the community. In other words, parties other than Asians talking about Asian-related issues seem to be defining what the news is. News from those sources has a much greater chance of being carried by the mainstream media.

Tangentially, when Asians are written about in the mainstream press, the news focus is often on how their presence affects the greater society around them.

For instance, one reads that "white shrimpers are at odds in Alabama with 1,000 Vietnamese, Cambodian and Laotian refugees."

Stories about the Hmongs relocating to pockets of Wisconsin, Colorado, Alabama, Georgia and California invariably deal with friction with the local community. (The Hmongs are among 100,000 Southeast Asians who arrived in the United States after they were forced to flee Laos in the 1970s because of the Vietnam War.)

Some papers have written about their problems in attempting to settle in the United States, but for the most part, their plight is brought to light mainly in terms of the conflicts created by their move into American communities.

In education and work ethics, Asians are often linked with phrases such as "model minority."

Increasingly, stories are appearing to pierce that myth, which is a good thing. But in the area of crime, it's a different story.

The stereotype of Asians as members of gangs/tongs/organized crime grows, as attested to by the types of stories reported.

Example: United Press International ran a story in January 1992 about raids focusing on Asian-American gambling networks. The story, filed from Fort Smith, Ark., reported that federal agents seized safe deposit boxes suspected to be holding proceeds of a "nationwide Asian-American crime network."

Along with the federal raid, what probably made this story newsworthy were the buzzwords "nationwide Asian-American crime network."

Whatever the rationale, crime is clearly a big chunk of the news diet. In this sense, stories about crimes involving Asians are not unfair. But what is clear in many stories about Asians and crime is that Asians more often are portrayed as suspects rather than as victims.

It is as though Asians as victims are not as newsworthy as Asians as perpetrators; only when the story involves gangs or the perception of Asians somehow threatening the system is it news of general interest to the mainstream press.

Group Formed for Asian Journalists

The Asian Studies Center of the Heritage Foundation, a conservative think tank in Washington, has formed the Washington Roundtable for the Asia-Pacific Press, a foreign correspondents association for Washington-based journalists from Asia and the Pacific Basin.

Membership also is open to U.S. reporters covering Asian affairs, said executive director Julian Weiss, who headed a similar organization that folded in the 1980s.

Questions for Critical Thinking and Discussion

1. The category called Asians is made up of a very wide variety of people from many distinct (and often dissimilar) cultural backgrounds or countries, such as China, Japan, Malaysia, Korea, and Vietnam. Why do you think these people are "lumped together" or categorized in this "Asian" way? That is, what characteristics are used to define membership to this category?

2. If there is such a great number of Asians in our society, why aren't they better represented in the media? Wouldn't it be to the media's economic advantage to reach as many people as possible?

Los Angeles *Times* Publisher Mark Willes in Praise of the "Cereal Killer"

DAVID PLOTZ

David Plotz is a senior writer for Slate *magazine.*

In this article, Plotz presents the latest murderer of the newspaper industry: the corporate bean counter. He profiles Mark Willes, former executive of General Mills (thus the "cereal killer" nickname). With only two years of newspaper experience, Willes was recently named publisher of the Los Angeles Times *and has been making big changes to the newspaper. Plotz analyzes the effects those changes are having on journalism and society.*

Newspapers are always dying, and someone is always killing them. Radio was supposed to bury them. So was television. So was their aging readership. So was *USA Today*. So was the Internet.

The latest murderer: the corporate bean counter. He breaches the Chinese Wall between business and editorial, cares more about the stock price than about the front-page lead, favors stories that focus groups want to read, and talks constantly about "product." To hear critics tell it, Times Mirror CEO Mark Willes, who just named himself publisher of the Los Angeles *Times*, is of that ilk. The greatest newspaper of the West is now being run by a man whose newspaper experience totals two years (much of it spent closing papers) and who passed the bulk of his career as an executive of General Mills, a breakfast-cereal company (or rather, a breakfast-cereal company, for chrissakes!).

[V]irtually every newspaper in the country has married some editorial and business functions, but Willes would go further. Rather than limiting business-editorial contact to the top of the masthead, he proposes to have each section of the *Times* (sports, business, etc.) operate as a more or less autonomous unit. Each will have its own "minipublisher" who will set profitability goals and consult with editors on general content (though not, Willes insists, on specific stories). Media critics are aghast. The *Wall Street Journal* calls it "a revolution in the newspaper business."

This article first appeared in *Slate.Com,* an online magazine (October 18, 1997).
www.slate.com

Willes is also pushing "hero" stories and civic journalism, the kind of pandering to readers that infuriates editors. He suggests that the *Times* introduce new sections aimed at Hispanic and female readers. Times staffers gripe that such sections would only ghettoize minority readers. Shelby Coffey, the *Times'* editor of nine years, quit . . . amid speculation that he couldn't stomach Willes' changes.

[T]he newspaper business has always been romantic, and few papers have been more romantic than the *Times*. For most of its life, it was a right-wing rag that rooted unapologetically for Republican politicians and local businessmen. Then in 1960, Otis Chandler, the surfing, antique-car–collecting scion of the Chandler family (which owns most of Times Mirror), took over as publisher. During the next two decades, Chandler and his editors transformed the *Times* into one of the best papers in the country. They hired talented writers by the score, ran the longest stories in the industry, and won Pulitzer after Pulitzer. The *Times* was profligate, editorially bold, and profitable. Otis Chandler's *Times*—like the Sulzbergers' *New York Times*, the Grahams' *Washington Post*, and all great newspapers—was as much grand adventure as business.

But Otis Chandler retired, the *Times* lost 300,000 subscribers, the stock went south, and Chandler's more conservative relatives demanded higher profits. The era of newspaper romance slipped away in Los Angeles (as it did everywhere else). Willes seems to embody the capitalist rationalism that has replaced it. A Utah native, he first made a name for himself in the late '60s as a conservative economist, touting "rational expectations" theory long before it became fashionable. In 1977, at age 35, he became the youngest president of a Federal Reserve Bank (in Minneapolis). In 1980, he jumped to General Mills, where he eventually served as president, chief operating officer, and vice chairman. General Mills, his critics note, is a company where marketing, rather than content, is king.

[T]wo years ago, the Chandler family picked him to run their $3.4-billion-but-still-sickly media company. (In addition to its flagship *Times*, Times Mirror owns half a dozen other newspapers, including the Hartford *Courant*, the Baltimore *Sun*, and *Newsday;* several magazines; and medical and legal publishers.) Within weeks, Willes had made himself one of the most detested men in journalism. In a now infamous interview, he compared newspapers to cereal. Then he shuttered the venerable Baltimore *Evening Sun* and *New York Newsday*, the much admired, much unread, much unprofitable downtown sister to *Newsday*. He also fired 175 members of the *Times* editorial staff. The paper, known as the "velvet coffin" because of its high pay and cushy working conditions, had not laid off reporters for decades. Predictably, Willes was nicknamed "Cereal Killer" and "Cap'n Crunch." Wall

Street loved what the newsroom loathed. Times Mirror's costs plummeted. Profits soared. The stock has tripled from $18 when Willes arrived to nearly $60 today—the best performance of any big media company. Publishing analysts say that Times Mirror is now one of the healthiest firms in the industry. The Chandler family has profited from the company's rising dividends and stock price.

[*T*]*imes*-philes do have some reason to worry about Willes as publisher. The idea of having ad salesmen and "minipublishers" help plan editorial sections is terrifying to anyone who's ever met an ad salesman. "Heroic" and civic journalism do often degenerate into idiotic rah-rah cheerleading. A push for shorter stories—also said to be in the works—may well vanquish the elegant, comprehensive (OK, long-winded) pieces for which the paper is famous. ("We'll just have to be famous for something else," snaps one *Times* vet.) But there is a more fruitful way to look at Willes: He is the first high-profile newspaper man in a long time who actually believes in newspapers. Newspaper profits may be at record highs, but the newspaper Zeitgeist is gloomy. Circulation has barely risen since World War II, and it's been falling for five years. Newspaper reporters increasingly feel themselves irrelevant—marginalized by TV news and the Internet, ignored by a younger generation of nonreaders.

[W]illes is an optimist. He's a proselytizer of newspapers. According to those who know him, he has learned why newspapers are a public trust since his unfortunate cereal interview. (He has forsworn cereal analogies.) Other papers are shrinking content; Willes wants to add sections and features. Other papers fear controversy; he proposes newspaper "crusades." His ideas may be terrible—some of them certainly are terrible—but at least they are new. Willes' boldest goal: to raise the *Times* circulation from 1 million to 1.5 million. No one thinks he can do it. Industry analyst John Morton says it would be "a miracle" if he pulled it off. But everyone wants him to try, because only new readers will save the industry in the long run. Willes recently halved the price of the *Times* to 25 cents to reach nonsubscribers. He's launched a huge ad campaign. The *Times* added 47,000 readers last year, more than any newspaper in the country—and about the same number the *New York Times* lost. To add half a million readers, or even half that number, Willes will need to steal subscribers from the 18 other newspapers in the Los Angeles area, including the Orange County *Register* and the Los Angeles *Daily News*. This raises an appetizing prospect. The *Daily News* is up for sale. Rupert Murdoch is rumored to be interested in buying it and turning it into a West Coast version of the *New York Post*. A circulation-hungry Willes vs. the rapacious Murdoch: That's just the kind of fight the American newspaper industry needs.

Questions for Critical Thinking and Discussion

1. Plotz admits that Willes has made changes that have increased profitability, but at what cost to journalism (credibility, content, etc.)?

2. Plotz writes that Willes "suggests that the *Times* introduce new sections aimed at Hispanic and female readers. *Times* staffers gripe that such sections would only ghettoize minority readers." How does creating special sections lead to ghettoization of minority readers?

3. Do you think Willes should be deemed "one of the most detested men in journalism"? Why or why not?

12

Holiness, Royalty, and Fame

JAMES MARTIN

James Martin, S.J., has been studying at the Weston Jesuit School of Theology in Cambridge, Massachusetts, in preparation for ordination to the priesthood. He is the editor of the book How Can I Find God? *(Triumph Books, 1997) and the winner of two Catholic Press Association awards for his writing in* America. *Mr. Martin is currently completing a book about his experiences working with refugees in East Africa.*

In this article, Martin compares news coverage of the deaths of Princess Diana and Mother Teresa. He discusses how these women were unique, cultural icons and how their media coverage reflected (or perhaps even created) their personas.

"Mother Teresa died a few hours ago," said Tom Brokaw in the middle of his coverage of another funeral a few weeks ago. "She was a friend of Princess Diana's."

There you have television news in a nutshell. Mother Teresa of Calcutta, a "living saint," one of the holiest women of our time—of any time—a Nobel Prize-winner, servant of the poor, missionary extraordinare, reduced to a walk-on in the life of the Princess of Wales.

But before you suspect a wholesale condemnation of the press for failing to cover Mother Teresa's funeral with the same verve as Diana's, we need to admit the radically different ways their lives ended. The short life of the Princess of Wales concluded horribly, in a gruesome and avoidable accident in a dark tunnel near the Seine, which is one reason for the attending shock, horror and attention afforded her tragic death. When Mother Teresa died, on the other hand, there was comparatively little shock—sadness, of course, that the world had lost perhaps its greatest contemporary saint, but also a certain gratitude and even contentment for the full and active life she had led for God. In part, this is the reason for the skewed media coverage of the coincident deaths.

Still, the often lackadaisical coverage of Mother Teresa's death, coming as it did in the middle of funeral preparations at Westminster, was remarkable even in an age noted for its celebrity worship. Tom Brokaw's comment

This article first appeared in *America* (October 4, 1997), Volume 177(9), pages 26, 28.

was but one example of many. Mark Harris wrote trenchantly (and accurately) in *Entertainment Weekly* (9/19), ". . . when news broke of Mother Teresa's passing, all of television paused for the approximate length of a sigh before getting back on the gravy train." On the day of Mother Teresa's funeral, *The New York Times* featured a minuscule front-page story on the event above a much larger column announcing: "Diana's Death Resonates Most Among Women in Therapy." Oh.

The striking contrasts between the coverage of the Princess and the saint were difficult to miss. Like many papers, *The New York Times* ran acres of worshipful articles about the Princess of Wales in the days leading up to her funeral. All well and good. But that same paper's coverage of Mother Teresa's life had an entirely different edge. Usually buried in the middle of the first section, articles about the Saint of the Gutters invariably mentioned her "sometimes controversial" teachings (presumably her pro-life stand, not the Gospels). Also inserted were snipings from one Indian journalist (whom the *Times* must have struggled mightily to find) that Mother Teresa had used the poor of Calcutta to—get this—advance her career. Somehow, though, Princess Diana's death insulated her from this type of criticism. Even Diana's friends would have admitted that she cannily used the media to her own advantage, though it was apparently deemed insensitive to mention this before her funeral.

The New York Times, in fact, continued its criticism of Mother Teresa even after her funeral. While other papers featured more positive coverage ("Mother of Poor Laid to Rest" read *The Boston Globe*'s one-inch headline), the *Times* stuck to its often snide tone. "Pomp Bars Poor From Mother Teresa's Rites" was how the *Times* summarized her funeral on its front page, suggesting perhaps that Mother Teresa herself was responsible for barring the poor from the liturgy. Inside the paper one could read about crowds that were "sparse" and "smaller than expected." (There was little mention of the hundreds of thousands who filed past her coffin in the motherhouse in the days before the funeral.) There were a number of important diplomats, but "not as many as expected," sniffed the *Times*.

The main difference in the coverage of Diana and Mother Teresa seemed to be that many felt obliged, in the case of Mother Teresa, to liven up their coverage with an abundance of criticism. This was, to put it mildly, far from the case with Diana. In short, while the Princess of Wales was laid to rest as a saint, Mother Teresa was exposed as a "complicated figure." Does this strike anyone as somewhat backwards?

For their coverage of the liturgy in Calcutta, ABC News decided to supplement their experienced "color" commentators with Christopher Hitchens, author of an execrable book on Mother Teresa entitled *The Missionary Position*, which attacked her for consorting with dictators and other less-than-perfect characters. (A certain carpenter from Nazareth, you will recall, was accused of similar crimes.) Mr. Hitchens also accused Mother Teresa of using the poor as a springboard for media attention. But Mr. Hitchens, with a book on Mother Teresa, a PBS documentary on Mother Teresa and articles on Mother Teresa in *The Nation* and *Vanity Fair,* seems quite content to use her as his own convenient springboard, even after her death. Mr. Hitchens' efforts, however, are not assisting many poor people.

At times, it seemed, the story of the Saint of the Gutters was all but buried under an avalanche of media attention for Diana. On the other hand, some noted that Mother Teresa's funeral itself might not have received as much attention as it did (live coverage, that is) had the news media not been so aware of their excesses with Diana. That is, they felt guilty. Indeed it seemed that the coverage of Mother Teresa's passing consciously aped that of the Princess of Wales, providing for some odd moments. One anchorman noted with apparent approval that a new song had been written for Mother Teresa to accompany the tune of Elton John's "Candle in the Wind" à la Princess Diana. It was called "Flame in the Gutter," a considerably less felicitous title.

But perhaps the fine art of balancing the coverage in such an extraordinary week would tax even the most thoughtful of television executives. Too much for Diana? Too little for Mother Teresa? It's difficult to say. And who knows if Mother Teresa herself might not have enjoyed the timing. Recently a friend remarked how upset she was that Mother Teresa had died so shortly after Diana. "What horrible timing!" she said, articulating the same reaction I had heard from a number of Catholics. "Now no one will notice!" But here, after all, was a woman who spent her life among the unnoticed, worked for decades in anonymity, shunned honors and said that she was "personally unworthy" of the Nobel Prize. So it was comforting to think that dying at a time that almost ensured she would receive as little attention as possible, while frustrating for her many admirers, might have pleased Mother Teresa immensely.

Questions for Critical Thinking and Discussion

1. James Martin analyzes the differences in the coverage of the deaths of Mother Teresa and Princess Diana. How do you think the coverage was handled? Do you think the coverage was fair and/or appropriate?

2. Do you think the juxtaposition of these two women was necessary? What value or purpose would comparisons between these women provide our culture?

chapter 5

Magazines

Girl Wide Web

NEVA CHONIN

Neva Chonin is Assistant Editor for the San Francisco Bay Guardian, *where she writes about music, arts, and culture.*

In this article, Chonin points out that print feminist media targeted at women and girls have always existed, but now they are more easily (and cheaply) produced as zines (on-line magazines). Thus new technology has made feminist messages more accessible. Chonin provides a general overview of woman-oriented networks and zines as well as a specific look at Maxi, *"strong, but feminine" and "the most absorbing girl-zine on the Web."*

Cyndi Lauper probably overstated the case when she sang "Girls Just Wanna Have Fun" back in 1983, but she did inadvertently voice some emerging truths for many girls coming of age in the wake of the '70s women's movement: mainly, that wearing makeup didn't preclude talking politics; that the fashion-conscious needn't become fashion victims; and that femininity and feminism weren't necessarily antipodes.

If only the mainstream media were as wise. Though femme feminists, lipstick lesbians, and flamboyant riot grrrls have ruled underground pop culture for years, magazines catering to hip young women have been rare to nonexistent since the demise of the original incarnation of *Sassy*. Startup costs for a publication remain formidable at a time when most women still lack the financial resources and connections to launch a fledgling enterprise. Many have responded with their own homemade zines, which are often inspired but woefully limited in circulation.

Now those looking for cool, women-based reading material have a third option. With some technical savvy and a few good friends, increasing numbers of women are launching online magazines with funky-but-chic graphics, vast editorial space, and virtually unlimited distribution. In a medium known for its gratuitous sexism, girl-zines are popping up like mushrooms, boasting brassy, facetious titles like *gUrl*, *Bust*, and *Postfeminist Playground*. And in an indie playing field dominated by publications from the East

This article first appeared in the A&E (arts and entertainment) section of the San Francisco *Bay Guardian* on-line edition (February 11, 1998). www.sfbg.com/AandE/32/19/maxi.html

Coast, San Francisco's *Maxi*, which launched at www.maximag.com in October 1996, is the star player.

Consumer Couture

On a rainy Sunday evening, *Maxi*'s West Coast founders—Janelle Brown, Molly Wright Steenson, and Rosemary Pepper (creative designer Heather Irwin works out of her home in Brooklyn, N.Y.)—are meeting in the apartment Pepper shares with her boyfriend, journalist Nick Tangborn, and their schnauzer, Estrogen N. Tonic. The *Maxi* machine is just kicking into high gear again after an autumn in which two of its editors were out of the country—Steenson in Bali, Brown in Thailand.

Helping herself to an Anchor Steam and a handful of potato chips, Brown excitedly describes an afternoon shopping at Circuit City. "There are these three teenage girls: one's got her raver clothing on, the other one's got this big, fuzzy fur coat, and one's got pink hair and platforms," she laughs. "And they're all running around going, 'Whoa, check out the female character in Virtua Fighter! She's so cool!' I thought that was really evocative of how girls are changing—I can't imagine having done that when I was 14. There wasn't this idea that women could be powerful, fighting creatures to be admired."

It was for girls like the Circuit City posse that *Maxi* was created. "We believed that if we built it, they would come," Steenson says, nibbling dreamily on a potato chip. "And they have."

In fact, they've come in droves: the site now averages 175,000 hits a month as surfers flock to read content that's girl-positive, politically savvy, and equally conversant in the latest shade of MAC lipstick and the pitfalls of patriarchal hegemony. Steenson, 26, says, "We grew up in this age of absolutely nothing. Fully Reaganomic. There was nothing I wanted to read, nothing that represented me. I'm smart and I care about feeding my intelligence. I'm an *Utne* and a *Harper's* reader. But there was nowhere where I could read about fashion and also find a decent critical article from a feminist standpoint that didn't take too much of a hard-core '70s-feminist-academic-radical approach."

Not that younger feminists don't feel indebted to '70s feminism, Brown, 24, adds—but in the '90s women's needs have changed. "A lot of what feminism did in the '70s was to reject the patriarchy and traditional women's roles, and ever since then there's been a floundering as to what a woman would be outside of that. And in the '90s, whether we like it or not, a lot of what's shaped culture and how women define themselves is consumerism. What we want to do with *Maxi* is to help women accept the multifaceted nature of being part of consumer culture, how to embrace it and embody it while being smart about it at the same time."

Steenson asserts, poker-faced, *"Maxi* is the manifestation of growing up watching *Free to Be You and Me.* Marlo Thomas would be proud."

Bitch Is Back

Maxi's roots run back to 1995, when *HotWired* coworkers Brown and Irwin decided that it was time for a little female-friendly content on the Web and teamed up with publisher Lisa Jervis to create an online version of her incendiary print zine, *Bitch.* "I had no background in graphics at the time," confesses Irwin, 27. "But I'd always been interested in design. It was really a learn-as-you-go experience." One of the Web's first independent women's zines, *Bitch* online quickly developed an avid readership with its critiques of pop culture and loud, rambunctious graphic design. Still, when Irwin relocated to New York and differences arose over editorial direction, *Bitch* deep-sixed in 1996.

Meanwhile, Pepper and Steenson were plotting their own online forum for cutting-edge commentary. "I was always complaining about how women's magazines sucked," laughs Pepper, 30. "It was like I only bought them so I could just throw them across the room. I wanted something that appealed to women in a way that was part educational, part entertaining, and part inspiring. So I decided to start my own, and nothing would stop me."

Pepper and Steenson met for their first brainstorming session at Sweet Inspiration on Market Street. "We were talking about things over tea and shortbread, and I was just saying, 'We should really talk to Janelle Brown,' when she walked in the door," Steenson remembers.

"It was fortuitous," Brown says. "I was just stopping in to buy a cookie."

A few cross-country conference calls later, Irwin joined the team, and the four women began strategizing a zine with a consumer-culture angle that focused less on polemics and more on critiques and witty explorations of gender politics in media and the arts. "We wanted it to be the smarter older sister of *Bitch*," Irwin explains, as her six-month-old son, Sam, squalls over the long-distance phone line. "Because I had no formal training when we started *Bitch*, it was a little raw. By the time *Maxi* started, I had refined my skills to the point where we could have a site that was warm, friendly, and easily navigated."

The change between the two zines can be summed up by their tag lines; while *Bitch* touted a "Feminist response to pop culture," *Maxi* declared itself "Pro-woman, post-grrl." "The grrrl thing has been appropriated too much," Steenson explains, "and it's also like, OK, been there, done that: angry feminism sitting out there saying fuck you to men. I think it's done wonders for the world; but we wanted to be positive, to show how you can take what you've learned from the grrrls and from being angry and move forward, take it to the next step. But 'post-grrl' doesn't mean 'anti-grrl.' We have riot grrrl to thank for the simple fact that *Maxi* can exist and do what it does."

Maxi's subject matter doesn't differ much from many riot grrrl zines of the early '90s—albeit with more of a sense of humor. The real difference comes in the size of its audience. Whereas a paper zine could only reach as far as the shelves of local independent stores or small mail-order houses, an online publication can reach ten thousand readers in a matter of minutes. "And this is without corporate sponsorship," Pepper notes proudly. "We're competing with sites that have giant budgets and advertising, but we have a loyal readership. This is a wholly volunteer effort; it just doesn't get more do-it-yourself than us."

Asked to explain the sanitary napkin–inspired moniker, Pepper laughs. "It came out of the blue. Janelle suggested it because I was complaining that there weren't enough words in the English language that were both feminine and strong."

By their own polls, *Maxi* has not only recaptured *Bitch*'s readership but broadened its audience to include everyone from professionals in their 40s to high school students. Most readers fall in the 22-to-30 age bracket and are college educated, technologically informed, career oriented, and unabashedly into fashion.

"I think the gap between teens and twentysomethings is closing," Brown says. "Teens are getting adult a lost faster, picking up the cultural accoutrements a lot earlier. And there's nothing out there that speaks to them anymore. You pick up *Seventeen* or *Teen* and it's tripe. *Maxi* is something that they can relate to."

Pepper says, "We get a lot of feedback in terms of E-mail, and it reinforces what we deeply believe—that we're doing something important, that we're getting other women to think critically about what's around them and being drilled into their heads every day."

Maxi Meme

. . . Like *Maxi*, EstroNet ["estrogen-powered web network"] was inspired by equal doses of dream and necessity. Soon after launching *Maxi*, its founders realized they weren't the only ones hatching a women-friendly Web site. "At first it was, like, 'Jesus! There's another site like ours! And another!'" Steenson says. "After a while I began wondering if we were some kind of meme, like a viral strain that was multiplying itself and spreading out. But it was just cultural synchronicity."

Minx appeared, then the *Women's Zone, Bust, gUrl, HUES*, and *Wench*. . . . Soon various editors began networking, swapping notes and tips. Finally they decided to pool their resources. "Back when Heather and I launched *Bitch*, the original idea was to get hundreds of Internet women's zines in one place as a kind of compendium of women's sites," Brown says. "So last October we got back to the idea, E-mailed everyone, and boom: EstroNet."

Irwin calls EstroNet an "incredibly empowering" concept. "Women like to congregate in communities, and that's one of the beauties of the Web—it brings women of all different ages and nationalities together in a way that no other medium can. With EstroNet, they can interact with each other and create a space outside the confines of forums of . . . guys who just want to flame everyone."

Questions for Critical Thinking and Discussion

1. A creator of *Maxi* was quoted as saying "We believed that if we built it, they could come. And they have." Do you think *more* women and men will become involved with feminist content now that it is more available or accessible?

2. When television was introduced to the public back in 1939, women's rights groups were very optimistic about its potential. They believed that television could be a tool to spread the "good word" of equal rights and that all the public needed was to be educated about such issues. Contemporary analysis of commercial media content has shown that women are often subordinated, are used as objects to market products, or are targeted themselves for products (for example, to obtain unreasonable beauty standards).

   Consider Internet content as it looks today. Again, there is great optimism about the Internet's potential for improving equality. In what ways are women positively represented or equally served on the Net? In what other ways can the Internet be detrimental to women's rights or their role/place in the culture and society?

14

The Color of Money, Part I

LORRAINE CALVACCA

Lorraine Calvacca is a writer for Folio *magazine.*

Here, Calvacca investigates why advertisers shy away from highly prolific and available minority periodicals when these titles so effectively reach their target audiences — audiences that are an economic gold mine.

Ad sales is, by any measure, a challenging profession. But for minority titles it can be downright Herculean. The struggle they face is not just to present dazzling demographics to clients and agencies, but simply to get a foot in the door.

Karen Wang's experience in trying to break the Visa account for the six-year-old *A. Magazine* is typical. "We don't do ethnic markets," she says she was told by an account representative at the agency. "I don't know what that means!" exclaims the flabbergasted ad sales rep, pointing to the affluent, well-educated, highly brand-loyal readership of the 100,000-circulation title.

Christy Haubegger, editor and publisher of the five-month-old bilingual title *Latina*, says she, too, has felt the crush of slamming doors with certain marketers. "Sometimes, they say, 'Your [readers] are not our market.' And I say, 'But you're selling *food!*'"

Advertiser resistance is by no means reserved for these relatively young start-ups. "I've been selling [the 26-year old *Black Enterprise*] for eight years," says executive VP/COO Earl G. (Butch) Graves Jr., "and in some ways, it is just as difficult today. Advertisers have been reluctant to understand or value the African-American market and what it means to the bottom line."

Graves cites, for example, the fact that Microsoft Corporation spent $600 million to introduce Windows 95, and "not a penny" went to *Black Enterprise* or any other minority media.

Rob Schoeben, group manager, marketing communications at Microsoft, responds that the month-long campaign precluded advertising in titles with longer lead times, and that the software publisher instead opted for weeklies and dailies like *Business Week, The Wall Street Journal* and *Newsweek*. "Minority publications are always in the consideration set. But [in this campaign] they weren't the best way to reach [Window 3.1 users and PC owners].

This article first appeared in *Folio* (November 1996), Volume 25(16), pages 44–46.

We're very committed to diversity in media buying and in our organization," he says.

Blacklist for Black Titles?

The relative dearth of African-American and other ethnic titles, says Graves, underscores the monumental selling difficulties they all face. Of the 4,000 consumer titles serving 264 million Americans, he notes, only four well-established books target the nation's 31 million blacks.

Time Inc. senior editor Roy S. Johnson's research for the still-pending start-up *Savoy* (described as a "black *Vanity Fair*") confirms Graves' view. That *Black Enterprise, Ebony, Essence* and *Jet* have survived—even thrived—he says, demonstrates "clearly that there's an ad base. But just as clearly it's a struggle to sell ads on a day-to-day basis."

Indeed, says Essence Communications, Inc., president Clarence Smith, the one million-circulation title for black women is flourishing. For 1996, ad pages are up 8 percent over 1995. Even with that significant increase, however, the monthly is far outweighed by most general-market women's books. "*Essence* is unique," says Smith. "Yet *Vogue* does more than half the business in one issue that we do all year. Is their reader a superior buy? Absolutely not. The reality is that doing business as a minority is harder than doing it as a majority."

Smith attributes advertisers' stonewalling largely to misperceptions about the buying power of the African-American market. "Our nation is in ethnic enclaves. When marketers look at African-American enclaves, they see poverty, not the affluence of the general markets, so they don't spend to market to them."

Yet statistics show a significant increase in black affluence and spending. According to Johnson's research, for example, the number of blacks who earn $50,000 or more has grown 41 percent since 1992, compared with the general population, which has grown 24 percent. Hispanic publications suffer from similar misperceptions, says Smith, whose Essence Communications, Inc., backed the launch of *Latina*. Census data show, for example, that Latinos' spending power will leap to nearly $300 billion in 2000, up nearly 27 percent from 1995.

Asian-American titles face a different hurdle, says Smith. Asians, he notes, are perceived as well educated and affluent. Advertisers' resistance here comes from the diversity in language and culture among the 51 subgroups of Asian-Americans, and from their relatively small population.

Excuses, Excuses

But the absolute focus on numbers, say ethnic-publication staffers, is off the mark. It's the ability to deliver a specialized, quality audience, not easily reached any other way, that matters, they contend. "Microtargeting is the wave of the future," asserts Joie Davidow, editor in chief and publications director of *Sí*, the one-year-old quarterly for Hispanic women.

"Agencies are so driven by numbers," agrees *A.*'s Wang. "If you're telling me that in the year 2020 there will be 20 million Asians, you're missing an opportunity to get in on the ground floor with a group that will be loyal consumers."

Agencies and clients, says Time Inc.'s Johnson, need to make decisions based on an understanding of the marketplace, its growth and its impact. If African-Americans or other minorities are spending disproportionately on consumer items, "they should see that as a wake-up call," he adds.

Advertisers dismiss ethnic publications, staffers claim, by saying advertising reaches minorities through general-interest publications or other media. Not surprisingly, the magazines' own studies show that people like to see themselves reflected in what they're reading. "I look at *Time, People* and fashion magazines, but they don't talk about things from an Asian-American perspective. I don't see 'me' covered in mainstream publications," says Wang.

Latina's Haubegger says: "You may reach me in *Glamour*, but you won't *move* me."

If You're Not Part of the Solution . . .

A significant part of the problem, all agree, is the racial make-up at ad agencies. "I'm rarely talking to someone who's part of our market," says Haubegger. What that means is a monumental educational task for minority sales reps. "It's a lot more work. I have to educate the food chain on the account side," says Haubegger.

"It's deplorable," says *Black Enterprises'* Graves. "Worse than in any other industry. General-market agencies must commit to hiring other than whites."

According to *Essence*'s Smith, board member of the Washington, D.C.–based American Advertising Federation, which tracks and advocates diversity in high-level marketing positions, there is no African-American senior marketing executive in an agency or company that is not black-owned. "That knocks me out," he says. But, he notes, people of color are becoming more visible on the corporate side in companies such as IBM and Xerox. Their input, says Johnson, can go a long way toward removing obstacles. "If CEOs of Fortune 500 companies stated that the products should be in the black market, it would be a step in the right direction."

In addition, says Graves, minority budgets are usually an afterthought to the general marketing plan. "I don't want to be treated like a sideshow when I'm bringing the main event," he says, referring to the title's 302,748 circulation of business people with an average income of $76,000. And relatively little business is going to black-owned agencies, he adds. "Even though we represent 13 percent of the population, the amount of dollars allocated to the market is less than 5 percent of a client's overall budget. That's an atrocity. That's basically institutionalized racism."

Moreover, the meager budgets must be divided among a sizable group. "Diversity now includes not just Hispanics, African-Americans, but gays, the disabled, and anybody else who's not mainstream," says Graves. So when dollars are allocated, they often go toward business-to-business or sporadic "feel-good" image ads.

Hispanic Business, a 17-year-old trade title, for example, has an impressive roster of clients that includes AT&T, IBM, Chevrolet and General Electric—but they are mostly image ads. "The struggle is to get general-market consumer ads that *Fortune* and *Forbes* have," says managing editor Hector Cantu. "There's a lack of understanding that our readers are comparable."

"A lot of these budgets are created as if they're a pot of gold. The mentality is, 'Let me show you that I care about blacks.' But if you spend $100 million in advertising and $750,000 is for African-Americans, then you're not serious," says Graves.

Nonetheless, there is some optimism among minority titles, whose executives observe that the cultural and business climate is warming up—albeit at a very slow simmer. Robert Filiatreaux, ad manager for *Hispanic Business,* notes an improvement in agencies' willingness to consider English-language publications aimed at Latinos.

Some forward-thinking industries are responding, not just in attitude, but in action. Auto advertisers are cited most often by Hispanic and African-American titles as able to recognize the potential value of their markets. Domestic automakers have been particularly visible in *Black Enterprise.* "We were ranked 16th by Publishers Information Bureau of all magazines receiving auto ads last year," says Graves. "That's not just window dressing. They're doing it because of viable demographics."

Cars are currently *Latina*'s largest ad category, says Haubegger, and include charter clients Ford, Chevrolet, Toyota, Honda and Saturn. "I am extremely encouraged by the ads we've gotten so far," she comments, citing, too, that cosmetics giant Revlon not only signed on for a six-time schedule with the June launch, but also ran the copy in Spanish. Time Inc.'s Johnson notes a positive trend in high-end advertisers, including Jaguar, Tiffany and Gianni Versache, showing up in a number of African-American titles that include *Black Enterprise* and the dual-race *Vibe.*

At *A. Magazine,* the trailblazers are financial and technology advertisers. Discover card, for example, joined the book last year with a six-time schedule, and again for 1996. AOL signed on in the August/September issue. "That Asian-Americans are technically literate and affluent is not an inaccurate perception," observes editor and publisher Jeff Yang.

Regardless of the roadblocks, a sense of optimism is also evident in the continued emergence of minority start-ups, among them newborns *Si* and *Urban: The Latino Magazine,* a service and lifestyle magazine; Forbes' *American Legacy,* a year-old title that covers blacks in history; and Rodale Press' *Heart & Soul,* a bimonthly health title for African-Americans. (*Heart & Soul's* circulation has grown 25 percent to 200,000 since its launch three years ago as a quarterly.) In addition, early next year, Chicago-based African-American publisher Sui Generis U.S., Inc., is launching domestic versions of two European books: *Visions in Black,* a beauty, fashion and health title; and *Savoire Faire,* described—like *Savoy*—by publisher Alan Thompson as "a black *Vanity Fair.*"

Still, says *Essence's* Smith, a lot of what is happening is "buzz rhetoric—and marketing behavior rarely follows." More often than not, advertisers and clients are dragging their feet, whether because of ignorance, misperceptions or outright racism. But the message from magazines to marketers is the same: "Get on the stick," as Graves so candidly puts it.

Down the road, minorities will constitute at least half of the marketing pie. In that context, says Haubegger: "Why would you give a client a pie with a big chunk missing?"

Questions for Critical Thinking and Discussion

1. As new technology brings more and more competitors into the business arena, it is possible that content will become more targeted to smaller, specific market groups. As ethnic populations increase, it seems that companies would benefit by addressing (reaching) these groups. According to Calvacca's article, why isn't big business targeting ethnic groups more than it is?

2. Should messages be altered or "customized" in order to reach various ethnic demographics? (a) If your answer is yes, choose a specific cultural or ethnic group and provide specific examples of how you would target this group with communication (images and words). (b) If your answer is no, consider how communication and culture must be homogenized in order to reach everyone the same way. What will this do to our melting-pot society?

15

The Color of Money, Part II

JENNA SCHNUER

Jenna Schnuer is the online editor for Publishers Weekly Interactive *and a senior editor for* Bookwire. *Schnuer continues with Part Two of this enlightening analysis of the economics, proliferation, and cultural impact of minority publishers and the hurdles they must face to succeed. She writes, "We're not blind to ethnic shifts, say advertisers. It's the minority magazines' own approach that makes them a hard sell."*

It's been a long time coming—and it's still not anywhere near perfect—but mainstream advertisers are acknowledging more and more their need and responsibility to market across cultural lines. "Many advertisers have come to realize that there are hardly any categories [of products or services] where minority influence isn't creeping up," says Doug Alligood, senior vice president, special markets for BBDO New York.

And Gwendolyn Kelly, associate media director of Burrell Communications Group, says that 25 years after the agency was started, staffers still invoke the founder's observation that "black people are not dark-skinned white people" when explaining to prospective clients why they need to enter new ethnic markets.

One of the first and most public statements in this arena came during the late 1980s when Procter & Gamble mandated that its advertising agencies have capabilities to market to Hispanic communities. Since then, a multitude of divisions have popped up at major agencies—along with an ever-expanding group of independent agencies—to focus on minority populations. But the one medium that advertisers who target minority populations remain wary of appears to be magazines.

Part of the problem for minority magazines is that advertisers are not fully comfortable with the variety of media habits that various cultures have. Historically, studies have suggested Hispanics gravitated more toward newspapers and television. "Marketing to Hispanics is still a very broadcast-dominant market," says Rochelle Newman, president of Hispanic advertising agency Enlace Communications, Inc.

Advertisers believe that Hispanics prefer the immediacy of those media and therefore invest their marketing dollars there. Also, Hispanic newspapers have a greater ability than magazines to target segments of the com-

---

This article first appeared in *Folio* (November 1996), Volume 25(16), pages 48–49.

munity. "People pick up the local community paper because it is much more culturally relevant. There has been a greater stratification of the newspaper media," says Shelly Lipton, president of Latin Reports, a new group set up to track Hispanic media. But there is a growing segment of the population that is integrating magazines into their daily lives.

No Audit, No Ads?

The most common reason advertisers give for avoiding titles in the African-American, Hispanic and Asian-American markets is that many of those titles are not audited.

"The importance of publishers contracting for circulation audits for their vehicles goes without saying: It is an investment by publishers in their own future; it provides credibility," reads a statement from Stacey Exposito, president and chief creative officer of the Bravo Group. "As more publications, and media in general, validate their audiences, the publications that don't will have less and less of a chance to make a buy list."

But some industry players say that response doesn't hold water for advertisers who want to increase marketshare; as competition heats up, advertisers who want to break into new markets are going to have to take some ad-dollar risks.

Nor does BBDO's Alligood believe that the demand for a circulation audit is entirely fair. "Auditing is a major drawback for Latino and black publications that are too small. It takes a while and costs money [to get an audit going]. Many of the big advertisers are holding up the standard and saying that if you're not audited, we're not going to use you."

Many ad agencies and advertisers are redefining how they evaluate minority magazines. "We tend to look at them as targeted magazines," says Newman. "We see them as targeted the way a bridal magazine or a fishing magazine is."

Allen Banks, executive vice president and executive media director for Saatchi & Saatchi North America, agrees that Newman's view of the titles is the appropriate one. "Those who see them as targeted magazines are looking at them in the right way. There is a greater realization that, as with other targeted markets, it makes sense to advertise in magazines that reach their needs," says Banks.

But even if it makes sense to use titles like *Latina, Si* or *A. Magazine* to prospect in new markets, many advertisers still refuse to do so on the basis of numbers. "There are just so many dollars," says Pam Becker, a spokeswoman for General Mills. "We look at ad buys for efficiency and reach. The circulations have to be there."

General Mills has not done much advertising in Hispanic publications, but Becker says the company has "dramatically increased the amount of advertising in African-American publications."

More Magazines; More Visibility

Another change that could help push aside objections is the use of a more professional look and attitude in magazine design and marketing materials. "In general, I think the more the publications take a professional publishing approach, the more credible they will be," says Newman. While many advertisers have not given a thought to minority publications for the past several years—opting instead to concentrate on radio or television advertising—a more polished approach could wake them up to some new possibilities. "The new vehicles coming into the market are making us rethink it," says Diane Labrizzi, president of Latino Media Source. She adds that the very high-profile launch of *People en Español* could do a great deal for the category. "*People* has an opportunity to build print advertising [in the category]."

Alligood adds, "I see tremendous shifts in terms of new magazines coming in. There's a new vitality, especially because they're targeting younger people."

The increased specialization among minority magazines may also attract advertiser attention to minority markets. As more and more titles are launched to target each population, their publishers are realizing that they must target their magazines more specifically in order to define a viable market. "We as an agency look at that as exciting news. It's really tapping into the richness of African-American culture and society," says Burrell Communications' Kelly. The Chicago-based Burrell handles advertising to the African-American community for such mega-marketers as Procter & Gamble, McDonald's, Sears and Coca-Cola.

In the end, the biggest change required within the advertising world is the realization that no matter what culture people come from, they do share one basic need when it comes to advertising. "We've been putting the focus on the media instead of who is using the media," says Alligood. "All people want the same thing, to know what is it about this automobile that is going to make me enjoy it."

Questions for Critical Thinking and Discussion

1. One of the problems facing corporate America is how to reach diverse ethnic groups. What are advertisers' problems with the approaches taken by minority magazines in order to reach specific ethnic groups?

2. Why is auditing so important to advertisers? Do you think auditing is a reasonable requirement or is it simply "a hurdle" used to limit membership into the mainstream majority influence and/or status quo?

chapter 6
Film

16

Hollywood Guilds Put the Moves on Multimedia

STANLEY KLEIN

Stanley Klein is a contributing writer for New Media *magazine.*

In this article, Klein presents the transition of entertainment content from film and television to new media/multimedia technology by addressing subjects such as unions, electronic rights, book publishing, cross-paradigm (medium) content, and spin-off deals.

The computer industry may wax starry-eyed over its new intimacy with Hollywood, but as multimedia developers employ more directors, script writers, actors and technicians, the industry is encountering a phenomenon all but unknown in Silicon Valley: labor unions.

"The impending growth of this new, interactive medium will create bountiful employment opportunities for our members," said Joel Block, who shepherds the Writers Guild of America's new Department of Industry Alliances. The department already has agreements with 50 companies, and Block is laying plans to aggressively recruit interactive writers, typically freelancers, into the 8,000-member guild.

The 10,000-member Directors Guild and 88,000-member Screen Actors Guild have also organized new-media departments. The Directors Guild's new-media efforts, which are run by Warren Adler, include a deal with Digital Pictures, and there are several other agreements in the works. The Screen Actors Guild, under Michael Prohaska, already has agreements with 20 game and multimedia companies that cover some 600 of its actors. Prohaska aims to sign up 100 more companies over the next six months.

For those already working under union agreements, interactive works will be business as usual. But in the laissez-faire computer world, unions are often viewed as a loathsome relic. "The Guild is a totally new concept for Silicon Valley," said Block.

Multimedia publishers may recoil at having to negotiate collective bargaining agreements covering compensation, working times and conditions. Perhaps most abhorrent is the prospect of paying royalties as well as fees,

This article first appeared in *New Media* (March 1994), page 25.

and sharing in revenues generated by ancillary products, such as merchandised products. A character created in traditional media by a Writers Guild author, for example, receives a 5 percent royalty on products merchandised around that character.

The issue of ancillary electronic rights is also being pressed by 10 members of the National Writers Union, who recently filed a lawsuit aimed at major publishers in the New York Federal District Court. They are arguing that the publishers routinely sold material to on-line services and other electronic venues even when electronic rights were not specified in the writer's contract. If the courts agree, many publishers could be forced to pony up large retroactive payments to writers.

In Hollywood, meanwhile, terms are still open for negotiation. The Writers Guild is trying to get a handle on interactive writing fees, job definitions, ancillary products and residual rights so that a more comprehensive contract can be formulated. Commented Block, "Our first goal is to understand the underlying economics in this new field."

The unionization campaigns by the guilds are in a honeymoon phase. While a traditional contract for the Writers Guild runs over 400 pages, for example, it has instituted a one-page "interim" agreement covering interactive projects. Its only requirement: a multimedia producer contributes 12.5 percent of a Guild writer's total compensation (negotiated solely by the writer and producer) to the Guild pension and health plan.

Many multimedia publishing companies are moving quickly to embrace the unions. Activision even relocated to Los Angeles just to be close to Hollywood's high-priced talent. "Having guild people on a project assures us of exceptionally qualified and professional talent," said Bobby Kotick, Activision's president and CEO.

Digital Pictures' president and CEO, Tom Zito, makes the same argument, having engaged guild directors and actors in *Ground Zero Texas*, *Double Switch* and *Prize Fight*. Zito will continue working with the guilds in six titles to be released in 1994. Brøderbund, Electronic Arts, Media Vision and Knowledge Adventure are among the companies using guild talent.

All of the players are keenly aware that megabucks are at stake, including the rights to cross-media ownership, royalty relationships and guaranteed fees. Multimedia publishing may soon go the way of theatrical movies, where profits often result only from pay-TV showings, video rentals and foreign releases. If compensation packages for creative types escalate, it will become tougher for the producer and investors to make a profit without spinoffs.

"A new economic paradigm is taking hold," said Joyce Schwartz, a Los Angeles entertainment and multimedia marketing consultant. "The negotiating power of the creative types is on the rise, even without the guilds, and to offset the high overhead wrought by stardom deal-making, the business game is to produce a title that can be parlayed into a feature film, theme park, cartoon series, or T-shirts and coffee mugs."

This strategy will be easier for larger publishers than for smaller ones. Many small shops will be hard pressed to pay union wages, let alone to make big-time spinoff deals.

Questions for Critical Thinking and Discussion

1. Labor unions seem like the best way to protect content creators in terms of compensation by big industry. At the same time, unions are a threat to smaller content production shops (because of high wages), which could lead to less independent productions and a smaller number of (perhaps only those mainstreamed) cultural voices. What is so important about the concept of "multiplicity of cultural voices"?

2. How far-reaching do you think union power should be? How can protection of workers *and* the development of culture be balanced?

Disney's All Smiles

DON L. BUROUGHS, DAN MCGRAW, AND KEVIN WHITELAW

Dan McGraw is a senior editor, Kevin Whitelaw is an associate editor, and Don L. Buroughs is a contributing writer for U.S. News & World Report.

In this article, these authors provide an in-depth look at the takeover of ABC by Disney and discuss the ramifications (cultural effects — positive and negative) of further concentration of ownership.

At about 7:30 in the morning last Monday, Charles Gibson was a half-hour into hosting ABC's *Good Morning America* when word came through his earpiece that the Walt Disney Co. was taking over Capital Cities/ABC. Within an hour, the show's surprise guests—Gibson's current boss, Capital Cities Chairman Thomas Murphy, and Gibson's future boss, Disney chief Michael Eisner—left the stunned interviewer at a loss for words on the air.

The shock waves of the deal will spread well beyond those wired into the media power structure. They will hit home in St. Louis, where 7-year-old Ryan McMillen played Simba in a *Lion King* skit at Corky's Preschool that very day; in Newtown, Conn., where Katie McMorran, 2, refused to eat her supper last Monday until her mother called her Pocahontas; and in Fort Worth, where Ashley Luke, 8, snuggled to sleep that night between Snow White sheets. And all because the corporation that most determines the characters America's children emulate, the songs they sing and the vacations they dream of is about to take control of the nation's most successful broadcast network and transform itself into the largest media company in the world. Indeed, the Disneyfication of America has reached a towering new height.

The $19 billion Disney-ABC transaction will be the second-largest corporate merger in U.S. history. But when Kohlberg Kravis Roberts swallowed RJR Nabisco for $25 billion, no one noticed a difference in his Triscuits or Winstons. By contrast, the prospect of Disney's blockbuster acquisition had its executives positively bubbling over with ideas for changes on television—from a Disney-dominated Saturday morning on ABC to sporting events hosted at Disney's future Florida sports complex that could be carried by ABC-owned ESPN. And in a dramatic sign of the increased interest

---

This article first appeared in *U.S. News & World Report* (April 14, 1995), pages 32–34, 43–44, 46.

in broadcast networks, CBS agreed to be purchased by Westinghouse for $5.4 billion, just a day after the Disney-ABC deal was announced. . . .

Disney's media merger caps both an astounding decade and a troubling year for the Burbank, Calif., company. Since Eisner was brought in to revive the moribund home of Mickey Mouse in 1984, revenues have shot up nearly sevenfold to more than $10 billion, with a hefty $1.1 billion in profits. In particular, Disney's filmed entertainment division, which had so lost its way that there was talk of abandoning the animation business, has been revived, accounting for nearly half of total revenues in 1994. The roaring success of *The Lion King* . . . — No. 1 in box office receipts, No. 1 album for the year and the bestselling video of all time — made it the most profitable motion picture in history. Today, Disney films account for seven of the 10 bestselling videos ever. The company's six theme parks attract more visitors than all 54 U.S. national parks combined. The Disney Channel is the second-largest pay channel on cable — after HBO — and the fastest growing. And the originator of the Mouseketeer's hat has become a major mover in the toy industry. . . .

New Math   The philosophy of the Disney deal can be summed up in one word: synergy. It is the belief that one plus one in this case will equal not two or even three, but four, says Eisner. For example, high-tech ESPN sports bars, such as the one planned for Disney World, can add cachet to both the cable network and the theme park. And "The Making of Pocahontas," a TV special that helped heighten anticipation of the film among the 14 million Disney Channel subscribers, can now be beamed to nearly every household in America. In addition to such cross-promotions, ABC provides another outlet for Disney's assets of content and characters. Joe Roth, head of Disney's film studios — including Touchstone and Miramax — notes that on the Arts & Entertainment cable channel, 37.5 percent owned by Capital Cities, "there's no reason to think you couldn't tune in every night from 10 to 12 and see a Miramax film, so we get another usage out of a library that we already own."

Disney's sense of synergy is well refined. What other company on earth could have taken a children's movie, *The Mighty Ducks*, parlayed it into a professional hockey team by the same name, broadcast games on its own KCAL-TV and sold Mighty Ducks jerseys in more than 400 of its own stores? "I think we wrote the book on synergy," says Judson Green, president of Walt Disney Attractions.

Access to ABC's prime-time audience opens an enormous door for Disney's television production business. The Magic Kingdom's TV studios currently produce the top-rated show, ABC's *Home Improvement*, and eight other series airing this fall on various networks. Dennis Hightower, chief of television for Disney, says that before last week, he had been hoping to produce a dozen shows within a couple of years, but with Disney helping to shape ABC's schedule, he will set his sights higher.

Disney was already a leading force in America's leisure pursuits before joining forces with ABC. Texas A&M University marketing professor James McNeal calculates that children's influence over family spending has tripled in the past 10 years, to $160 billion. And Disney is taking in a growing share of those dollars. In a typical Toys "R" Us store in Maryland, a Pocahontas display area near the entrance carries more than 100 Pocahontas toys, from bead kits to tepees, made by Disney licensees. Twenty feet away, in the racks of coloring books, parents can choose among 23 Disney coloring books, including four Beauty and the Beast compilations. Those who might want a selection of basic pictures like apples and sailboats have only three options. By working closely with toymakers and stores, and by creating its own Disney Stores, the company has swollen its consumer product revenues from $110 million to $1.8 billion in the past decade.

Values   But the cultural impact of Disney is much larger than any numbers could indicate. Jamie O'Boyle, an analyst with the Philadelphia-based Cultural Studies & Analysis who has spent much of his career studying the influence of the company, notes that unlike the films that come out of other studios, Disney's products consistently echo the same themes and values. The ideas that everything is going to be OK, that risks are required to make progress and that outsiders have a contribution to make run through virtually all the studio's films. "Consistency is what gives them the clout they have," notes O'Boyle. "They've really set the tone for our mainstream mythology." Roy Disney, current head of animation and nephew of cofounder Walt Disney, says such themes are very consciously built into the story lines of his films. "We almost start from there," he explains. And with the addition of ABC, he expects Disney's influence to grow.

Playtime   The dominance of Disney is visible everywhere in the nation's schools. Within two weeks of the release of *The Lion King*, "everyone had seen it," says Lyn Tanner, the director of Corky's Preschool. "Everybody acts like a lion; they make the faces and the sounds." By the time children have tired of one story line, Disney has introduced the next. Sales of the new Pocahontas toys are now apace with their leonine predecessors. Adds O'Boyle: "[Kids] can keep their play based around Disney's version of American values for most of their childhood."

That thought makes some observers uncomfortable. "I don't mind Disney having its view," declares Benjamin Barber, a Rutgers University professor of political science. "It's when Disney's view becomes *the* view and the only view that I get worried." But to others, Disney's ubiquity acts as a bridge across America's divisions. "It constitutes a common culture for most Americans and their parents," argues Karal Ann Marling, who teaches an annual course on Disney at the University of Minnesota. "It's one of those things that hold us together." David Britt, president of the Children's Television Workshop, seems neither distraught nor elated by Disney's swelling role in TV. Although he would rather see more educational fare like *Sesame Street*, which CTW produces, he is more disturbed by violent kids' programs, such as *Mighty Morphin Power Rangers*. Contemplating Disney's control of ABC's Saturday-morning schedule, Britt says, "in comparison with what is generally around on Saturday morning, I would expect that would be an improvement."

But the expectations Disney creates also make it a lightning rod for controversy. When Disney's Miramax subsidiary announced earlier this year that it would release *Priest*, a film about a gay clergyman, on Good Friday, the Catholic League called for a boycott against all of Disney. Miramax postponed the debut by a week. More recently, Disney forced Miramax to sell the rights to *Kids*, a film about an HIV-infected teenage boy who has sex with teenage girls. The rights went to a company formed by the co-chairmen of Miramax, who went on to release the film. Some analysts believe that under the Disney aura, ABC will also attract protest, with critics holding it to a higher standard than the other networks. Such scrutiny "goes with the territory" at Disney, explains film chief Roth. "Nothing's free."

Ambassador Disney's cultural influence is spreading even more rapidly overseas than at home. International revenues shot up from $142 million in 1984 to $2.4 billion last year, almost a quarter of the company's total business. And Disney's new TV assets could accelerate that growth. Eisner wants to pair the Disney Channel with ESPN to gain entry into China, India and other parts of the world. The Disney Channel is now plugged into a few countries; ESPN is established in more than 100. Eisner's expectations don't stop with cable, however. He calls an ESPN-Disney pairing the "opportunity that opens the door for the rest of our products, movies and everything else." Capital Cities' Murphy told *U.S. News* last week that his company's 80 percent ownership of ESPN is "the No. 1 reason" that Disney fits better with ABC than with any other network.

Back in America, Disney intends to spread its influence well beyond film, television and toys. The company of late has become a dabbling duck, experimenting with Broadway theater, professional sports, cruise ships, adult education and residential real estate. The entertainment giant even emerged last week as a potential bidder for Rockefeller Center in New York. Late this year, the company will begin selling homes in Celebration, a Florida town of 20,000 that Disney is building from the ground up, complete with houses, shops and schools. The Disney cruise line is set to launch in 1998.

And the Disney Institute will begin offering educational vacations for adults this winter.

When its experiments succeed, the company is not shy about expansion. The stage version of *Beauty and the Beast* opened in April of last year to become one of the hottest tickets on Broadway. By the end of this year, Belle will be falling for the Beast on eight stages, from Osaka, Japan, to Vienna, Austria. Disney is also refurbishing the New Amsterdam Theater on 42nd Street in preparation for its next Broadway show. Current plans call for three or four New York productions running concurrently by the turn of the century.

Disney's mark on the sports world is also growing. The Mighty Ducks of Anaheim, Calif., are considered one of the most profitable teams in hockey, selling out their last 47 home games despite a second-season record of only 16 wins and 27 losses. Ducks merchandise is the best-selling in the league, and Disney has every intention of making it the nation's team. Now it is trying the same formula in baseball, awaiting approval of its bid to buy a 25 percent share of the California Angels and an option to buy the rest of the team. With a bat-swinging parent company, all eyes will be on ABC Sports to see if it will break its oath to abandon baseball for the rest of the decade. Disney is also looking into opportunities for Southern California teams in professional football and basketball.

Sports World   In Florida, Disney has broken ground on a 1.1-mile oval track that will open the 1997 Indy car season, broadcast live on ABC. That same year, the company's 200-acre Florida sports complex will open. The Amateur Athletic Union last week announced it is moving its headquarters to the facility, and by the end of the decade, Disney hopes to host 60 AAU national championships. The ABC-ESPN-Disney combination has complex director Reggie Williams filled with ideas such as made-for-TV competitions for pro athletes at the facility. Declares Bill Robertson of Disney Sports: "With the merger, we have become the premier sports company."

For all the excitement in Burbank over the opportunities in television, there is plenty of potential for static in Disney's new future. Size is no guarantor of creativity, a crucial determinant of entertainment success. And in addition to the usual hazards of merging two distinct cultures and managements, the future in electronic media is anything but clear. Predicting that an interactive information superhighway will carry a nearly infinite amount of entertainment, George Gilder, a senior fellow at the Discovery Institute in Seattle, cautions that the benefits of combining content with broadcast capability "are going to evaporate in the next few years."

Momentarily casting his eyes toward the past, rather than the future, Roy Disney, 65, savored the irony of the ABC acquisition last week. Back in

1954, the company solicited a $500,000 investment from ABC that it desperately needed in order to build Disneyland. "It's a very sweet circle to have come around," muses the company's head of animation. And Roy Disney is certain that his uncle would have approved of the purchase. "Walt's basic ambition was to own the whole damn world," Disney recalls. "It's just that he couldn't afford it." But the Walt Disney Co. can afford the world now. And the world is buying Disney.

Questions for Critical Thinking and Discussion

1. Consider the wide variety of sources provided by Disney (e.g., films, television, music, clothing, toys). What do you think about this overwhelming reach of Disney?

2. What are the positive and negative aspects of the Disney experience? Consider the big money spent to produce very popular, arguably high-quality products versus the economic *cultural* costs involved with participating in the Disney experience.

chapter 7

Radio and Sound Recording

Radio Activity

CHARISSE JONES

Charisse Jones is a contributing writer for several periodicals, including Vibe *and the* New York Times.

Vibe introduced this article perfectly when it asked, "Why are radio stations playing the same songs over and over? Why can't you hear Seal, Raekwon, and MC Lyte on the same station? Charisse Jones delves into radio's ultra-competitive universe and finds out that it's not always about the music — but it is always about the money."

"Radio used to be *dope*," says Ed Lover, morning jock on New York's Hot 97 and a former host of *YO! MTV Raps*. "Now urban radio beats kids in the head with the same 12 hip hop records, and they have no appreciation for anything else."

Turn to a radio station that gears itself toward what has come to be known as an urban audience — a group of people 60 to 80 percent black — and you'll be hard-pressed to find the folkie songs of Tracy Chapman or Maxwell, the bouncing rhythms of go-go, or the plaintive trills of the blues. In urban radio's major markets — Atlanta, Los Angeles, New York, Chicago, Dallas, and San Francisco among them — a listener must turn to one part of the dial to hear the Dells, another to hear Rick James, and another to hear 2Pac or Mary J. Blige.

In an effort to hold on to a targeted audience, many urban stations have sacrificed the variety and adventurousness that characterized old-school black radio in favor of the new niche programming, which "superserves" a specific audience by giving them an overabundance of a certain kind of music — rap, smooth jazz, pop, whatever. And for better or for worse, based on the high ratings of niche-formatted stations like New York's Hot 97 and 92.3 the Beat in Los Angeles, as well as "power" country and "power" alternative formats across the U.S., radio audiences seem to like "certain kinds" of music a lot.

"Being all things to all people just doesn't cut it anymore," says Lover's boss, Steve Smith, program director at the highly rated, Emmis Broadcasting–owned WQHT (Hot 97). Why? In a word: competition. It began to escalate

This article first appeared in *Vibe* (October 1996), pages 89–90, 92.

during the late 1980s when investors such as Evergreen (which now owns 32 stations) and Clear Channel Communications (over 100) noticed that stations playing music created by African-Americans often had the highest ratings in their markets—and the potential to bring in millions from advertisers. The number of urban stations jumped from 284 in 1989 to 347 in 1995, and urban radio saw a 27.1 percent increase in revenue between January 1993 and December 1995.

While the final decision about what music gets played ultimately rests with the listeners, the pool of music from which they choose has grown increasingly narrow. Most top stations have a playlist of no more than 20 to 30 songs. "A station as narrow-minded as this is going to, at best, only promote music from that genre," says one disgruntled Hot 97 listener on the World Wide Web, "and make its listeners intolerant of other kinds of music. At worst it will flood the industry with substandard product and corrupt the very music it's claiming to promote." Ed Lover hates niche (he calls it "narrow-minded") programming. "There is *no reason in the world*," he says via cell phone, "that Dionne Farris or Seal should have a problem getting their songs played on urban radio. It's *sickening*."

But there's a belief among radio consultants and program directors that the fewer songs a station plays, the higher the ratings will be. "People want to turn on the radio and hear songs they're comfortable with," says Keith Naftaly, vice president of A&R at Arista Records and award-winning former program director of San Francisco's KMEL and L.A.'s 92.3 the Beat. "People say they like variety, but if they liked it as much as they claim, you'd hear more of it on the radio."

Ratings back up Naftaly's claim. "We all live and die by a service called Arbitron," Hot 97's Smith says. Arbitron is a nationwide company that measures how many people are listening to a given station, and for how long they are listening. The higher the Arbitron ratings, the more money a station can charge advertisers for airtime. The loss or gain of a single rating point can translate into millions of dollars. In 1994 one New York City radio station rating point was worth $3.9 million in advertising revenue.

Smith says it's most effective to maintain a core of listeners for long periods of time—and his station, one of the highest-rated in New York, does this extremely well playing the hip hop and hip hop–influenced R&B they've determined urban listeners ages 18 to 34 want to hear. "It's a benefit of niche programming," he says.

And niching brings in the dough, especially if a station appears to be more mainstream than urban. "Black radio" became "urban radio" in the late 1980s—to make it more salable by deemphasizing blackness, radio watchers say. A new category, "churban" (crossover hits urban), also came into existence at the same time. Those stations, which may have slightly broader playlists—they play the occasional R.E.M., say, or Madonna, in addition to Monica and the Notorious B.I.G.—are perceived by record companies and advertisers as having even more of a crossover appeal. Quincy McCoy, urban editor at *Gavin Report*, the radio industry's most prominent industry trade magazine, says the logic to the changing identifications is simple.

"People who own and format the stations get money from agencies who represent companies like Budweiser and Chevrolet," he says from his San Francisco office. "And blackness traditionally gets the low part of the buy. If you're a 'black' station in the market, the advertiser skips you and goes to another station. How do you clean that up? You're not 'black' or 'urban' anymore. You're 'churban.' You send your white people into the advertising agency, and you get a better part of the buy."

There is a lot of money on the line, but still, some music personalities, radio executives, listeners, and music critics argue that the result is that listeners aren't challenged, talented artists aren't exposed, and radio will become stagnant as rigidity prevails. "The kind of music that comes from artists like Des'ree and Seal is only one form of African-American–based music that has experienced a woeful absence on R&B stations," says J. R. Reynolds, R&B editor at *Billboard*, who has proposed in his The Rhythm and the Blues column a new radio format called "rhythm alternative," which would make a place for artists like Lenny Kravitz, Dionne Farris, Maxwell, Tricky, and other performers who fall outside of conventional rhythm and blues.

"What about the people who grew up on hip hop but who can appreciate the Ornette Colemans?" Ed Lover asks rhetorically. "Everybody should be able to enjoy all kinds of music on one station. Don't you think it would help close the generation gap if you could hear, right after A Tribe Called Quest song, where A Tribe Called Quest got their music and ideals from?"

Thembisa Mshaka, rap editor at *Gavin Report*, feels that the lines of definition as far as what black music is and isn't are too severely drawn. "If you're encouraging people over 35 to listen to songs recorded between 1965 and 1985, and encouraging the kids to listen to songs recorded from 1985 to 1996, that's two generations of African-Americans that are never meeting over the airwaves," says Mshaka, who enjoys Al Green as much as E-40. "You need the elders to be on the air with the hip hop heads."

But it's not the stations' job to close the generation gap—it's their job to make money. "We tend to hold on to this thing of 'Back in the day, you could hear everything from a rock record to a dance record on the same station,'" says Hot 97's Smith. "I think most people would argue that radio is better now. There are more choices. Back in the day, there was less competition. In many markets there was just one station playing black music, so the ratings were automatically competitive with pop stations. But when black music be-

came a hot commodity, firms invested in the places that played it, more stations came into being, and the competition got fierce."

"It's not about what we *want* to do, it's about what we *gotta* do," says
Maxx Myrick, program director of Chicago's WVAZ (V103), an urban/adult
contemporary station. He's been in radio since 1978. "What we gotta do is
make money and get ratings, or we aren't going to have these jobs. These are
public companies, and the board of directors want to hear that they're making a return on their investment." He sighs. "It's just not possible to play a
lot of the great music. You just can't take the chance."

Cliff Winston, morning personality and program director of Los Angeles'
KJLH (Kindness, Joy, Love, and Happiness), an urban/adult contemporary
station owned since 1979 by Stevie Wonder, says, "You *could* go from Jimi
Hendrix to R. Kelly to B. B. King—and you wouldn't have any listeners.
That's what college radio is for. And just because an artist is black doesn't
mean the artist is playing black music." He notes that there have always
been black artists, from Richie Havens to Joan Armatrading, who didn't get
played on black/urban radio. "Many black-owned stations are struggling to
compete with their pop and corporate-owned counterparts," he says. "They
must cater to a particular age/income/sex demographic that is appealing
to advertisers who want to target a particular audience—if they're going to
survive. Black media enterprises are not missionaries, they're businesses."

At Chicago's V103, Herb Kent, the station's legendary "King of the Dusties,"
plays a wide variety of music—from the Impressions to the Time to Anita
Baker to the Fugees. Here, new songs are played for a few weeks so listeners can become familiar with them, and then the records are tossed into the
hands of audience researchers. What they find out determines a song's fate.

"We spend several hundreds of thousands of dollars a year on research,"
says V103's Myrick, whose format is No. 1 with Chicago listeners ages 25 to
54, the key demographic for companies selling cars, credit cards, and other
high-end products. "There are some records that just don't work," he says,
citing Tony Rich's "Nobody Knows" as an example; people simply were not
checking for it when the research was done. "But Brandy's 'Sittin' up in My
Room' was a hit, even though music from younger artists tends to burn out
quickly here. We don't ask people why they don't like it. We ask them if they
like it, how much they like it, and if they don't."

Once upon a time, radio programming was all about instinct. Program
directors or disc jockeys would put a record on because they liked the way
it sounded. If the request lines lit up, they knew they had a hit. No more. Ed
Lover says that what's happened in radio is the same thing that happened
when he cohosted *YO! MTV Raps.* "When black music became a billion-
dollar baby, radio got crazy political. Like at MTV—at first it was just us

programming the show. As soon as it became a million-dollar show, our power was taken away."

Stuff got real scientific, just as it already had with general market stations. "Call-out" research is one of the most important tools: Researchers telephone members of the station's target audience once a week and play hooks from the songs on their playlist. The audience members rate them, and then the station's program director reviews the data to determine how often a given song should be played. Besides monitoring request lines, some stations have street researchers who poll people randomly, or researchers who go to dance clubs to see what listeners are getting into. Stations look at record sales and peruse industry publications to find out what songs are working for stations elsewhere. But some in the record industry complain that such heavy reliance on research can send a good song to a premature death.

"Before you had the consolidation of stations into these large conglomerates, before you had consultants, you had radio guys who knew and felt the music," says Tom Bracamontes, vice president of promotions/urban music for Sony 550 Music, the home of R&B alternative artists like Des'ree, George Clinton, and Vernon Reid. "A lot of it was a gut check."

It could be said that Frankie Crocker, legendary DJ and program director for New York's WBLS, an urban/adult contemporary station, is, as far as radio is concerned, the progenitor of the "gut check." In 1971, when Crocker was named the voice of 'BLS, the former jazz station became the first FM R&B station in the world. Over the next 20 years, the station was responsible for launching nearly every major black R&B and dance artist—from Barry White to Prince. Even now, Crocker's got his own style. "I hear something I like; it's mostly by ear," Crocker says. "Afterward, I look at research, but sometimes, I just put it on because I know it's good. That's how most of the black artists today got their start."

But today music selection has become so restrained that Hector Hannibal, program director for Washington, D.C.'s popular WHUR/the Adult Mix, says that some of his fellow programmers refuse to play certain artists on the strength of looks alone. "I think Maxwell's CD cover may have scared people off," says Hannibal, who has played Maxwell, Me'Shell Ndegé-Ocello, and other artists not usually heard on urban radio. "I asked one person in particular if he listened to the album and he said no—because he thought it was something that he couldn't use. He was basing it on the look of the artist."

Keith Naftaly says any kind of radio is a "delicate dance, a science. Even Babyface's acoustic ballad, 1993's 'When Can I See You Again,' was considered risky by urban radio." But programmers, won over by Babyface's track record and familiar voice, took a chance. "It was accepted," he admits, "and that's what moves the format forward."

Nelson George, screenwriter/music historian/VIBE contributor, and author of the award-winning *The Death of Rhythm & Blues*, says that Hannibal is right. "The mentality is very reductive," George says from his Brooklyn home. "Program directors now are going for something easy to maintain." And the growing presence of white PDs—as urban stations are increasingly owned by white corporations—worries some who believe it's having a negative impact on what gets on the air. But Hot 97's Smith says that "there hasn't been a lot of flack" about the station having a white PD. "We provide a service to the audience and play what they want to hear. We listen and care enough about the audience to superserve it. I'd like to believe the other issues are not that important."

Ultimately, audiences and stations are going to have to meet each other halfway if the sounds on urban radio are going to be as diverse as the voices resonating throughout black America. But as long as money continues to speak the loudest, stations will only remain stratified, if not actually get more so. "Radio programmers, in their heart of hearts, know that average R&B listeners would be open to artists like Des'ree or Us3," says J. R. Reynolds. "But they would have to sacrifice I don't know how many rating points to get their audience accustomed to listening to those different sounds." He admits that listeners do usually like what they are used to. "But every once in a while, something new will come along that the kids get into, and the music will go off in new directions. That's what you saw with hip hop."

And it can happen again. Popular Bay Area DJ Michael Erickson, whose KMEL plays a mixture of pop, dance, and rap, says he once slipped in a Green Day song—and played it for three months—and the listeners dug it big-time. "When you play Green Day and then you put on Dionne Farris after, it doesn't sound as extreme anymore," he says.

He's right. There's a lockstep that prevails among many urban listeners, making them resistant to new sounds not quite funky enough, rhythmic enough, or conventionally black enough. If a guitar-laced ballad by Tracy Chapman follows an R. Kelly groove, it *is* likely some will flip the dial. But it's also true that young blacks are the ones who created and supported music as varied as dancehall, hip hop, and house, and some would presumably appreciate a little Me'Shell Ndegé-Ocello thrown in with their Method Man. Stations might lose some listeners by becoming more eclectic, but they stand to gain others who are interested in an old-fashioned idea known as variety.

Ingenuous? Maybe. But that's what people thought kids were in 1979 when they were scratching records and spinning on swatches of linoleum. They were a tiny minority, and the beginning of a new way of dealing with music no one could have predicted. They are the reason urban music is making so much money now. The backward-cap-wearing early B-boys and B-girls, however subconsciously, changed radio, music, and, many would argue, American culture. Perhaps what urban radio—all radio—needs is some of that spirit. "A really good station follows its listeners," says Erickson. "But occasionally a station asserts itself and leads them."

Questions for Critical Thinking and Discussion

1. Just as television became more "niched" because of cable, radio has become more "niched" because of competition. Radio can no longer be all things to all people. Jones discusses the splintering of the urban format to meet the needs of smaller subgroups of listeners. Could it be that the urban format (category) was too general or too homogenized to begin with? Weren't a very wide variety of types of music all labeled "black music" or "urban" just a decade ago?

2. If radio programmers play only "what the people (market) want," how will new music or new ideas make it into the cultural mix? How will the culture grow or progress if new ideas aren't tried (whether they succeed or fail)? What does it do to our culture if we let money drive innovation instead of cultural creativity?

19

Reading Between the Lines:
Let's Stop Crying Wolf on Censorship

JONATHAN ALTER

Jonathan Alter is a contributing writer for Newsweek *magazine.*

In this article, Alter presents a passionate comparison of censorship with "good judgment" or "editing." He addresses the political ramifications of defining and applying censorship within our society.

Imagine that a big record-company executive discovered a new skinhead band called Aryan Nation and distributed 2 million copies of a song with the lyrics: *Rat-a-tat and a tat like that / Never hesitate to put a nigga on his back.* This frank call for whites to kill blacks might run into a few problems around Hollywood. It's not likely, for instance, that Bill Clinton's advisers would recommend that their man appear at a gala fund-raiser at the executive's house. If radio stations declined to air Aryan Nation's songs advocating lynching, no one would scream "censorship."

Those lyrics in fact come from a rap song by Dr. Dre, whose label is Death Row/Interscope, which is part owned by Time Warner. Interscope is headed by Ted Field, a movie-and-record mogul who hosted Bill Clinton's big Hollywood fund-raiser last year. "A lot of this [criticism of rap] is just plain old racism," Field told the *Los Angeles Times* last month. "You can tell the people who want to stop us from releasing controversial rap music one thing: Kiss my ass."

Since Hollywood already has enough people who spend their days eagerly taking Ted Field up on that offer, I thought I'd try a different tack. It is Field and other phony liberals of his ilk, wrapping themselves in constitutional pieties, who are applying the racial double standards and devaluing legitimate civil-liberties concerns. It is they, more than the rappers themselves, who are responsible for spreading irresponsibility. And it is those who oppose them—private citizens rebuking or boycotting sociopathic entertainment—who are engaged in free expression in its best, most democratic sense.

That word—censorship—has been thrown around much too casually in recent years. If a record-company executive or an art-gallery owner or a

---

This article first appeared in *Newsweek* (November 29, 1993), page 67.

book publisher declines to disseminate something, that's not censorship, it's judgment. It might be cowardly judgment or responsible judgment, but it is what they are paid to do. Garry Trudeau makes this point whenever some wimpy newspaper decides not to run a controversial *Doonesbury* strip: his fans say he was censored; he rightly calls it bad editing.

How did we get to a point where "art" became a code word for money? As record executive David Geffen said last year about Time Warner chief Gerald Levin's lame rationalizations for Ice-T's "Cop Killer," "To say that this whole issue is not about profit is silly. It certainly is not about artistic freedom." In other words, the Constitution guarantees all Americans the right to rap, but it says nothing about Dr. Dre's right to a record contract.

In fact, if censorship means companies like Sony and Time Warner and Capitol Records begin to think harder about the messages they're sending young African-Americans, then maybe we need more of it. If censorship means executives bear greater personal accountability for what their companies produce—if it means that when Ted Field walks into a Beverly Hills restaurant, the patrons turn around and say with disgust, "Hey, that's the guy who tells blacks to shoot each other"—then it could help.

But that's not what the word means. Real censorship is when the government—*the government*—bans books in school libraries, prosecutes artists and writers for their work, seizes pornography, exercises prior restraint. And there's the whiff of censorship when the government hints at future action, as Janet Reno did last month with the TV networks. The line here gets tricky. Tipper Gore was way ahead of her time, and she never advocated censorship, only voluntary labeling of albums. But as the wife of the vice president, she's probably wise to go light on the issue now. Otherwise it might begin to feel censorious. A few private institutions—like schools that try to punish offensive student speech—could also be categorized as engaging in real censorship.

Beyond that, let's give the word a rest. I was once a judge for a journalism contest sponsored by a group called Project Censored. The goal was to identify underreported or ignored stories, not officially censored ones. Such casual use of the word demeans victims of real censorship, here and abroad. So does describing the battle over government funding of controversial art as a "censorship" issue. This is loopy. Declining to use taxpayer dollars to fund art is hardly the same as suppressing it. When Los Angeles radio station KACE-FM recently took the commendable step of banning "socially irresponsible" music from its format, this, too, was attacked by some other radio stations as censorship. These other stations routinely fail to play any folk music. Are they censoring Peter, Paul and Mary? Of course not. They're simply making a business assessment that folk is a ratings loser. What's annoying is the implicit assumption that choosing songs on the basis of what sells is somehow superior to choosing them on the basis of what's responsible.

If an editor wants to change the text of an article about ghetto life, that's editing. But if a rap producer wants to change sociopathic lyrics, that's seen as censorship. Even if you assume that rap is superior esthetically to journalism, is it really more worthy of protection? Is rap an inherently more valid form of expression than prose with no beat behind it? After all, they are both "voices of the community," waiting to be heard. So is Aryan Nation.

This is not an argument for applying a harsh moral standard to art, for easy listening everywhere on the dial, for record-company executives to sponsor nothing that they don't personally embrace. But even at its grimmest, music is meant to enhance life. Like tobacco executives, artists and record moguls who market death bear at least some responsibility for the consequences of their work. Let's confront that—and stop crying wolf on censorship.

Questions for Critical Thinking and Discussion

1. Censorship is based on laws defining obscenity and profanity, which are based upon "contemporary standards"—a slippery notion at best. The First Amendment is based on the idea that if everyone has a fair chance to participate, good ideas will survive and bad ideas will fail. Do you think that content should be censored? Under what circumstances?

2. Who should decide what content is okay for public consumption and what content is too dangerous for people to consume? The government? The content producers? The audience? Or some other person or group (explain)?

chapter 8

Television

Call It Courage

DAN RATHER

In the form of a tribute to Edward R. Murrow, Dan Rather, a top network news anchor and correspondent for CBS News, provides a very stern, critical analysis of the performance of news in contemporary society. Rather asks the tough questions about journalism's outward and inward effects on privacy, credibility, responsibility, and ethics.

> Men at some times are masters of their fates:
> The fault, dear Brutus, is not in our stars,
> But in ourselves. . . .
> CASSIUS, *JULIUS CAESAR*, ACT I, SCENE 2

Part I
Introduction to a Video

Thank you. And thank you, members of the Radio and Television News Directors Association. This is an honor for me, and I am grateful. It is humbling to be asked to speak on this night to this group. On this night, because it is the time when the late, great Ed Murrow has a commemorative stamp issued in his name. . . .

He was the best reporter of his generation. The best reporter in broadcasting or print. He reported, he led, he made the best broadcasts of his time, both in radio and television. And those broadcasts remain, to this day, the best of all time. They include the "This Is London" broadcasts from the Battle of Britain, the radio reports from the death camp at Buchenwald, and the television programs on Joseph McCarthy and "Harvest of Shame."

. . . .

But we should, we must remember this: he was a real, flesh-and-blood, flawed, vulnerable, mistake-making hero.

With all of his triumphs, many and mighty, he also fought some fights he should not have fought, and he sometimes, often times, lost. Including losing at the end. In the end, his bosses and his competitors—inside as well as outside his own network—cut him up, cut him down, and finally cut him out.

Dan Rather gave this speech at the annual convention of the Radio and Television News Directors Association (September 29, 1993), in Miami, Florida.

And not long after that, he died. Cancer was the cause, they say.

. . . .

Ed Murrow said of television: "This instrument can teach, it can illuminate; yes, and it can even inspire. But it can do so only to the extent that humans are determined to use it to those ends. Otherwise, it is merely wires and lights in a box. There is a great and perhaps decisive battle to be fought against ignorance, intolerance, and indifference. This weapon of television could be useful."

What follows now is a tribute, a biography and a fond remembrance, prepared by CBS News, to Edward R. Murrow—a commander in the battle against ignorance, intolerance, and indifference.

Part II
Call It Courage

The speech Ed Murrow gave at the RTNDA convention in Chicago, 1958, was a risky speech, and he knew it. It was a bold shot, and he knew it. That was part of the Murrow style, and part of what has made the Murrow mystique: the bold, brave shot.

He began that speech with the modest speculation that, and I quote, "This just might do nobody any good." I don't think Ed Murrow believed that. It was a call to arms—the most quoted line is the one about "wires and lights in a box," but the more important line is "this weapon of television." Ed Murrow had seen all kinds of battles, and if *he* lifted *his* voice in a battle cry, surely some of his own colleagues would hear him and heed him.

As with many television and radio news people of my generation, that speech has criss-crossed the back-roads of my memory through a lifetime in the business.

. . . .

As he had been for many others, Murrow had been my hero when I was just a boy. . . . Murrow told me tales of bravery in time of war, tales more thrilling than "Captain Midnight" or "Jack Armstrong" because these were *true.*

He talked about the bravery of soldiers and citizens. He never made a big fuss about his own bravery. But even as a little boy, I knew it took bravery just to stand on that rooftop, with the bombs raining down thunder and lightning all around him . . . or to go up in that plane—"D-for-Dog"—with the ack-ack and the messerschmidts all about. And I never forgot that Murrow did all this because he wanted me and my family, and all of us back home in America, to know . . . the truth. For *that*, for our knowledge of the truth, he risked his life.

In my mind, then and now, neither Achilles nor King Arthur—not Pecos Bill or Davy Crockett—surpassed a hero like that.

The Murrow I met years later—person to person, if you will—the real Ed Murrow was everything I wanted that hero to be. He was a quiet man: tall, strong, steady-eyed, not afraid of silence.

What separated Ed Murrow from the rest of the pack was courage.

. . . .

Ed Murrow had courage. He had the physical courage to face the Blitzkrieg in London and to ride "D-for-Dog." He had the professional courage to tell the truth about McCarthyism. And he had the courage to stand before the Radio and Television News Directors Association, and to say some things those good people didn't want to hear, but needed to hear.

In our comfort and complacency, in our (dare we say it?) cowardice, we, none of us, want to hear the battle cry. Murrow had the courage to sound it anyway. And thirty-five years later, however uncomfortable, it's worth pausing to ask—how goes the battle?

In the constant scratching and scrambling for ever better ratings and money and the boss' praise and a better job, it is worth pausing to ask— how goes the real war, the really important battle of our professional lives? How goes the battle for quality, for truth, and justice, for programs worthy of the *best* within ourselves and the audience? How goes the battle against "ignorance, intolerance, and indifference"? The battle *not* to be merely "wires and lights in a box," the battle to make television *not* just entertaining but also, at least some little of the time, *useful* for higher, better things? How goes the battle?

The answer we know is "Not very well." In too many important ways, we have allowed this great instrument, this resource, this weapon for good, to be squandered and cheapened. About this, the best among us hang their heads in embarrassment, even shame. We all should be ashamed of what we have and have not done, measured against what we could do . . . ashamed of many of the things we have allowed our craft, our profession, our life's work to become.

Our reputations have been reduced, our credibility cracked, justifiably. This has happened because too often for too long we have answered to the worst, not to the best, within ourselves and within our audience. We are less because of this. Our audience is less, and so is our country.

Ed Murrow had faith in our country, and in our country's decision to emphasize, from the beginning, *commercial* broadcasting. He recognized commercial broadcasting's potential, and its superiority over other possibilities. But even as he believed in the strength of market values and the freedom of commercial radio and television, Ed Murrow feared the rise of a cult that worshipped at the shrine of the implacable idol Ratings. He feared that the drive to sell, sell, sell — and nothing but sell — was overwhelming the potential for good, the potential for *service* of radio and television.

He decried the hours of prime-time as being full of (quote) "decadence, escapism, and insulation from the realities of the world in which we live." As you let that sink in, let's remember that he was talking about programs like *I Love Lucy* and *The Honeymooners,* that are now esteemed on a par with the best comedies of Plautus and Molière; Murrow singled out the *Ed Sullivan Show,* which is now studied and praised as a modern-day School of Athens, peopled by all the best minds and talents of the time. These are the programs that had Ed Murrow worried.

He wasn't worried about, didn't live to see *Full House* or *America's Funniest Home Videos* or *Fish Police.* He wasn't worried about, didn't live to see the glut of inanities now in "Access" time. He never lived to see the cynicism and greed that go into the decisions to put on much of that junk.

In 1958, Murrow was worried because he saw a trend setting in . . . avoiding the unpleasant or controversial or challenging . . . shortening newscasts and jamming them with ever-increasing numbers of commercials . . . throwing out background, context, and analysis, and relying just on headlines . . . going for entertainment values over the values of good journalism . . . all in the belief that the public must be shielded, wouldn't accept anything other than the safe, the serene, and the self-evident.

Murrow knew that belief was wrong, and contrary to the principles on which this country was founded. He'd seen how honest, mature and responsible American listeners and viewers could be when programming itself was honest, mature and responsible. Reducing the amount of real-world reality on television, Murrow argued, was unconscionable.

But Murrow did not just offer criticism. He also offered solutions. Importantly, Murrow proposed that news divisions and departments not be held to the same standards of ratings and profits as entertainment and sports. He recognized that news operations couldn't be run as philanthropies. But, he added (quote) "I can find nothing in the Bill of Rights or the Communications Act which says that [news divisions] must increase their net profits each year, lest the Republic collapse."

Murrow saw turmoil, danger, and opportunity in the world; and the best means of communicating the realities to the public — the communications innovation called television — was increasingly ignoring the realities. And those few Americans who had been given the privilege of owning and operating television stations and networks, the privilege of making great wealth from them, were beginning to reduce if not downright eliminate their responsibilities to public service.

Private profit from television is fine, but there *should be* a responsibility to news and public service that goes with it; this was the core of Murrow's case.

These were words which needed to be heard. Then, and now. . . .

When Murrow spoke to your predecessors at RTNDA, he knew that *they* were not his problem. The people he wanted most to hear and heed his speech were not in that Chicago ballroom. They worked in boardrooms, not newsrooms. Murrow's Chicago speech was a brave, bold bid to persuade corporate executives, both at stations and networks and at the advertising agencies and corporate sponsors.

He failed. Not long afterward, his position inside his own network was diminished. And not long after that, he was out.

Little has changed since Murrow gave that report from the battlefield and issued that call to arms. And much of what *has* changed has not been for the better. More people in television now than then are doing things that deny the public service of television, that ensure that the mighty weapon of television remains nothing more than wires and lights in a box.

Even the best among decision-makers in television freely take an hour that might have been used for a documentary, and hand it over to a quote-unquote "entertainment special" about the discovery of Noah's Ark—that turns out to be a one-hundred percent *hoax*.

And the worst among the decision-makers have got us all so afraid of our own independence and integrity that at least one news director recently planned to have all his hirings reviewed by radical ideological and highly partisan political groups. (And he bragged about it.)

They've got another news director telling his staff that he didn't want stories on the Pope's visit—he wanted stories—plural—on Madonna's Sex Book. It's the ratings, stupid.

And they've got us putting more and more fuzz and wuzz on the air, cop-shop stuff, so as to compete not with other news programs but with entertainment programs (including those posing as news programs) for dead bodies, mayhem, and lurid tales.

They tell us international news doesn't get ratings, doesn't sell, and, besides, it's too expensive. "Foreign news" is considered an expletive best deleted in most local station newsrooms and has fallen from favor even among networks.

Thoughtfully-written analysis is out, "live pops" are in. "Action, Jackson" is the cry. Hire lookers, not writers. Do powder-puff, not probing, interviews. Stay away from controversial subjects. Kiss ass, move with the mass, and for heaven and the ratings' sake don't make anybody mad—certainly not anybody that you're covering, and especially not the mayor, the governor, the senator, the President or Vice-President or *anybody* in a position of power. Make nice, not news.

This has become the new mantra. These have become the new rules. The post-Murrow generation of owners and managers have made them so. These people are, in some cases, our friends. They are, in all cases, our bosses. They aren't venal—they're afraid. They've got education and taste and good sense, they care about their country, but you'd never know it from the things that fear makes them do—from the things that fear makes them make *us* do.

It is fear of ratings slippage if not failure, fear that this quarter's bottom line will not be better than last quarter's—and a whole lot better than the same quarter's a year ago.

A climate of fear, at all levels, has been created, without a fight. We—you and I—have allowed them to do it, and even *helped* them to do it.

The climate is now such that, when a few people at one news organization rig the results of a test to get better pictures—and are caught and rightly criticized—there's no rejoicing that a terrible, unusual journalistic practice has been caught, punished, and eradicated. Because we all know that, with only a slight relaxation of vigilance and a slight increase of fear, those journalistic sins could be visited upon us—we know that, as honorable and sensible as we, our friends and our colleagues try to be—it could happen to us.

Now you would be absolutely justified in saying to me right now—"Excuse me, Mister Big Shot Anchor Man, but what the hell do you expect me to do about it? If I go to my boss and talk about television as a weapon, and why don't you take *Current Affair* or *Hard Copy* or *Inside Edition* off the air next week and let me put on a tell-it-like-it-is documentary about race relations—I *know* they're gonna put me on the unemployment line, and I'll be *lucky* if they don't put me on the funny farm."

Well, none of us is immune to self-preservation and opportunities for advancement. I'm not asking you for the kind of courage that risks your job, much less your whole career.

Ed Murrow had that kind of courage, and took that kind of risk several times. But you and I, reaching deep down inside ourselves, are unlikely to muster that kind of courage often, if ever.

But there are specific things we can do. They won't cost us our jobs. But they will make a difference—a start—a warning shot that the battle is about to be joined.

Number one: Make a little noise. At least question (though protest would be better) when something, anything incompatible with your journalistic conscience is proposed. When it comes to ethics and the practice of journalism, silence is a killer.

No, you won't always be heeded or heard. And yes, even to question may be a risk. But it is a wee, small risk, and a tiny price to pay to be worthy of the name "American journalist." To be a journalist is to ask questions. All the time. Even of the people we work for.

Number two: In any showdown between quality and substance on the one hand, and sleaze and glitz on the other, go with quality and substance. You know the difference. Every one of us in this room knows the difference because we've been there. We've all gone Hollywood—we've all succumbed to the Hollywoodization of the news—because we were afraid not to. We trivialize important subjects. We put videotape through a Cuisinart trying to come up with high-speed, MTV-style cross-cuts. And just to cover our asses, we give the best slots to gossip and prurience.

But we can say, "No more." We can fight the fear that leads to Show-bizzification. We can *act* on our knowledge. You know that serious news—local and regional, national and international—doesn't have to be *dull*, not for one second. People *will* watch serious news, well-written and well-produced. The proof—it's all around, but I'll give you two examples. Look at *Sunday Morning* and *Nightline*. No glitz, no gossip. Just compelling information. You can produce your own *Nightline* or *Sunday Morning*—all that's required of you is determination and thought, taste and imagination. That's what Tom Bettag and Ted Koppel, that's what Linda Mason, Missie Rennie, Charles Kuralt and their teams bring to work.

Number three: Try harder to get and keep minorities on the air *and* in off-camera, decision-making jobs. Try—and be determined to succeed.

I know that there are market survey researchers who will bring you confusing numbers and tell you they add up to one thing: your audience wants to see Ken and Barbie, and your audience *doesn't* want to see African Americans, or Arab Americans, or Latinos, or Asian Americans, or Gays or Lesbians, or Older Americans or Americans with Disabilities. So we give our audience plenty of Ken and Barbie, and we make the minorities we *have* hired, so *uncomfortable* that they hold back on the perspective, the experience, the intelligence, the talent that they could have offered to make us wiser and stronger.

Those market researchers, with their surveys and focus groups, are playing games with you and me and with this entire country. We actually pay them money to fool us—money that I submit to you could be better spent on news coverage. Their so-called samples of opinion are no more accurate or reliable than my grandmother's big toe was when it came to predicting the weather. Your own knowledge of news and human nature, your own idealism and professionalism will guide you more surely than any market researcher ever will. You and I know that market research can and often does cripple a newscast—pronto. But the market researchers will keep getting away with their games so long as you and I and the people we work for, let them.

If we change the voice and the face of broadcasting, honestly and fairly, on the basis of excellence and ethics, talent and intelligence, we can shatter false and cheap notions about news, we can *prove* that our audience wants electronic journalism that is ethical, responsible, and of high quality—and that is as diverse, as different, as dynamic as America itself.

There is another thing we all can do, a difference we can make. One Word. *More.*

Let's do more to think more. Let's bring all the brilliance and imagination this industry has to bear. *That's* what Ed Murrow was talking about. Let's phase out fear. If we've got an idea, let's not hide it out of fear—the fear of doing things differently, the fear that says, "Stay low, stay silent. They can't fire you if they don't know you're there." That fear runs rampant through the corridors of radio and television today.

The people we work for are more fearful than we are. Fear leads them to depend on thoughtless, lifeless numbers to tell them what fear convinces them are facts. "American audiences won't put up with news from other countries. Americans won't put up with economic news. Americans won't put up with serious, substantive news of any kind."

Bull-feathers. We've gone on too long believing this nonsense. We've bought the lie that Information Is Bad for News. We are told, and we are afraid to disbelieve, that people only want to be entertained. And we have gone so far down the Info-Tainment Trail that we'll be a long time getting back to where we started—if ever.

The more the people we work for believe this kind of nonsense, the less inclined we have been to prove them wrong. We go about our days, going along to get along. The fear factor freezes us.

The greatest shortage on every beat, in every newsroom in America, is courage.

I believe, as Ed Murrow did, that the vast majority of the owners—and executives and managers we work for are good people, responsible citizens, and patriotic Americans. I believe that the vast majority of the people in this room also fit that description. We all know what's at stake. We know that our beloved United States of America depends on the decisions we make in our newsrooms every day.

In the end, Murrow could not bring himself to believe that the battle about which he spoke so eloquently could be won. He left the electronic journalism he helped to create—believing that most, if not all, was already lost, that electronic news in America was doomed to be completely and forever overwhelmed by commercialism and entertainment values.

About that, I hope, I believe Murrow was wrong. What is happening to us and our chosen field of work does not have to continue happening. The battle is dark and odds-against. But it is not irreversible, not—not yet. To prevent it from being so requires courage.

A few, just a few, good men and women with courage—the courage to practice the idealism that attracted most of us to the craft in the first place—can make a decisive difference. We need a few good men and women . . . with the courage of their convictions, to turn it around. We can be those men and women. If the people in this room tonight simply agreed, starting tomorrow, to turn it around—we would turn it around. What is required is courage.

I don't have to tell you, you already know, but it is important for me to say it to you anyway—I haven't always had that courage.

I said earlier that to talk about Ed Murrow before you tonight was *humbling*. And perhaps that's true most of all in this respect: it is humbling to realize how little courage I have, compared to Murrow who had so much, and how many opportunities I have already wasted.

But tomorrow is a new day. We toil and are proud to be in this craft, because of the way Edward R. Murrow brought it into being. We can be worthy of him—we can share his courage—or we can continue to work in complacency and fear.

Cassius was right: "Men at some time are masters of their fates: The fault, dear Brutus, is not in our stars, but in ourselves. . . ."

Questions for Critical Thinking and Discussion

1. Rather tells us that Ed Murrow "feared that the drive to sell, sell, sell—and nothing but sell—was overwhelming the potential for good, the potential for *service* of radio and television." How do you think television has fared during your lifetime? In what ways has it served you, and in what ways has it sold you?

2. Can you think of examples where news has, according to Rather, put "more fuzz and wuzz on the air, cop-shop stuff, so as to compete not with other news programs but with entertainment programs (including those posing as news programs) for dead bodies, mayhem, and lurid tales"?

3. Rather provides the following list of things news programming can do to improve itself:

   a. Make a little noise.

   b. Go with quality and substance.

   c. Try harder to get and keep minorities on the air and in off-camera, decision-making jobs.

   d. Do more and think more.

   Can you add to Rather's list?

21

The Rich Tapestry of Hispanic America Is Virtually Invisible on Commercial Television

PAUL ESPINOSA

Paul Espinosa is an independent producer in San Diego. He has produced a PBS series on the Mexican War of 1846–48, an armed conflict between the United States and Mexico. Espinosa discusses the slanted or lack of presentations of Hispanic films and programs on commercial television stations and what effect this has on the Hispanic community and the society at large.

I recently had the good fortune of being honored with a film festival bearing my name. The Paul Espinosa Film Festival wasn't held in the south of France, and no Hollywood big-wigs attended—if they did, they didn't identify themselves.

Presented in the Porter Troupe Art Gallery in San Diego, the festival showcased 10 films that I have produced over 15 years for public television dealing with different facets of the Mexican-American experience. One film (*The Lemon Grove Incident*) dramatized the nation's first successful legal challenge to school segregation, a little-known case involving Mexican-American children in 1930. Another (. . . *and the earth did not swallow him*) examined one traumatic year in the life of a Mexican-American boy and his family, who migrated north every year to pick crops in the Midwest. A third (*The Hunt for Pancho Villa*) profiled Villa's infamous raid on a small New Mexican town in 1916 and the so-called "punitive" expedition sent to capture him.

These films were as well received at the festival—we actually had to turn away folks—as they had been during their original PBS broadcasts. Diverse audiences—Latino, black, white, and Asian—responded enthusiastically to a wide range of depictions of Hispanic life in America—from Guillermo Gómez-Peña's wonderful portrayal of a Mexican-American father concerned about his child's education to the fearful testimony of undocumented immigrants worrying daily about being apprehended by the Immigration and Naturalization Service; from the colorful exploits of an

This article first appeared in the *Chronicle of Higher Education* (October 3, 1997), Vol. 44(6), pages B7–B8.

86-year-old veteran of the Mexican Revolution to the earnest reflections of a 12-year-old about the nature of God and the devil.

Unfortunately, life as depicted in these films, the rich tapestry of Hispanic America, isn't finding a regular home on television, especially commercial, English-language television. For Hispanics, TV *is* the vast wasteland that Newton N. Minow, a former chairman of the Federal Communications Commission, predicted. With a few notable exceptions—Jimmy Smits's layered performances on *NYPD Blue*, Liz Torres's antics on the now-defunct *John Larroquette Show*—you have to watch a lot of television to find Hispanic characters.

Sure, a few show up from week to week as drug pushers, pimps, maids, gardeners, and Latin-American drug lords. But the absence of textured Hispanic characters is remarkable, particularly when you consider the size of the Hispanic population in the United States. Currently numbering over 28 million people—the majority of whom are of Mexican origin—Hispanics will become the nation's largest ethnic group by 2005. (If they made up a separate nation, it would be the fifth largest Spanish-speaking country in the world.)

A study done last year by the Center for Media and Public Affairs for the National Council of La Raza was aptly titled "Don't Blink: Hispanics in Television Entertainment." The study reported that representation of Hispanics on television had actually decreased during the last 30 years. Although they constitute about 10 per cent of the country's population, Hispanics accounted for only about 2 per cent of all characters depicted in the 139 prime-time series studied.

How is it that the entertainment industry, located in a city whose official name is Nuestra Señora la Reina de Los Ángeles de Porciúncula, manages either to exclude or to represent poorly such a large segment of the population?

This situation invites comparisons with the depiction of African Americans on commercial television. These days, there is no paucity of black characters and programs—although some of the depictions are so demeaning as to make one wonder whether it is better to be invisible than to be caricatured. Nevertheless, African Americans clearly have made significant progress in television in the past 20 years. Why have Hispanics not been able to achieve the same high visibility that African Americans have, both on television and in other forms of popular culture?

My own theory is that when Americans think of race and ethnicity—a subject that most of us would rather not think of at all—we can't get beyond the bipolar model of black and white. Maybe there is something archetypal about this model; the reality is that nearly all national discussions around the issue of race have been dominated by this black-white divide. It is doubly ironic that the black-white model is so pervasive in California, where Hispanics far outnumber African Americans and where so much television is actually produced. While it is no doubt true that Hispanics have not pressed the entertainment industry as hard or as energetically as African Americans have, it is also true that the industry, like much of the rest of white America, often has responded to African-American demands with a sense of historical guilt, which has not characterized its relationship to other ethnic groups.

Despite the fact that, demographically, we are experiencing a dramatic shift in the racial make-up of our population, national consciousness hasn't yet caught up with the great diversity of race in America. Perhaps we can hardly expect television, by any measure a medium that follows rather than leads, to act any differently.

But why should we care at all if Hispanics are not presented on television? What does it matter if some people, young or old, rarely see themselves represented there?

I believe it matters deeply—both for the larger society and for the Hispanic community itself. So much of what the public knows or thinks it knows about Hispanics comes directly from television, the principal symbolic system of our times. This is particularly true for those viewers who have limited contact with real-life Hispanics. Even a casual viewer realizes that the world of Hispanics depicted on television is a bleak and dangerous place. Too often, they are portrayed only as criminal, violent, or otherwise-dysfunctional individuals whom the public should fear.

Although the "Don't Blink" study found that this situation was slowly changing, roles portraying criminals were still 50 per cent more likely to be filled by Hispanics than by whites. Given the way Hispanics are portrayed on television, it is no accident that recent political campaigns in California have gone out of their way to use negative images of Hispanics to make easy points with the public—to create a not-so-subtle relationship between economic problems and crime, and the growing presence of Hispanics.

The long-term impact on the Hispanic community of being misrepresented or not represented at all on television cannot be known with any certainty, because no reliable studies have been done on this topic. Nevertheless, it does not take a rocket scientist to verify how important symbols are to all of us. It may be an exaggeration to suggest that the soaring high-school dropout rate for Hispanics is related to their viewing of television, where they encounter a symbolic world with no place for them. Yet if their future looks anything like our current television universe, it should come as no surprise that they do not want to pursue learning and living in a world in which they don't exist or in which they are relegated to the bottom of society.

We don't really know what happens when a significant group in our society consistently perceives that no one in the larger world hears its stories, no one knows its heroes, no one paints its pictures, no one sings its songs. But surely the damage to the human soul wounds us all.

Let me offer a few modest suggestions about the role that educators can play in addressing this problem. First, they can help their students—and, really, all of us—to analyze the nature of the problem. What, exactly, are the impacts on the Hispanic community of being ignored or misrepresented? And why are Hispanics so poorly represented? The answers to those questions are diverse, from poor decision making at top corporate levels to a lack of recognition that different stories need telling.

Educators at both the high-school and college levels need to help their students think critically about the construction and presentation of televised images, especially images of race and ethnicity. Most of today's students have been heavy consumers of television for their entire lives, but they may not have developed the analytical tools that allow them to evaluate how television does its work. The possibilities for critical analysis of television are endless. Students could do comparative analyses of how television and print cover the same stories in their own communities; or, around election time, they could deconstruct political advertisements to see how they work.

Faculty members in communications and fine-arts departments can help by committing themselves to develop more Hispanic producers, writers, directors, and actors to become part of the next generation in television. Part of this task is to nurture the imagination of students, to keep alive the creative impulses of young Hispanics who may feel disheartened by what they see around them.

Furthermore, students need to gain an understanding of the larger socioeconomic system within which television operates, and they need suggestions about ways to challenge entrenched attitudes. Over the last 20 years, I have seen a remarkable number of highly talented, creative Hispanics working in various jobs in film and television leave the business after hitting the "glass ceiling." Although increasing numbers of Hispanics have managed to break into the business, many discover that key decision-making positions are simply not open to them.

By educating our students about how and why Hispanics are misrepresented or made invisible by the media, educators can begin showing them where and how change can occur. Students also need to be made aware of the complexity of the process of change. It will require building coalitions both inside and outside the industry to force television and other media to confront the mechanisms of their own institutional racism.

Aside from their direct responsibilities to students, educators often have the chance to interact with professionals working for newspapers, television, radio, or other media. They need to use these encounters to enlighten key decision makers about the importance of improving representation of Hispanics on television.

Over the course of the 10-week festival showcasing my work, I was surprised and delighted by the response. Students and parents, professionals and lay people, young and old, Hispanic and non-Hispanic, the viewers clearly were interested in learning more about the Hispanic experience in America. The festival developed a loyal following of folks who returned, week after week, for the screenings and the lively discussions that followed.

Although the current television landscape is disheartening, I have hopes that we are turning a corner, about to enter an era in which Hispanics will begin to be seen in all their rich diversity. If we cannot close the gap between that world and the present television universe, all of us will be poorer for it, and in the long run, suffer the consequences of stories left untold.

Questions for Critical Thinking and Discussion

1. Espinosa considers the representation of Hispanics on television from the outside with his question, "Why should we care at all if Hispanics are not represented on television?" Then he considered the issue from the inside, "What does it matter if some people rarely see themselves represented there?" Answer these questions based upon your own experiences and consumption of television.

2. Are there other cultural or ethnic groups that are ignored or negatively stereotyped by television? Provide specific examples to support your answer.

22

TV Could Nourish Minds and Hearts

FATHER ELLWOOD KIESER

Father Kieser produced Insight *and* Romero *and heads the Humanities Prize organizations.*

Kieser claims that "The problem of American television is not the lack of story-tellers of conscience but the commercial system within which they have to operate." He considers the cultural and spiritual effects of accepting the "fact" that television is a profit-seeking industry just like any other business.

Despite questions of the motivation behind them, the attacks by the President [George Bush] and the Vice President [Dan Quayle] on the moral content of television entertainment have found an echo in the chambers of the American soul. Many who reject the messengers still accept the message. They do not like the moral tone of American TV. In our society only the human family surpasses television in its capacity to communicate values, provide role models, form consciences and motivate human behavior. Few educators, church leaders or politicians possess the moral influence of those who create the nation's entertainment.

Every good story will not only captivate its viewers but also give them some insight into what it means to be a human being. By so doing, it can help them grow into the deeply centered, sovereignly free, joyously loving human beings God made them to be. Meaning, freedom and love—the supreme human values. And this is the kind of human enrichment the American viewing public has a right to expect from those who make its entertainment.

It is not a question of entertainment *or* enrichment. These are complementary concerns and presuppose each other. The story that entertains without enriching is superficial and escapist. The story that enriches without entertaining is simply dull. The story that does both is a delight.

Is that what the American viewing public is getting? Perhaps 10% of prime-time network programming is a happy combination of entertainment and enrichment. I think immediately of dramas like *I'll Fly Away* and *Life Goes On* or comedies like *Brooklyn Bridge* and *The Wonder Years*. There used to be television movies rich in human values, but they have now become an endangered species. Sleaze and mayhem. Murder off the front page. The

This article first appeared in *Time* (September 14, 1992), page 80.

woman in jeopardy. Is there too much sex on American TV? Not necessarily. Sex is a beautiful, even holy, part of human life, a unique way for husband and wife to express their love. No doubt there is too much dishonest sex on TV. How often do we see the aching emptiness, the joyless despair that so often follows sex without commitment? And certainly there is too much violence. It desensitizes its viewers to the horrors of actual violence and implies that it is an effective way to resolve conflict. I seldom see the dehumanization that violence produces, not only in its victims, but also in its perpetrators. And I never see the nonviolent alternative—the way of dialogue and love—explored. Jesus has much to teach us here. So do Ghandi and Martin Luther King. Ninety-four percent of the American people believe in God; 41% go to church on any given Sunday. But you'd never know it by watching American TV. We seldom see TV characters reach for God or fight with Him, despite the theatricality latent in their doing so. Why is that? I find television too much concerned with what people have and too little concerned with who they are, very concerned with taking care of No. 1 and not at all concerned with sharing themselves with other people. All too often it tells us the half truth we want to hear rather than the whole truth we need to hear.

Why is television not more fully realizing its humanizing potential? Is the creative community at fault? Partially. But not primarily. I have lived and worked in that community for 32 years, as both priest and producer. As a group, these people are not the sex-crazed egomaniacs of popular legend. Most of them love their spouses, dote on their children and hunger after God. They have values. In fact, in Hollywood in recent months, audience enrichment has become the in thing. ABC, CBS and NBC have all held workshops on it for their programming executives. A coalition of media companies has endowed the Humanitas Prize so that it can recognize and celebrate those who accomplish it. And during the school year, an average of 50 writers spend a Saturday a month in a church basement discussing the best way to accomplish it. All before the Vice President's misguided lambasting of *Murphy Brown*.

The problem with American TV is not the lack of storytellers of conscience but the commercial system within which they have to operate. Television in the U.S. is a business. In the past, the business side has been balanced by a commitment to public service. But in recent years the fragmentation of the mass audience, huge interest payments and skyrocketing production costs have combined with the FCC's abdication of its responsibility to protect the common good to produce an almost total preoccupation with the bottom line. The networks are struggling to survive. And like most businesses in that situation, they make only what they feel the public will buy. And that, the statistics seem to indicate, is mindless, heartless, escapist fare. If we are dissatisfied with the moral content of what we are invited to watch, I think we should begin by examining our own consciences. When we tune in, are we ready to plunge into reality, so as to extract its meaning, or are we hoping to escape into a sedated world of illusion? And if church leaders want to elevate the quality of the country's entertainment, they should forget about boycotts, production codes and censorship. They should work at educating their people in media literacy and at mobilizing them to support quality shows in huge numbers.

That is the only sure way to improve the moral content of America's entertainment.

Questions for Critical Thinking and Discussion

1. Father Kieser finds television:
   a. "too much concerned with what people have"
   b. "too little concerned with who they [people] are"
   c. "very concerned with [people] taking care of No. 1"
   d. "not at all concerned with sharing themselves with other people"
   e. "tells us the half truth we want to hear rather than the whole truth we need to hear"
   Can you think of specific examples of television content that demonstrate these ideas?

2. Kieser argues that the industry *and* the audience are responsible for what content appears on television. Briefly explain how this shared responsibility works.

chapter 9

Public Relations

PR! A Social History of Spin

STUART EWEN

Stuart Ewen teaches in the doctorate program in sociology at the City University of New York Center and is Professor and Chair of the Department of Communications at Hunter College.

Ewen explains how the splintering of society into target demographic groups or markets is antithetical not only to the basic concept of democracy but to its practical application as well. His call is for all of us to remember the old adage "United we stand, divided we fall."

Looking at the historical development of public relations as a force in American society, one sees that a consequential change has taken place, one that throws simplistic pendulum theories into question. Coinciding with recurrent swings between public relations as a response to democratic mobilizations and as an attempt to colonize the horizons of public expression, there has been a parallel development. Over the course of this century, while arenas of public interaction and expression have become scarce, the apparatus for molding the public mind and for appealing to the public eye has become increasingly pervasive, more and more sophisticated in its technology and expertise. Economic mergers in the media and information industries, in particular, are only reminders that though many are touched by the messages of these industries, fewer and fewer hands control the pipelines of persuasion.

At the dawn of a new millennium, particularly in the face of this communications imbalance, pivotal questions become more urgent:

- Can there be democracy when the public is a fractionalized audience? When the public has no collective presence?
- Can there be democracy when public life is separated from the ability of a public to act—for itself—as a public?
- Can there be democracy when public agendas are routinely predetermined by "unseen engineers"?
- Can there be democracy when public opinion is reduced to the published results of opinion surveys, statistical applause tracks?

This piece was excerpted from Ewen's latest book, *PR! A Social History of Spin!* (Basic Books, 1996) and appeared in *Adbusters* (Spring 1997), Vol. 5(1), pages 33–36.

- Can there be democracy when the tools of communication are neither democratically distributed nor democratically controlled?
- Can there be democracy when the content of media is determined, almost universally, by commercial considerations?
- Can there be democracy in a society in which emotional appeals overwhelm reason, where the image is routinely employed to overwhelm thought?
- What developments will emerge to invigorate popular democracy this time around? What will move us beyond prevailing strategies of power that are aimed at managing the human climate?

These are big questions. Their answers, if they are to come, lie beyond the scope of any book. For those who continue to cherish democratic ideals, however, these questions point to an agenda for the future.

In thinking about ways to reawaken democracy, we must keep in mind that the relationship between publicity and democracy is not essentially corrupt. The free circulation of ideas and debate is critical to the maintenance of an aware public. The rise of democratic thinking, in fact, cannot be explained apart from the circulation of pamphlets, proclamations, and other literary documents that provided a basis for public discussion and helped to transform once-heretical ideas into common aspirations.

Publicity becomes an impediment to democracy, however, when the circulation of ideas is governed by enormous concentrations of wealth that have, as their underlying purpose, the perpetuation of their own power. When this is the case—as is too often true today—the ideal of civic participation gives way to a continual sideshow, a masquerade of democracy calculated to pique the public's emotions. In regard to a more democratic future, then, ways of enhancing the circulation of ideas—regardless of economic circumstances—need to be developed.

We need to imagine what an active public life might look like in an electronic age. We need to discover ways to move beyond thinking of public relations as a function of compliance experts and learn to think of it as an ongoing and inclusive process of discussion. Ordinary people need to develop independent ways and means of understanding and airing public problems and issues and of acting on them.

In 1927—just as public relations and the modern media system were coming of age—John Dewey remarked that "[o]ptimism about democracy is to-day under a cloud." With its bounteous amusements, he argued, a modern consumer culture was deflecting people from the functional responsibilities of citizenship. While "we have the physical tools of communication as never before," he maintained, the public had minimal access to them and was "so bewildered that it cannot find itself." "There is too much public, a public too diffused and scattered and too intricate in composition."

To move beyond this predicament and to rediscover itself as a social force, Dewey asserted, the public must move beyond its status as an audience of consumers and learn to communicate actively with itself.

> Without such communication, the public will remain shadowy and formless, seeking spasmodically for itself, but seizing and holding its shadow rather than its substance. Till the Great Society [then a common phrase for mass industrial society] is converted into a Great Community, the Public will remain in eclipse. Communication can alone create a great community.

To a disturbing extent, Dewey's speculations on "the public and its problems" continue to resonate. In our commercial culture, the extent to which the public engages in an ongoing and dynamic process of communication — unassisted by the methods and devices of opinion experts — is virtually nil. To move beyond this circumstance, a number of changes need to be made.

Present inequities regarding *who has a say? who gets to be heard?* need to be corrected. The vast power of the commercial communications system today lies in its unimpeded control over the avenues of public discussion. For this situation to change, the public sphere — currently dominated by corporate interests and consciously managed by public relations professionals — must revert to the people.

Though camouflaged by business as usual, the capacity to make such a change is within sight. Ironically, the enormous authority of a business-centered worldview is derived from the fact that large corporations have been permitted to occupy and impose upon public properties — such as the broadcast spectrum — without paying any significant rent to the public. For a negligible licensing fee, private corporations harvest an incessant windfall of public influence.

If this practice was to change — if a fund to support public communication, for example, regularly received a fair rent from those who were permitted to exploit public properties commercially — funding for noncommercial venues of expression and for noncommercial arenas of public education would be plentiful. If 15–25 percent of all advertising expenditures in the United States were applied this way, the crisis in funding for public arts and education would evaporate. New visions would flourish. Locally based community communications centers — equipped with up-to-date technologies and opening new avenues for distribution — would magnify the variety of voices heard. Schools could more adequately prepare their students for the responsibilities of democratic citizenship.

This issue of education is pivotal, since it has often been a casualty of public relations reasoning. In 1947, Bernays acknowledged this danger when he proclaimed that "[u]nder no circumstances should the engineering of consent supersede or displace the functions of the educational system." Then — contradicting his own admonition — he added that in most situations, an educated public will only interfere with leaders' ability to act. Leaders "cannot wait for the people" to understand issues fully. To harvest public support efficiently, he advised, it is crucial for leaders to arm themselves with the implements of "mass persuasion" and look to the engineering of consent as a strategy of first resort.

Epitomizing public relations doctrine that had been germinating since the First World War, this perspective has had dire consequences for the caliber of public discourse in the United States, particularly in the decades since the end of the Second World War. Inasmuch as public relations is rarely intended to inform the population about the intricacies of an issue and is more often calculated to circumvent critical thinking, it has meant that much of what is put forth for public consumption is intentionally indecipherable on a conscious level. The growing primacy of the image—as the preferred instrument of public address—is predicated on the assumption that images work on people enigmatically, that they affect people without their even realizing that a process of persuasion is going on.

The implications of this predilection, particularly for the ways in which we think about education, are considerable. We live in a world where the modern media of communication are everywhere and inescapable. Instrumental images vie for nearly every moment of human attention. Therefore, it is essential for our schools to move toward the development of critical media and visual literacy programs from the early grades onward.

The systematic examination of media institutions and the forces that influence them will encourage students and teachers to look behind the messages they receive, to uncover what, today, is a predominantly secret world. A better understanding of public relations practices will allow students to see that unconventional categories, such as "news" and "entertainment," do not adequately describe the forces at play within them.

In a society where instrumental images are employed to petition our affections at every turn—often without a word—educational curricula must also encourage the development of tools for critically analyzing images. Going back some time, the language of images has been well known to people working in the field of opinion management. For democracy to prevail, image making as a communicative activity must be understood by ordinary citizens as well. The aesthetic realm—and the enigmatic ties linking aesthetic, social, economic, political and ethical values—must be brought down to earth as a subject of study.

The development of curricula in media and visual literacy will not only sharpen people's ability to decipher their world, but it will also contribute to a broadening of the public sphere. Literacy is never just about reading; it is also about writing. Just as early campaigns for universal print literacy were concerned with democratizing the tools of public expression—the written word—upcoming struggles for media literacy must strive to empower people with contemporary implements of public discourse: video, graphic arts, photography, computer-assisted journalism and layout, and performance. More customary mainstays of public expression—expository writing and public speaking—must be resuscitated as well.

Media literacy cannot simply be seen as a vaccination against PR or other familiar strains of institutionalized guile. It must be understood as an education in techniques that can democratize the realm of public expression and will magnify the possibility of meaningful public interactions. Distinctions between publicist and citizen, author and audience, need to be broken down. Education can facilitate this process. It can enlarge the circle of who is permitted—and who will be able—to interpret and make sense of the world.

One last point. As a precondition for other changes, we need to question demographic categories of identity that, at present, divide the public against itself and separate people who—when viewed from a critical distance—may share common interests. Demographics is a powerful tool of divide and rule. To combat it, we need to rediscover a sense of social connectedness. Beyond looking out for ourselves—as individuals or as members of a particular group—we must also learn to rediscover ourselves in others, to see our concerns and aspirations in theirs.

At present, the champions of vested power insolently claim to be acting in the name of public opinion. Engineers of consent—armed with sophisticated demographic tools—continue to dictate public agendas. For this situation to change, we need to rethink those habits of mind within ourselves that disunite ordinary Americans along lines of class, race, ethnicity, gender, and persuasion, encouraging us to fight it out over increasingly insufficient crumbs. Until a sense of difference is balanced by a sense of commonality, a democratic public will be unattainable. *For the greater good to prevail, we need to imagine ourselves as a greater public.*

Questions for Critical Thinking and Discussion

1. According to Stuart Ewen, under what circumstances is publicity a contributor to democracy? And when can publicity become an impediment to democracy? Provide examples of television (publicity) content that you think help and/or hurt democracy.

2. What are some ways we can "rethink those habits of mind within ourselves that disunite ordinary Americans along lines of class, race, ethnicity, gender, and persuasion, encouraging us to fight it out over increasingly insufficient crumbs" as Ewen suggests?

24

Smokers' Hacks

WARREN BUFFETT

Warren Buffett was once R. J. Reynolds's largest shareholder, but now he's one of its strongest critics. He provides a chronology of public relations' involvement in the selling of tobacco to the American public.

I'll tell you why I like the cigarette business. It costs a penny to make. Sell it for a dollar. It's addictive. And there's fantastic brand loyalty.

One of the PR industry's first major clients was the tobacco industry. In the early twentieth century, the tobacco companies used PR's psychological marketing skills to first hook women and then children on their drug. Edward Bernays, Ivy Lee and John Hill all worked on PR for tobacco, pioneering techniques that today remain the PR industry's stock in trade: third party advocacy, subliminal message reinforcement, junk science, phony front groups, advocacy advertising, and buying favorable news reporting with advertising dollars.

Prior to World War I, smoking cigarettes was considered unrefined for women and effeminate for men, who either smoked cigars or stuck to tobacco of the chewing variety. The war brought cigarettes into vogue for men, and during the Roaring Twenties, the American Tobacco Company turned to PR to develop a vast new market—American women—for sales of its Lucky Strike brand. The company first hired adman A. D. Lasker, who portrayed Lucky Strikes as a healthy cigarette by concocting surveys using spurious data to claim that doctors preferred Luckies as the "less irritating" brand. Lasker also developed an advertising campaign featuring female Metropolitan opera stars, their soprano voices somehow unaffected by smoking, giving testimonials such as "Cigarettes Are Kind to Your Throat" and "I Protect My Precious Voice With Lucky Strikes."[1]

Edward Bernays was hired by Liggett & Myers, the maker of Chesterfields. To spoof their rivals at American Tobacco, Bernays created an organization called the "Tobacco Society for Voice Culture" to "establish a home for singers and actors whose voices have cracked under the strain of their cigarette testimonials." The satire was successful enough that American To-

This article first appeared in *Toxic Sludge Is Good for You* (chapter 3, pages 25–32), edited by John Stauber and Sheldon Rampton (Common Courage Press, 1995).

bacco President George Washington Hill hired Bernays away from Liggett & Myers. Some time later, Bernays learned that Hill had also hired Ivy Lee's PR firm a year earlier. When Bernays asked Hill about this, he replied, "If I have both of you, my competitors can't get either of you."[2]

To persuade women that cigarette smoking could help them stay beautiful, Bernays developed a campaign based on the slogan, "Reach for a Lucky Instead of a Sweet." The campaign played on women's worries about their weight and increased Lucky sales threefold in just twelve months. (The message, "cigarettes keep you thin," reverberates today in the brand name Virginia Slims.)[3]

But smoking remained a taboo for "respectable" women, and Bernays turned to psychoanalyst A. A. Brill for advice. Brill provided a classic Freudian analysis:

> Some women regard cigarettes as symbols of freedom. . . . Smoking is a
> sublimation of oral eroticism; holding a cigarette in the mouth excites the oral
> zone. It is perfectly normal for women to want to smoke cigarettes. Further
> the first women who smoked probably had an excess of masculine components
> and adopted the habit as a masculine act. But today the emancipation of
> women has suppressed many of the feminine desires. More women now do
> the same work as men do. . . . Cigarettes, which are equated with men, become
> torches of freedom.[4]

Brill's analysis inspired Bernays to stage a legendary publicity event that is still taught as a model in PR schools. To sell cigarettes as a symbol of women's liberation, he arranged for attractive debutantes to march in New York's prominent Easter parade, each waving a lit cigarette and proclaiming it a "torch of liberty." Bernays made sure that publicity photos of his smoking models appeared world-wide.[5]

Decades of saturation cigarette advertising and promotion continued into the 1950s via billboards, magazines, movies, TV and radio. Thanks to Bernays and other early pioneers of public relations, cigarettes built a marketing juggernaut upon an unshakable identification with sex, youth, vitality and freedom. The work for the tobacco industry, in turn, earned PR widespread credibility and launched the rise of today's multi-billion dollar public relations industry.

The Truth Hurts

In the early 1950s, the first scientific studies documenting tobacco's role in cancer and other fatal illnesses began to appear. In 1952, *Reader's Digest* ran an influential article titled, "Cancer by the Carton." A 1953 report by Dr. Ernst L. Wynder heralded to the scientific community a definitive link between cigarette smoking and cancer. Over the next two years, dozens of articles appeared in the *New York Times* and other major public publications: *Good Housekeeping,* the *New Yorker, Look, Woman's Home Companion.* Sales of cigarettes went into an unusual, sudden decline.[6]

The tobacco czars were in a panic. Internal memos from the industry-funded Tobacco Institute refer to the PR fallout from this scientific discovery as the "1954 emergency." Fighting desperately for its economic life, the tobacco industry launched what must be considered the costliest, longest-running and most successful PR "crisis management" campaign in history. In the words of the industry itself, the campaign was aimed at "promoting cigarettes and protecting them from these and other attacks," by "creating doubt about the health charge without actually denying it, and advocating the public's right to smoke, without actually urging them to take up the practice."[7]

For help, the tobacco industry turned to John Hill, the founder of the PR megafirm, Hill & Knowlton. Hill designed a brilliant and expensive campaign that the tobacco industry is still using today in its fight to save itself from public rejection and governmental action. Hill is remembered today as a shrewd but ethical businessman. In a letter, he once stated, "It is not the work of public relations . . . to outsmart the American public by helping management build profits." Yet Hill's work to save tobacco in the 1950s is such an egregious example of "outsmarting the American public . . . to build profits" that Hill & Knowlton is still in court today answering criminal charges.[8] The company's role is described as follows in a 1993 lawsuit, *State of Mississippi vs. the Tobacco Cartel:*

> As a result of these efforts, the Tobacco Institute Research Committee (TIRC), an entity later known as The Council for Tobacco Research (CTR), was formed.
>
> The Tobacco Industry Research Committee immediately ran a full-page promotion in more than 400 newspapers aimed at an estimated 43 million Americans . . . entitled "A Frank Statement to Cigarette Smokers." . . . In this advertisement, the participating tobacco companies recognized their "special responsibility" to the public, and promised to learn the facts about smoking and health. The participating tobacco companies promised to sponsor independent research. . . . The participating tobacco companies also promised to cooperate closely with public health officials. . . .
>
> After thus beginning to lull the public into a false sense of security concerning smoking and health, the Tobacco Industry Research Committee continued to act as a front for tobacco industry interests. Despite the initial public statements and posturing, and the repeated assertions that they were committed to full disclosure and vitally concerned, the TIRC did not make the public health a primary concern. . . . In fact, there was a coordinated, industry-wide strategy designed actively to mislead and confuse the public about the true dangers

associated with smoking cigarettes. Rather than work for the good of the public health as it had promised, and sponsor independent research, the tobacco companies and consultants, acting through the tobacco trade association, refuted, undermined, and neutralized information coming from the scientific and medical community.[9]

Smoke and Mirrors

To improve its credibility, the TIRC hired Dr. Clarence Little as director. Previously, Little had served as managing director of the American Society for the Control of Cancer, forerunner to today's American Cancer Society.[10] Little promised that if research did discover a direct relationship between smoking and cancer, "the next job tackled will be to determine how to eliminate the danger from tobacco." This pretense of honest concern from a respected figure worked its expected magic. Opinion research by Hill & Knowlton showed that only 9% of the newspapers expressing opinions on the TIRC were unfavorable, whereas 65% were favorable without reservation.[11]

There is no question that the tobacco industry knew what scientists were learning about tobacco. The TIRC maintained a library with cross-indexed medical and scientific papers from 2,500 medical journals, as well as press clippings, government reports and other documents. TIRC employees culled this library for scientific data with inconclusive or contrary results regarding tobacco and the harm to human health. These were compiled into a carefully selected 18-page booklet, titled "A Scientific Perspective on the Cigarette Controversy," which was mailed to over 200,000 people, including doctors, members of Congress and the news media.

During the 1950s, tobacco companies more than doubled their advertising budgets, going from $76 million in 1953 to $122 million in 1957. The TIRC spent another $948,151 in 1954 alone, of which one-fourth went to Hill & Knowlton, another fourth went to pay for media ads, and most of the remainder went to administrative costs. Despite TIRC's promise to "sponsor independent research," only $80,000, or less than 10% of the total budget for the year, actually went to scientific projects.[12]

In 1963 the TIRC changed its name to the Council for Tobacco Research. In addition to this "scientific" council, Hill & Knowlton helped set up a separate PR and lobbying organization, the Tobacco Institute. Formed in 1958, the Tobacco Institute grew by 1990 into what the *Public Relations Journal* described as one of the "most formidable public relations/lobbying machines in history," spending an estimated $20 million a year and employing 120 PR professionals to fight the combined forces of the Surgeon General of the United States, the National Cancer Institute, the American Cancer Society, the American Heart Association and the American Lung Association.[13]

The tobacco industry's PR strategy has been described by the American Cancer Society as "a delaying action to mislead the public into believing that no change in smoking habits is indicated from existing statistical and pathological evidence."[14] In the 1990s, medical studies estimated that 400,000 of the 50 million smokers in the United States were dying each year from tobacco-related diseases, and that smoking was likely to be a contributing factor in the deaths of half the smokers in the country.[15] Tobacco opponents lobbied for public education and strict new regulations to prevent youthful addiction and to protect the public's right to a smoke-free environment. But despite smoking's bad press, tobacco profits have continued to soar, and the industry is opening new, unregulated mega-markets in Asia, Eastern Europe and the Third World.[16] Even in the US, most attempts at serious federal or state regulation or taxation are swatted down by tobacco's skilled army of highly paid lobbyists.

Snatching Victory from the Ashes

One way the cigarette industry intends to keep winning is by escalating to unprecedented levels its use of front groups such as the "National Smokers Alliance," an ambitious and well-funded "grassroots" campaign developed by Burson-Marsteller PR with millions of dollars from Philip Morris.

The National Smokers Alliance (NSA) is a state-of-the-art campaign that uses full-page newspaper ads, direct telemarketing, paid canvassers, free 800 numbers and newsletters to bring thousands of smokers into its ranks each week. By 1995 NSA claimed a membership of 3 million smokers. The campaign's goal is to rile up and mobilize a committed cadre of foot soldiers in a grassroots army directed by Philip Morris's political operatives at Burson-Marsteller. Philip Morris knows that to win politically it has to "turn out the troops," people who can emotionally battle on its behalf. The NSA is a sophisticated, camouflaged campaign that organizes tobacco's victims to protect tobacco's profits.

In the past, the tobacco industry attempted, not too convincingly, to distance itself from pro-smoking forces. The Tobacco Institute's Brennan Dawson told the *Congressional Quarterly* in 1990, "If we were to fund smokers' rights groups and bring them to Washington, wouldn't they then be viewed as an arm of the tobacco industry?"

Apparently desperate times require more obvious measures. In 1994, *National Journal* writer Peter Stone observed that NSA "is increasingly looking like a subsidiary of Burson-Marsteller," and noted that the PR firm "used its grassroots lobbying unit, the Advocacy Communications Team, to start building membership in the group last year." Thomas Humber, a Burson-Marsteller vice-president, is president and CEO of NSA. Burson executives Kenneth Rietz and Pierre Salinger are active, as is Peter G. Kelly, a prominent Democrat with the firm of Black, Manafort, Stone & Kelly, which is owned by Burson-Marsteller.[17]

How does the NSA recruit smoking's victims into becoming its advocates? Through a combination of high-tech direct marketing techniques and old fashioned "feet in the street" community organizing. Like every good grassroots group, the National Smokers Alliance has a folksy but strident newsletter for its membership, called *The NSA Voice*. According to its June 1994 issue, the NSA pays hundreds of young activists to sign up members in bars and bowling alleys in cities around the country. Eric Schippers, in charge of the membership drive, reported that "during only the first two months of activity, the Chicago campaign put 180 recruiters on the street and enlisted more than 40,000 members."

Many NSA members are first recruited via full-page ads with 800 numbers that exhort puffers to stand up for their rights. Everyone who calls receives the NSA newsletter free for three months, along with 10 membership recruitment cards and stickers to place in stores and restaurants that say, "I am a smoker and have spent $_____ in your establishment." NSA members who sign up another ten people at $10 each can win a free NSA t-shirt. The committed and informed pro-smoking advocate can also call a free 800 number to order more sign-up cards and stickers, or get the latest marching orders regarding which bureaucrats or politicians need nudging from Marlboro's masses. One recent NSA mailing, sent first class to hundreds of thousands of smokers, urged them to write letters to the Occupational Safety and Health Administration (OSHA) to defeat new regulations that would "ban smoking in any site where work is conducted."

Burson-Marsteller's propagandists have even coined a clever play on words that questions the patriotism of anti-smokers by calling them "anti Americans." NSA's newsletter advises, "If 'Anti' America is pushing a discriminatory smoking ban in your workplace, speak up," and "check the laws in your state with regard to the protection of individual rights."[18]

Bringing in the Sheaves

In recent years California has been the front line of the tobacco wars and the state where the industry has suffered its worst setbacks. In 1988 the cigarette companies spent more than $20 million in a failed effort to defeat a major anti-smoking initiative. Since then health activists have passed hundreds of local smoking bans. As a result, California has seen a 27% decrease in cigarette consumption, the most success of any state in reducing tobacco's deadly toll.[19]

Philip Morris is fighting back through a California PR firm called the Dolphin Group. Dolphin CEO Lee Stitzenberger used a half-million dollars from Philip Morris to set up a front group called "Californians for Statewide

Smoking Restrictions." Using this deceptive name, NSA members gathered signatures to put a referendum on the California ballot in November 1994, which the Dolphin Group promoted with billboards reading, "Yes on 188 — Tough Statewide Smoking Restrictions — The Right Choice."[20]

In reality, Proposition 188 was a *pro*-tobacco referendum which, if passed, would have undermined 270 existing local anti-smoking ordinances in California cities, as well as the state's new statewide smoke-free workplace law.[21] Anti-smoking groups charged that many of the people who signed petitions in favor of the referendum were led to believe that they were supporting a measure to protect nonsmokers and youths. After the public learned about the funding source behind "Californians for Statewide Smoking Restrictions," opinion turned decisively against the referendum and it was voted down. "The $25 million smokescreen the tobacco industry created to dupe Californians into voting for Proposition 188 has cleared, and the voters have spoken," declared the American Cancer Society.[22]

The tobacco industry's PR campaign is not really about swaying public opinion, a battle which the industry has already lost. Even half of smokers favor stricter government regulation of their deadly habit.[23] The industry's goal is not to win good PR, but to avoid losing political and legal battles. The survivalist strategy has served the cigarette industry well for forty years. At a PR seminar in May 1994, Tom Lauria, the chief lobbyist for the Tobacco Institute, pointed out that tobacco sales continue to grow worldwide. He dismissed tobacco critics as simply a "political correctness craze" and ridiculed predictions of tobacco's demise, saying that the media has been preparing smoking's obituary for decades. Tobacco may be fighting for its life, but Lauria reminded the assembled PR practitioners that his industry has been fighting and winning that battle for a long time.[24]

Hazy Ethics

Sixteen thousand PR practitioners (including Harold Burson and Lee Stitzenberger) belong to the Public Relations Society of America (PRSA) and pledge to abide by its seventeen-point "Code of Professional Standards." The code states that a PRSA member "shall conduct his or her professional life in accord with the public interest."

PR legend Edward Bernays, who designed the "torches of liberty" parade that made smoking socially acceptable for American women, later said if he'd known of the dangers of tobacco he would have refused the account. "When the profession of public relations was first outlined," Bernays stated, "it was envisioned as other professions functioned: that is, as an art applied to a science, in this case social science, and in which the primary motivation was the public interest and not pecuniary motivation. . . . No reputable public relations organization would today accept a cigarette account, since their cancer-causing effects have been proven."[25]

These ethical qualms in his later years made Bernays a minority voice within the public relations industry. In 1994, an informal survey of 38 PR firms revealed that only nine would decline a contract to represent the tobacco industry.[26]

Bernays, a nonsmoker, lived to be 103 years old, passing away in March 1995. His final years were spent fruitlessly appealing to the PRSA to police its own ranks. "Under present conditions, an unethical person can sign the code of PRSA, become a member, practice unethically—untouched by any legal sanctions," Bernays observed. "In law and medicine, such an individual is subject to disbarment from the profession. . . . There are no standards. . . . This sad situation makes it possible for anyone, regardless of education or ethics, to use the term 'public relations' to describe his or her function."[27]

Notes

1. Richard W. Pollay, "Propaganda, Puffing and the Public Interest," *Public Relations Review*, Vol. XVI, No. 3, Fall 1990, p. 40.
2. Ibid., p. 41.
3. Ibid., p. 40.
4. Stuart Ewen, *Captains of Consciousness: Advertising and the Social Roots of Consumer Culture* (New York: McGraw-Hill, 1976), p. 160.
5. Pollay, p. 41.
6. Ibid., p. 42.
7. Ibid., p. 50.
8. Scott M. Cutlip, "The Tobacco Wars: A Matter of Public Relations Ethics," *Journal of Corporate Public Relations*, Vol. 3, 1992–1993, pp. 26–31.
9. Mike Moore, Attorney General, State of Mississippi in lawsuit filed on May 23, 1994.
10. Cutlip, "The Tobacco Wars," p. 28.
11. Cutlip, *The Unseen Power*, p. 488.
12. Pollay, pp. 45–49.
13. Cutlip, *The Unseen Power*, p. 501.
14. Ibid., p. 497.
15. Michael Evans Begay et al., "The Tobacco Industry, State Politics, and Tobacco Education in California," *American Journal of Public Health*, Vol. 83, No. 9, Sept. 1993, p. 1214.
16. Carolyn Henson, "World Health Organizations No Tobacco Day," Associated Press, May 30, 1994. See also Robert Evans, "Third World, Women Boost Smoking Death Forecasts," Reuters wire service, May 30, 1994.
17. Peter H. Stone, "It's All Done With Some Smoke and Some PR," *National Journal*, May 28, 1994, pp. 1244–1245.
18. "Anti-America," *The National Smokers Alliance Voice*, Vol. 2, Issue 4, June-July 1994.

19. John Schwartz, "California Activists' Success Ignites a Not-So-Slow Burn," *Washington Post*, May 29, 1994.
20. "State Official Challenges Tobacco Firm, California Initiative Said to Be Deceptive," *The Washington Post* wire service, June 2, 1994.
21. B. Drummond Ayres, Jr., "Philip Morris on Offensive in California," *New York Times*, May 16, 1994, p. 1.
22. Gaylord Walker, "Smoke Hits the Fan—American Cancer Society Thrilled," PR Newswire, Nov. 9, 1994.
23. Advertising Age Gallup poll, quoted in "Tobacco Industry's Own Health is the Latest Victim of Marketing Practices," *Inside PR*, April 1994, p. 6.
24. "Tobacco Institute Relies on PR to Help Smoke Out P.C. Police," *O'Dwyer's Washington Report*, Vol. IV, No. 12, June 1994, pp. 1, 7.
25. Bernays, *The Later Years*, p. 115.
26. "3 of 4 Flacks Agree: No Ifs About Butts," *PR Watch*, Vol. 1, No. 4, Third Quarter 1994, p. 2.
27. Bernays, *The Later Years*, p. 139.

Questions for Critical Thinking and Discussion

1. It's difficult to believe that decades ago cigarette smoking was considered a bad thing to do (Buffett says that before World War I it was "unrefined for women and effeminate for men" to smoke). Can you think of other products (or services or industries) that were once thought of negatively but have now gained public favor through publicity?

2. Who is responsible for health problems caused by smoking? Discuss how culpability might be shared by the following: the manufacturers (who haven't been forthright about the dangers of smoking); the PR firms that sold "the bill of goods" to the public; the smokers, themselves, because they could have chosen *not* to smoke in the first place; and/or the general public for allowing controlled substances to be sold to the public and perhaps even for providing some "permission" through sexy cigarette media images or advertising.

25

Targeting Minority Publics

LINDA P. MORTON

Linda P. Morton is associate professor at the University of Oklahoma's H. H. Herbert School of Journalism and Mass Communication.

Morton claims that public relations fail to distinguish important differences among and within minority publics. She provides a brief characterization of three ethnic groups (African Americans, Asian Americans, and Hispanic Americans) and discusses how these groups (and their subgroups) are stereotyped or homogenized by targeted messages.

As public relations practitioners, we represent our organizations to many publics. We must segment these publics if we are to maintain mutually beneficial relationships with them.

Minority publics are no exception. Yet too often, we fail to distinguish important differences among and within minority publics. A recent *USA Today* article notes that advertisers must overcome five myths to effectively target minority publics. The myths apply as much to public relations practitioners as to the advertisers.[1]

The myths include: (1) Minorities are the same as Caucasians. (2) Minorities are homogeneous. (3) Organizations can reach minorities through the mass media. (4) Language isn't important. (5) Minorities are only interested in certain products.

USA Today continued by providing evidence that burst the myths. Thus, minorities are not the same as Caucasians. Yet, neither are they homogeneous. Practitioners shouldn't target them all as though they are the same any more than they would target them as though they are Caucasians.

This article attempts to answer that article's call to determine "minorities' differing preferences," and to keep us from offending minority publics or overlooking "important minority segments altogether."[2] It provides information on three major minority groups in the United States—African Americans, Asian Americans, and Hispanic Americans. It distinguishes each from Caucasians and provides information about targeting them as groups and as subgroups within each group.

This article first appeared in *Public Relations Quarterly* (Summer 1997), Vol. 42(2), pages 23–28.

One marketer who specializes in targeting African Americans provides principles to guide communications with African Americans. These principles apply as well to Asian and Hispanic Americans, and I refer to them throughout this article.

- Provide relevant information,
- Recognize them by portraying them in non-stereotypical ways,
- Show respect for their culture and values, and
- Recognize them as loyal consumers.[3]

African Americans

African Americans number almost 30 million and comprise more than 12% of the U.S. population and 14% of its work force.[4] Any organization hoping to influence policy must deal with the African American public. The average income for African Americans in 1995 was $18,600, just 60% of Caucasian income.[5]

We can provide relevant information to them by communicating about causes that involve them. For instance, a chamber of commerce could produce a flyer or folder that lists local businesses supporting causes such as the United Negro College Fund, the Sickle Cell Disease Foundation and Just Say No to Drugs.[6] Sponsoring special events for Black History Month and Dr. Martin Luther King's Birthday provide another way to provide relevance to African Americans.

AT&T recently recognized African Americans in a nonstereotypical way. It featured a family viewing a photograph of Egyptian pyramids on an AT&T desktop system.[7] However, just adding photographs of African Americans will not do the job. Practitioners must also consider African Americans' values, which differ from Caucasians'.

Showing respect for African American values includes recognizing their attitudes about family, religion and self-image. African Americans value families. They average four people per household with almost half of their households headed by women. They also value religion, blending traditional Christianity with their tradition of gospel music. They value self-image, style, and personal elegance more than Caucasians, making them trendsetters especially among the young.[8]

We can increase message effectiveness if we recognize these values when communicating with African Americans. For instance, photographs that portray the African American family as it is should fare better than ones that picture a father, mother, two children and a dog. The latter is a traditional Caucasian family. Assuming that it represents "family" for African

Americans and other minorities will prove ineffective or worse offensive. Similarly, photographs of African Americans should portray their sense of style and personal elegance.

Those of us who represent businesses must also recognize African Americans as consumers. As a group, they spend $350 billion annually.[9] They like to shop, considering it a social event. They buy name brands, educational equipment and reference books. They are particularly interested in finances and investing.[10] They desire recognition and select brand products, premium liquors, new cars, expensive clothes and jewelry as affordable status symbols.[11] We can increase message relevance for African Americans by including these products as props in visual communications and referring to them in verbal communications. Coupons and samples also work effectively with them.[12]

Successfully targeting African Americans also demands that practitioners recognize differences between them. They differ by socio-economic class. Poor African Americans mostly live in the poor inner cities. Wealthier African Americans live in the suburbs, own homes, and are frequently well-educated professionals.[13] Most (53%) still live in the South, where they earn low incomes.[14] However, 75% are above the poverty level, and 13% have annual incomes of $50,000 or more.

Communicating with African Americans in different socio-economic classes requires different verbal and visual messages. Those in lower socio-economic classes are most likely to respond to "images of black unity and Afrocentric identity." Those in the lower and lower-middle classes respond favorably to black slang. However, middle-class African Americans respond less favorably to Afrocentricity and are often offended by black slang. They prefer blending African American culture with middle-class lifestyles. Independent and self-confident, middle class African Americans don't need to impress Caucasians.[15]

Even middle-class African Americans are not all alike. More than a third (38%) work in white-collar jobs with slightly less (36%) working in blue collar jobs. A factory worker making $40,000 a year is quite different from an accountant earning the same income.[16]

Including African American practitioners as a part of a public relations staff and piloting messages and designs to subgroups of African Americans can increase practitioners' effectiveness in relating to them.

Asian Americans

The 1990 census counted more than seven million Asian Americans for 3.5% of the U.S. population.[17] Some researchers claim that the census underrepresented Asian Americans and that ten million more accurately reflects this

---

Asian American Subgroups

- Vietnamese, Cambodians, and Laotians are below the average annual income.

- Asian Indians are highly educated and more evenly distributed across the nation than other Asian Americans. Many of them are professionals, with 10% anesthesiologists.

- Many Japanese are in the U.S. on assignment. They tend to live around New York, while born-in-the-U.S. Japanese cluster around California. Most Japanese are managers and work for one company for life.

- Koreans also tend to work for one company for life. However, many own their own businesses such as grocery markets and dry cleaners. They cluster in large metropolitan areas.

- Filipinos are the largest and best-assimilated subgroup of Asian Americans. Many of them are professionals.

- Vietnamese compose the fastest growing subgroup, with a third of them living in California.

- Chinese are composed of two groups. Those in the first group were born in the U.S. and tend to be well off and well assimilated. They live primarily in the suburbs and speak English. The second group are recent immigrants who work in blue-collar jobs and are conservative and patriarchal. Chinese frequently speak their native language for generations, cluster together in Chinatowns, eat traditional Chinese food and support Chinese and Chinese-American businesses. Chinese white collar workers are usually professionals.[45]

---

population.[18] According to one marketer, Asian Americans represent the nation's fastest-growing market.[19]

Much of this growth comes from immigration. Of the 30% that moved to the U.S. since 1970, 75% immigrated from 1980 to 1990. Most (69%) live in 25 metropolitan areas, with 39% living in California.[20]

As consumers, Asian Americans have good purchasing power. They are the wealthiest of all minorities, averaging annual incomes of $38,500 in 1995 compared to $31,000 for Caucasians.[21] They are the only minority to earn more than Caucasians.[22] According to *Time* more than 32% of Asian Americans have family incomes exceeding $50,000 compared to only 29% of Caucasian families.[23] In 1992, Asian Americans spent $120 billion.[24] Only 11% of Asian American families live in poverty.

One reason Asian Americans fare so well economically is that most are married, and both husband and wife work.[25] Almost three-quarters of Asian

Americans are employed with 80% of those employed working in white collar jobs. Another reason they fare well economically is that they value education, with 74% completing college.[26]

Asian Americans' share many values that provide guidelines to targeting them as a group. Most (80%) are married. They do not believe in divorce so their divorce rate is low. They respect older people. Often several generations live together, making for large families. The average household size is 4.1.[27] Relationships are extremely important to Asian Americans, making public relations particularly important in keeping those relations positive and mutually beneficial.

However, Asian Americans include many different subgroups—Asian Indian, Chinese, Hawaiian, Japanese, Korean, Philippine, Vietnamese and others. Providing relevant information to Asian Americans requires that we recognize subgroups' differences in language, culture and demographics. The sidebar on Asian Americans notes some of these differences. These subgroup differences require that public relations practitioners consider each subgroup separately.

As practitioners, we can more effectively reach Asian Americans through news releases than any other minority groups. However, we need to write news releases in the language of subgroups and publish in their newspapers. Most (94%) read newspapers with 82% reading newspapers in their native languages.[28]

We can also reach Asian Americans through their television programs and sub-carrier radio channels. Japanese and Indians own five television companies that produce programming in New York. *The Pacific Century*, a PBS program, reaches Asian Americans. Sinocast Radio, a national broadcast, reaches Chinese.[29]

We can also effectively reach Asian Americans through events and community organizations. Asian Pacific Heritage month in May provides an event celebrated by all Asian American subgroups. Local cherry-blossom festivals reach Japanese. Supporting such festivals provide the relevant involvement necessary to reach any minority group.[30]

Asians fly and make many long-distance telephone calls.[31] Thus, we can reach them with relevant articles in airline companies' on-board magazines and through inserts in long-distance telephone bills.

Hispanic Americans

The Hispanic American population is predicted to grow to 30 million by the year 2000 and 41.2 million by 2020.[32] This population is about 75% (13 million) Mexicans who live mostly in southwestern states, with the remaining 25% Cubans (1 million) who live primarily in Florida; Puerto Ricans

---

Employment of Hispanic Americans by Country of Origin

More than half of Mexican American males work in either precision production, craft and repair jobs (20%) or as operators, fabricators and laborers (29%).
Only 9% hold managerial or professional positions. Contrary to the stereotypes,
more Mexican American females work in technical, sales or administrative
support jobs (39%) than work in service occupations (25%). Like the males,
many (16%) of females also work as operators, fabricators or laborers. More
females (14%) than males work in managerial or professional positions.

Puerto Rican American males divide quite equally among four areas of
employment: operators, fabricators and laborers (24%), precision production,
craft and repair (18%), service (22%), and technicians, sales and administrative
support (23%). Only 11% hold managerial and professional positions. The
largest percentage (48%) of Puerto Rican American females work in technical,
sales or administrative support. Another 21% hold managerial and professional
positions, 18% work in service occupations, and 11% work as operators,
fabricators, and laborers.

Cuban American males are almost equally divided among three areas of
employment: technicians, sales and administrative support positions (25%),
operators, fabricators, and laborers (23%), managerial and professional
positions (21%). Of the remaining minority 15% work in precision production,
craft and repair and 12% work in service occupations. The largest percentage
(49%) of Cuban American females work in technical, sales or administrative
support. Another 27% hold managerial and professional positions, 13% work
in service occupations, and 10% work as operators, fabricators, and laborers.

The largest percentage (27%) of Central South Americans work as
operators, fabricators, and laborers. The remaining majority are divided
among four areas of employment: service (22%), precision production, craft
and repair (18%), and technicians, sales and administrative support (17%).
Only 14% work as managers or professionals. The largest percentage (35%)
of Central South American females work in service occupations. Another 30%
work in technical, sales or administrative support; 16% work as operators,
fabricators, and laborers, and 15% hold managerial and professional positions.

(2.5 million) who live mainly in New York, New Jersey and Chicago; and
others (2.2 million) who primarily come from Central and South America.[33]
In 1990, Hispanics lived primarily in California, Texas, New York, Florida,
and Illinois.[34] They live in intergenerational families that include children,
adults and grandparents.[35]

As consumers, Hispanic Americans together spend about $200 billion
annually.[36] In 1995, they earned an average income of $22,000, better than
African Americans, but only 72% of Caucasians' annual income.[37] They re-

spond well to samples, which they consider gifts. We can reach them better with door-to-door sampling than in-store or newspaper sampling.[38]

Hispanic Americans as a group share several characteristics. Two of the most important are language and religion. Although many are bilingual, most speak only Spanish. Practitioners will have little success communicating with Hispanic Americans through the mass media. Less than 10% use mass media, and only 50% read English. Minority newspapers such as *La Opinion*, and radio and television stations such as Telemundo reach many,[39] but direct mail in Spanish reaches them better.

Although Protestantism is the fastest growing religion among Hispanics, most are Catholics. They value family, children, traditional middle-class values, aesthetics, emotions and appearance. Communications that emphasize these values provide relevance and increase effectiveness of public relations messages.

They want to keep their ethnicity, including holidays, rituals, and festivals. Sponsoring or participating in these events demonstrates support for and builds relationships with Hispanic Americans. Major events occur annually in Miami, New York, Washington, D.C., Chicago, Houston, San Francisco and Brownsville, Texas. The top three—Calle Ocho in Miami, Puerto Rican Day and Hispanic Day Parades in New York—each reach more than a million Hispanic Americans annually.[40]

Hispanic Americans look at work differently than Caucasian Americans, mixing in pleasure throughout their workday rather than working all day before allowing time for pleasure. This has contributed to an incorrect stereotype of Hispanics as unmotivated.[41] Avoiding this stereotype and all stereotypes of minority groups is fundamental to building positive relationships with them.

Rossman, author of *Multicultural Marketing*, contends that each segment of the Hispanic American population deserves individual attention, saying that "It would be a mistake to pitch . . . to a racially mixed Puerto Rican market by using only white Cuban models in a South Florida setting."[42]

Another marketing study notes differences between Uruguayans, Cubans and Panamanians. It notes that each are enthusiastic shoppers with largest percentage preferring small, personalized stores to convenience and department stores. However, their differences provide insights into reaching them.

- Uruguayans are the most innovative and self-confident shoppers and the most comfortable with English of the three subgroups.
- Cubans are more likely than the others to shop in large department stores and prefer English mass media. They also believe that knowing English is important to succeed in the U.S.

- Panamanians prefer neighborhood stores, are the least likely to use credit cards, and most prefer communications in Spanish.[43]

Practitioners can successfully reach many Uruguayans and Cubans through English mass media. However, direct mail publications will be more successful in Spanish.

Practitioners should assume that this applies to public relations as well as marketing, and target specific segments of the Hispanic-American population. Each differs by country of origin, culture, beliefs, opinions and purchasing decisions. The sidebar provides differences in employment.

Conclusions

The many groups and subgroups of American minorities require that public relations practitioners use techniques that marketers and advertisers have already begun to use:

- Cater different messages to the tastes of each group or subgroup.
- Communicate in each group's native tongue. (This is especially important for Hispanic and Asian Americans.)
- Use ZIP-codes to target groups with direct mail.[44] One source for targeting minorities with direct mail is *Book of Demographics and Buying Power for Every Zip Code in the USA* (Arlington, VA: CAC).
- Make design decisions based on psychographic and sociographic information inferred from demographic information.

Notes

1. "Minority Consumers Grow in Importances," *USA Today,* April 1992, 10–11.
2. Ibid.
3. Marlene L. Rossman, *Multicultural Marketing: Selling to a Diverse America* (NY: Amacom, 1994), 124.
4. Marilyn Kern-Foxworth, "Black, Brown, Red and Yellow Markets Equal Green Power," *Public Relations Quarterly,* Spring 1991, 27–30.
5. Kathy Bodovitz, "Black America," *American Demographics* (Desk Reference #1, Reprint #906, 1991).
6. Loro, "Minority Promotions Pick up the Pace," *Advertising Age* 66 (March 20, 1995), S4 & S6.
7. Ibid., S4.
8. Rossman, *Multicultural Marketing.*
9. Loro, "Minority Promotions Pick up the Pace," S4.
10. Rossman, *Multicultural Marketing,* 125.
11. Ibid.

12. Loro, "Minority Promotions Pick up the Pace," S4–S5.

13. Rossman, *Multicultural Marketing*, 123.

14. Kathy Bodovitz, "Black America," 7.

15. Rossman, *Multicultural Marketing*.

16. Ibid.

17. Kathy Bodovitz and Brad Edmondson, "Asian America," *American Demographics*, 10–11.

18. Rossman, *Multicultural Marketing*.

19. Ibid.

20. Paul Sladkus, "Affluent Asian Consumers," *American Demographics*, *** 1992, 10.

21. Loro, "Minority Promotions Pick up the Pace," S6.

22. Bodovitz and Edmondson, "Asian America," 10–11.

23. Thomas McCarroll, "It's a Mass Market No More," *Time*, Fall 1993, 80–81.

24. Loro, "Minority Promotions Pick up the Pace," S4–S5.

25. Rossman, *Multicultural Marketing*.

26. Paul Sladkus, "Affluent Asian Consumers," *American Demographics*, *** 1992.

27. Ibid.

28. Sladkus, "Affluent Asian Consumers," 11.

29. Ibid., 12.

30. Ibid., 11.

31. McCarroll, "It's a Mass Market No More," 81.

32. Loro, "Minority Promotions Pick up the Pace," S4.

33. Ibid.

34. Kathy Bodovitz, "Hispanic America," *American Demographics*, 8–9.

35. Loro, "Minority Promotions Pick up the Pace," S4.

36. Loro, "Minority Promotions Pick up the Pace," S4.

37. Bodovitz and Edmondson, "Asian America," 10–11.

38. Ibid.

39. McCarroll, "It's a Mass Market No More," 81.

40. "It's Carnival Time," *Adweek's Marketing Week*, Oct. 30, 1989, 14–15, cited in Kern-Foxworth, 29.

41. Rossman, *Multicultural Marketing*, 46.

42. Ibid.

43. E. Lincoln James and Louisa Ha, "Media Language Choice and Shopping Orientation Among Hispanics," in *Business Research Yearbook: Global Business Perspectives*, III, International Academy of Business Disciplines, 1996, 33–37.

44. McCarroll, "It's a Mass Market No More," 80–81.

45. Rossman, Multicultural Marketing, 86–87: Sladkus, "Unaffluent Asian Consumers," 11.

Questions for Critical Thinking and Discussion

1. Though Linda Morton calls for PR firms to adjust their thinking away from ethnic stereotypes, she seems to provide new stereotypes to take the place of traditional stereotypes (based on poll information). Find specific examples where Morton might be defining group characteristics too narrowly and stereotypically (again).

2. If PR firms are doing such a bad job at reaching minority ethnic groups, what makes us think they are doing such a great job reaching white ethnic groups? Do you think white society is homogenized and accurately or effectively defined and reached by PR firms? Can you think of instances where this group's perceptions and desires are stereotyped or perhaps artificially created to sell products or ideas?

chapter 10

Advertising

26

"Buy Nothings" Discover a Cure for Affluenza

CAREY GOLDBERG

Carey Goldberg is a staff writer for the New York Times.

  November 28, 1997, was Buy Nothing Day. Goldberg looks at the public's attempt to break the stronghold of advertisers during the biggest holiday season — Christmas — and provides a shopping checklist and other strategies to help people avoid overspending.

BOSTON, Nov. 28 — News flash: Dozens of people did not shop today.

And not only did those people pointedly refrain from buying anything themselves, but they also dared to challenge publicly the very institution of the Christmastime consumption season on this, the day it traditionally begins.

To the tune of "Rudolph the Red-Nosed Reindeer" they caroled, "Uh oh, we're in the red, dear." They passed out "gift exemption certificates." And they suggested sweetly to shoppers that they spend their time with loved ones or resting instead of herding automatically to the stores.

From Vermont to Seattle, these shopping-mall subversives advocated a new designation for the Friday after Thanksgiving: Buy Nothing Day.

Well, maybe Buy Nothing Day activities did not stretch all the way from Vermont to Seattle in one great anticonsumerist wave. In fact, the Buy Nothing Day action was largely limited to utopian-tinted places like Vermont and Seattle — and the handfuls of quixotic counterpropagandists were outnumbered nationwide perhaps one million to one by glassy-eyed shoppers.

But there were signs that six years after it was originated by the Media Foundation, a group based in Vancouver, British Columbia, that is bent on fighting consumer culture, Buy Nothing Day was starting to take on a life of its own, and a certain momentum.

"All I know is that there are these spontaneous outbursts of street theater, of mall invasions, of pranks and shenanigans of all kinds," said Kalle Lasn, director of the Media Foundation. "And this is nothing we're pushing heavily; it's just happening spontaneously."

This article first appeared in the *New York Times* (November 29, 1997), page A7.

There were scattered reports today of Buy Nothing Day posters, which could be downloaded from the Media Foundation's Web site, (http://www.adbusters.org) cropping up on college campuses around the country, and of related events, from seminars to singalongs, in a dozen spots, Mr. Lasn said. Anticonsumers in more than a dozen other countries put on similar events, he said.

In Vermont, Chapin Spencer, a part-time carpenter, said he had not heard of Buy Nothing Day until he recently saw a public television program about "affluenza," the spiritual and environmental ills brought on by American-style overconsumption.

Then Mr. Spencer and a friend who is a college professor quickly cobbled together a group in the Burlington area that drafted a couple dozen people, Quakers, college students and others, to staff tables outside stores. Braving the slush today, they passed out about 600 "gift of time" certificates that offered the recipient a block of the giver's time instead of a material gift, he said.

At the Church Street Marketplace in downtown Burlington, merchants concerned that the protest would hurt their sales asked the Buy Nothing demonstrators to move from their entrances to a vacant Woolworth's storefront, which they did. But in general, there was little negative reaction, Mr. Spencer said.

"The message is a positive one, not a confrontational one," Mr. Spencer said. "We're not telling people we shouldn't buy what we need, but we need to look at what we're buying and what the effect of that is personally, socially and environmentally."

In downtown Seattle, where "Buy Nothing" activities were held at the Westlake Mall, an ad-hoc singing group calling itself "The Frugalettes" crooned satirical carols with lyrics like "Big business has been telling us what Christmas means today" and "shopping like Santa's zombies." Their version of "God Rest Ye Merry, Gentlemen" began, "Slow down, you frantic shoppers, for there's something we must say."

Some Buy Nothing advocates passed out checklists to help shoppers buy more consciously; they included questions like "Do I need it?", "How many do I already have?" and "Can I do without it?" And others dispensed advice from a booth much like the one Lucy occupied in the comic strip Peanuts, under a sign reading "The affluenza doctor is in."

"We can take control of how we celebrate this holiday," said Vicki Robin, co-author of *Your Money or Your Life*, a bible of the "Voluntary Simplicity" movement, which advocates consuming less.

"If you weigh the amount of press for Buy Nothing Day against the wad of ads that came in yesterday's paper, it's no contest," said Ms. Robin, who lives in Seattle. "But ideas planted on Buy Nothing Day can make a difference in people's lives."

Checklist for Shopping

The Buy Nothing Day campaign in Seattle distributed this checklist to let shoppers evaluate things they were thinking of buying.

- Do I need it?
- How many do I already have?
- How much will I use it?
- How long will it last?
- Could I borrow it from a friend or family member?
- Can I do without it?
- Am I able to clean, lubricate and/or maintain it myself?
- Am I willing to?
- Will I be able to repair it?
- Have I researched it to get the best quality for the best price?
- How will I dispose of it when I'm done using it?
- Are the resources that went into it renewable or nonrenewable?
- Is it made of recycled materials, and is it recyclable?
- Is there anything that I already own that I could substitute for it?

It was Ms. Robin who suggested to the Media Foundation that it move Buy Nothing Day from its original date in September to the day after Thanksgiving, which it did last year, Mr. Lasn said. Since then, it has taken off, he said.

Among passers-by who stopped to take in the Buy Nothing tableaux in Burlington and Seattle, virtually none had ever heard of the holiday-in-the-making. While a few grumbled at it, most caught its gist quickly and seemed to agree.

"Ads just try to get you on a guilt trip to come in and start running up your credit card," said Paul Byron Crane, 46, an environmental planner in Seattle.

Opponents complained that Buy Nothing Day was a guilt-inducer as well, and that retailers provide the economy millions of jobs and billions of dollars in income.

"It doesn't make any sense," said Allen Parker, a 39-year-old dishwasher in Burlington. "People should be able to buy whatever they want without being made to feel guilty about it. To do for others, you have to spend money."

Still, many would like to spend less. The Center for a New American Dream, a group in Burlington that advocates "sustainable consumption," recently commissioned a survey that found that most Americans would welcome lower spending and less emphasis on gifts during the holidays.

The survey, conducted last month, found that 15 percent of its 800 respondents were still paying off their 1996 holiday bills.

Questions for Critical Thinking and Discussion

1. Define "affluenza." Can you identify (with specific examples) any affluenza in your own life? Use the shopping checklist to help you with your task.

2. Do you agree with the passerby who said, "People should be able to buy whatever they want without being made to feel guilty about it. To do for others, you have to spend money"? What are some ways to "do for others" *without* spending money?

Move Over Boomers, the "Xers" Are Here! (Or Are They?)

Generational Identity

BEYOND THE RATINGS STAFF

Ever wonder how the advertising industry defines the demographic that has been nicknamed "Generation X"? Straight from the "horse's mouth," here is a thorough elaboration on the subject provided by Arbitron, one of the two major companies (Neilsen being the other) that has provided ratings service to the broadcasting industry. This interview was conducted with Don Easdon, former executive creative director of Backer Spielvogel Bates, Inc., an international advertising agency with billings of $5.1 billion. This article summarizes how Gen Xers are researched, analyzed, defined, and, ultimately, sold.

Recently, a number of trade magazines have featured articles calling attention to "Generation X." This is a group that TV station personnel and ad agency media staffers have also referred to as "Xers," "post-boomers," "twentysomethings," "baby busters," or "the shadow generation."

Whatever they're called, there are several facts that pertain to them about which everyone can agree: that this generation consists of persons 18 to 29 years of age; that there are about 44 million of them; that they have an estimated spending power of $125 billion a year; that three-quarters of the males are still living with their parents; that the group's loyalties to brands have yet to be entrenched.

And more to the point—as Don Easdon, former executive creative director of Backer Spielvogel Bates, has observed—psychographically they perceive themselves to be truly unique: not only different from the boomers who preceded them, but from all other 18- to 29-year-olds who have lived in the past.

The above statement is just one of Easdon's observances from his study of Generation X. It, along with others, was recently presented to some of BSB's clients, and more recently to *BTR* during an interview with Easdon.

This article first appeared in *Arbitron's BTR (Beyond the Ratings)* (Spring 1993), pages 8–9.

BTR: *What prompted you to study these 18- to 29-year-olds, the so-called Generation X?*

EASDON: Several months ago the head of one of Backer's overseas clients announced he would be visiting the agency's New York office. He said he wanted to be brought up to date on the latest trends in American advertising, especially as to what kinds of TV commercials young adults were watching. So I began to read everything I could about them. I also started to interview them, mostly the ones in their mid-20s. My goal was to get to understand their basic values and attitudes so that I could figure out a way to create ads for them.

BTR: *And what did you find out?*

EASDON: They're driven in four different ways, which I'll get to in a minute. Right now what I want to say is, if there's one thing that makes this group distinct, say, from my or any other generation, it is their lack of identity. People have called them the "indifferent generation" because they've been perceived as not being involved in political activity. But that's changing. And they've been called "the shadow generation" because they came after the boomers.

What's more, this is a group made up of what I call "survivors." They have a high suicide rate, and more accidents and murders have occurred among them than among any other age group in modern history. If that's not enough, there's AIDS. AIDS has robbed them of many lives. And when you think about it, AIDS has done something else: It's also created stars like Madonna and Marky Mark. Fantasy sex symbols—blatantly so, not subtly so; not laid around; nothing deeper. And that's important to this twentysomethings generation. Those two performers turn them on sexually vicariously. It's all very direct, which is significant when one looks at some of the advertising this group respects. They want to be told that one and one equals two. They want to be free for today, and they don't have time to sit with some image for more than right now. I think that's why Madonna appeals to them. She's constantly changing her image.

BTR: *You mentioned four things that drive them. What are they?*

EASDON: Number one, they really don't see a reason to pay extra for status, like having to own a BMW or spending on something they really don't need.

Second, they really appreciate life on a different level than we do. I think that's because, as I said, they've survived a lot of things that we have not had to face.

Third, they don't need to stand out, while at the same time they don't need to fit in. What I mean is, my generation felt it needed to be accepted, to be part of a crowd. With Xers there's still a lot of that. At the same time, they want to be accepted for their originality. It's very important to them as to how they feel inside rather than what they're letting other people know about themselves.

Fourth—and this relates to advertising—they're ready to penalize advertisers who they believe only stand for making a profit. But they're willing to reward companies that exhibit a sense of social consciousness.

BTR: *Do you have any thoughts about this group's future?*

EASDON: You know, there's another title we might give this group, and that's to call them the "question generation." Because with them, everything has to have an answer. They don't accept anything at face value. They question everything and then come to their own individual conclusions. And it's this that's going to make it hard for advertisers to group them. Nonetheless, I believe they're going to dominate media and advertising in the not-too-distant future in the same way boomers do now. In fact, it's already beginning to happen.

The first person to define Generation X was Douglas Coupland, whose 1991 book, *Generation X: Tales of an Accelerated Culture*, became a best seller. Another book within this genre is *Generations*, coauthored by the historian Neil Howe.

Last February 11 Howe appeared on the PBS TV show *Adam Smith's Money World*.

During the broadcast, Howe pointed out that instead of just two generations, the old and the young, there are four age groups, each vying with each other for economic and political power.

The oldest of these, he claims, is the "G.I. Generation": 25 million living Americans born between 1901 and 1924. Next in line is the so-called "Silent Generation," the organization men of the '50s and '60s. There are 40 million of them, born between 1925 and 1942. According to Howe, this generation experienced the fastest income growth and the greatest accumulation of wealth of any generation before or since.

Following that group come the boomers, President Clinton's generation, made up of 69 million living Americans born between 1943 and 1960. This is the generation of rock-and-roll, Woodstock and sexual freedom.

Last, there's what Howe calls the "13th Generation": 80 million young Americans born between 1961 and 1981. Not only are they the MTV generation, they're the poorest since the 1930s Depression; the generation of "McJobs," jobs that pay the minimum wage. Howe has named them the

13th Generation because they're the 13th since the first U.S. generation appeared with Benjamin Franklin.

Of note, it took the G.I. Generation a relatively few years to double its standard of living. According to the TV show's Adam Smith, the 13th Generation won't see that doubling in their lifetimes. Said Smith, "It will take an incredible 240 years for them to double theirs."

Questions for Critical Thinking and Discussion

1. What are some of the social and environmental phenomena that have affected Generation X's perceptions and aspirations (both positively and negatively)?

2. Neil Howe divides the U.S. population into four age groups: (a) the G.I. Generation; (b) the Silent Generation; (c) the baby boomers; and (d) the 13th Generation (Gen Xers). Briefly describe what characterizes each of these groups.

3. What do you think about the prospect that "while it took the G.I. Generation only a few years to double its standard of living, the 13th Generation (Gen Xers) won't see that doubling in their lifetimes"? Should the possibility of acquiring a better standard of living be guaranteed? Isn't that the American way (i.e., work hard and you will be rewarded)? Or were the other generations just simply lucky and, therefore, future generations are unlucky but shouldn't complain about it?

28

Tuning In to Generation X

They Are 44 Million Strong, Invisible, Overshadowed by the Boomers, Culturally Diverse, Socially Aware, Survivors

JOSEPH SCHWARTZ

Joseph Schwartz is a journalist specializing in reporting the impact of demographics on the business community.

Schwartz provides further analysis of the demographic group nicknamed Generation X. He explains the economic and population circumstances that have left advertisers scurrying to understand this large group in order to target them with marketing messages.

On college campuses today, radio stations play "classic rock" from the 1960s and 1970s. Reruns of *Star Trek, Gilligan's Island* and other favorite 1960s television shows are common on cable channels.

Baby boomer music. Baby boomer TV. The 78 million baby boomers, born between 1946 and 1964, are less than a third of the U.S. population, yet they garner more than their share of media time.

The generation born after the boom has largely been ignored by the media. It is a smaller generation, close to 44 million people who were born between 1964 and 1975. The boundaries of this newer generation define a lull in national birth rates that began at the end of the baby boom and halted when the national birth rates began ticking up as baby boomers began producing their own babies.

Even the names that this fresh crop of young adults are called sound disparaging: the "Baby Bust," "Generation X." . . .

Today, the members of this Generation X range in age from 18 to 29 years old. In spite of the lack of attention paid to them, they are the next generation of leaders and high earners.

Defining Characteristics

Many of the demographic characteristics that older baby boomers experienced in their 20s probably will be followed by Generation X: They will marry

---

This article first appeared in *Arbitron's BTR (Beyond the Ratings)* (Spring 1993), pages 10–12.

late, postpone having children and worry most about establishing careers. As they approach their 30s, the share who are married will steadily increase, along with the presence of children in the home and household income. However, marketers who assume that their lifestyles automatically will follow in the steps of the baby boom are mistaken.

The era during which twentysomethings came of age could be defined as the 1980s. Unlike the baby boomers, who grew up with mass-marketed network television, Generation X came of age with the explosion of channels on cable television and the growing penetration of the VCR. Generation X had infinitely more media choices than the baby boomers and it never retained loyalty to particular shows or networks as much as the baby boomers did.

Older baby boomers grew up in an era of 35-cent gasoline; Generation X grew up in an era of overflowing landfills. The baby boomers have been tagged as the generation that started the sexual revolution, while Generation X grew up with AIDS.

Obviously, age-related characteristics alone cannot determine the values and lifestyles of a generation. There also is what demographers call a "cohort" effect that takes the experiences of a generation into account.

. . . .

As television gets better at attracting Generation X through television shows and cable channels such as MTV and E! Entertainment, consumer product manufacturers are following suit by changing their television advertising formats.

"We've been talking in terms of 18- to 29-year-olds, in a new type of advertisement," notes Mike Moran, manager for public affairs at Ford Division of Ford Motor Company in Detroit. "We've been focusing our efforts on that age group."

Ford's Mustang, Escort GT and Ranger are targeted toward young adults in a new television ad that "breaks the mold" of traditional Ford ads, Moran says. The ad includes quick shots of young adults in a "whole barrage of settings with music and lifestyles of people in that age category."

Why do Mustang, Ranger and Escort GT appeal to twentysomethings? "It's a matter of affordability and lifestyle," says Moran. People in their 20s and late teens usually have a tight budget, they often are single and have few, if any, children. Sporty yet small, economical two-door vehicles often appeal to them, while people aged 30 and over often want larger, four-door cars, such as the Taurus, for business or family use, Moran explains.

. . . .

At Ford, executives are learning that they don't have to like an advertisement for that ad to be effective. "They obviously are not in that age category. If they like an ad targeted toward youth, they probably won't use it because it won't work," explains Ford's Moran.

"The basic premise of advertising is to target your message to the target group," agrees Blaise Newman, an executive at the Detroit office of J. Walter Thompson. "If you hate an ad, you probably are not the target audience."

Targeting the twentysomethings is especially difficult. "It is a cohort of changing values and lifestyles. The variety of choices that young people have intrinsically makes them harder to reach," Newman says.

Demographic Density and Diversity

Many people call it choice. Some call it change. Others call the tumult of the twentysomethings "Demographic Density."

"Demographic density means that a population is rapidly changing its demographic status. From the time someone graduates from high school at the age of 18 until they turn 30, their lives typically transform from dependents living with parents to workers supporting themselves, to married couples and, often, to parenthood," says Thomas Exter, president of TGE Demographics, Inc. "In the span of about a decade, young adults undergo a host of demographic changes more rapidly than at any other stage of their lives. They are a moving target and therefore they are very hard to hit."

. . . .

Demographic density underlines the challenge of marketing to people in their 20s. Yet learning about people in their 20s will help businesses understand changes in store for the entire nation.

The U.S. population is growing by about one percent annually, but the mixture of cultures and races among America's 247 million residents is rapidly changing.

Younger Americans may be the hardest to target because not only are they undergoing changes, they also are the most demographically diverse group of adults. Compared to the baby boomers and older generations, Generation X is the most diverse crop of young adults ever.

Non-Hispanic whites account for about 76 percent of the total U.S. population. African-Americans account for 12 percent, Hispanics account for nine percent and Asian-Americans are about three percent of the total population, according to the Census Bureau and TGE Demographics, Inc.

. . . But among people aged 20 to 29 years, 72 percent are non-Hispanic whites, 14 percent are African-Americans, 11 percent are Hispanic and about three percent are Asian-American.

Demographic diversity is even more apparent among the youngest Americans: Among the 15- to 19-year-olds, 71 percent are non-Hispanic whites, almost 15 percent are African-American, 12 percent are Hispanic and about three percent are Asian-American.

Using projections from the Urban Institute, Market Segment Research predicts that "by the year 2010, minority shares of the population under 30 will be even more dramatic. Asian-Americans are expected to more than double their share of the under-30 crowd from three percent in 1990 to seven percent in 2010. Hispanics should increase their share from 12 percent to 16 percent of people under 30 in 2010. African-Americans, in contrast and in part because of the low rates of immigration, will remain 14 percent of the population under 30 over the next 20 years."

As a harbinger of the future, Generation X is a crucial group of people for businesses to understand.

Marketing to Generation X

Traditionally, television has targeted a broad swath of young adults, aged 18 to 34 years. Many researchers are discussing whether to tighten the focus of marketing efforts to a smaller 18- to 29-year-old age group. By reducing the target size, young adults experiencing the years of demographic density— 18 to 29 years—would be one target market. Meanwhile, the 30- to 34-year-olds, who are the youngest baby boomers, would be included along with the older members of their generation.

Focusing marketing efforts on a group of 44 million people can never be an exact science. The target simply must be the age group where a set of values and experiences tends to be clustered, not confined. Hence, reducing that target market to people in their 20s would increase efficiencies.

The argument about what to do with people aged 30 to 34 years could be answered with the same solution: Tighten the focus on the baby boom just as it is being tightened on Generation X. The baby boom itself spans nearly 20 years and it includes far more people than California, New York and Florida combined. It certainly is not a monolith of values or lifestyles.

Journalists often mention the Beatles and the Vietnam War as the defining characteristics of the baby boom generation. They are wrong. When leading-edge baby boomers were fighting in the Vietnam War (or protesting it) or listening to the Beatles, most of the youngest trailing-edge baby boomers were in kindergarten or grade school. The baby boom generation, born between 1946 and 1964, was defined by elevated birth rates, not by overall cohesive experiences and values. Just take a look at two of today's most famous baby boomers: Bill Clinton and Rush Limbaugh. Making broad assumptions about the baby boom generation—or Generation X—is about as useful as lumping the population of Florida into a single cohort.

Preferably, marketers should tighten their focus on cohorts within the baby boom, just as they should tighten their focus on Generation X.

Questions for Critical Thinking and Discussion

1. According to Joseph Schwartz, there are several reasons why Generation Xers are so difficult to target. List three of those reasons.

2. Do you think Generation Xers are accurately characterized? If your answer is yes, would you add anything to this article's Gen X description? If your answer is no, how would you define the Generation X demographic?

3. Based on your answers to questions 1 and 2, what approach do you think would be effective in reaching the Gen X demographic?

Now Worse Than Ever!
Cynicism in Advertising!

MARK LANDLER

Mark Landler is a staff writer for the New York Times.

The media and associated industries (public relations and advertising firms) sometimes have difficulty in reaching certain segments of the consuming audience (see the previous article "Tuning In to Generation X" by Joseph Schwartz). So how are advertisers trying to reach demographic groups that are anti-affluence and anti-consumerism (like Generation Xers are supposed to be)? Landler investigates ABC's promotional attempt that trashes both the process of hucksterism and the product itself: TV. His question is whether such cynicism will backfire.

Television networks enter a special kind of purgatory in August, when they start flogging their new fall shows even though they're still serving up reruns from last winter. Now ABC has come up with a solution to this annual problem: an advertising campaign so unorthodox and subversive that it diverts attention from any shows—new or old.

It's not just the look of these ads, though their mustard-yellow color has driven more than a few commentators to distraction. It's not the flip, ironic language, though the tone of the campaign has elicited a flurry of meditations on the state of advertising.

What has turned ABC's ads into a genuine pop culture event is their message: Television rots your brain, and that's just fine.

Winks and Nods

Irony has been a tool in Madison Avenue's bag of tricks for at least a decade; its roots go back to the creative revolution of the 1960s, when the ad agency Doyle Dane Bernbach sold Volkswagens in a big-car market by running a tiny photo of the Beetle above the phrase "Think Small." With the emergence of young consumers, jaded by a bombardment of marketing messages, advertising with a wink and a nod is seen as a way to establish rapport between buyer and seller.

This article first appeared in the *New York Times* (August 17, 1997), pages E1, E6.

But ABC has taken this concept into entirely new, and risky, territory. Even the most glib advertising has been predicated on the idea that—while the process of selling may be distasteful—the product being pushed is essentially good. ABC's ads, however, lampoon both the process and the product. The only thing worse than ads about TV, the campaign seems to be saying, is TV itself.

In doing this, the advertising crosses the line from irony to cynicism, said Stuart Ewen, a professor and chairman of the film and media studies department at Hunter College and the author of *PR! A Social History of Spin* (Basic Books, 1996). "It's like the people at the network, who have been saying these things for years at cocktail parties or in psychiatrist's offices, are now leaking their thoughts into the public," Mr. Ewen said.

To be sure, ABC is not the only company to use a mocking tone. Miller Lite, Mercedes-Benz, Boston Market and Sprite all use satire to push their products. In a recent Sprite ad, some teen-agers are partying on the beach while drinking a soft-drink called Jooky. As the camera pulls back, one sees that this is a fictional TV ad being watched by two teens, who open their own cans of Jooky and experience absolutely nothing. "Image is nothing; thirst is everything," says the slogan, in a sly nod to Sprite.

But unlike Sprite's, ABC's $40 million campaign concedes that watching the tube is basically bad—a corrosive habit that alienates people from society, nature, even their families. "Hobbies, Schmobbies," reads the copy on one ad. "It's a beautiful day, what are you doing outside?" asks another. "You can talk to your wife anytime," says a third.

"The intention of the campaign is to be clever and hip," Mr. Ewen said, "but it speaks to a truth that people would rather not see. While they spend a lot of time watching TV, they feel guilty about it."

Adding Attitude

For ABC's advertising agency, TBWA Chiat/Day, such analysis amounts to psychobabble. Bob Kuperman, the agency's chief executive, said Chiat/Day was simply trying to set ABC apart from the other networks, which promote themselves with hyperactive music, whirling logos and banal slogans like "Welcome Home" (CBS) or "Must See TV" (NBC).

The networks each devote $500 million a year worth of advertising time to promote themselves. Yet Mr. Kuperman said a telephone poll of 1,000 consumers conducted for Chiat/Day found that few people could recall the slogans the network used. "None of the networks has an identity," he said. "Part of the idea is to develop an attitude for ABC."

Chiat/Day knows a little about attitude. The agency, which is based in Venice, Calif., produced attitude-laden ads for Nike and Apple, including the computer maker's legendary "1984" commercial, with its haunting image of a young woman hurling a hammer at a Big Brother image on a flickering screen. The ad, which was broadcast just once, during the 1984 Super Bowl, is considered by some advertising critics to be the best commercial in history.

Along with other upstart shops, Chiat/Day introduced a whole new vernacular to advertising. Rather than pitching products overtly ("buy this, and you will have a better sex life"), such agencies tacitly acknowledged the superficiality of consumer society and let the consumer in on the joke ("We know this is shameless hucksterism; you know this is shameless hucksterism. But you should buy this product anyway.").

Pitching Self-Parody

Self-parody as a marketing strategy came of age in 1986, when the ad executive Jerry Della Femina introduced Joe Isuzu, the oleaginous car dealer played by actor David Leisure. Joe, you may recall, made extravagant claims about Isuzu automobiles, while the phrase "He's lying" flashed on the screen just under his leering grin. To anyone who ever left a used-car lot feeling gulled, the ads hit home.

Another hot agency, Wieden & Kennedy, took self-conscious advertising to a new level in 1987 in a campaign for Nike that paired Michael Jordan with the film maker Spike Lee. In one spot, Mr. Lee interrupts the filming of the ad to walk to the window and holler at his noisy neighbors: "Shut up! I'm doing a Nike commercial here."

Chiat/Day has gone in a different direction in its campaign for Nissan. Convinced that viewers tune out most car ads, the agency has banished images of the car in favor of a fictional character named Mr. K, who symbolizes the original leader of Nissan's American sales operation. The commercials encourage viewers to "enjoy the ride," but say little about why Nissan's ride is any better than Honda's.

Despite the attention ABC has gotten for its campaign, many ad people say the approach is old hat.

"I don't see it as any kind of a breakthrough," said Donny Deutsch, the chairman of Deutsch, a New York agency that has produced witty ads for the home-furnishing chain Ikea. "This is only an issue because the networks are in the 1950's in terms of how they sell themselves. In any other category, this kind of advertising would be seen as derivative."

Martin Puris, the head of Ammirati Puris Lintas, goes even further — saying that such ads betray a creative exhaustion on the part of ad agencies: "The advertising industry has allowed itself to be on the trailing edge of the communications industry, rather than on the leading edge, as it was in the 1960's."

Measured by their effect on sales, self-consciously hip ads have an uneven track record. Wieden & Kennedy's work for Nike helped turn the shoemaker into a global powerhouse. But Chiat/Day's elliptical ads for Nissan haven't lifted the Japanese car maker's torpid sales. Partly it's a case of baffling the consumer: in subway cars where ABC has plastered its ads, riders often stare at them blankly for minutes before getting the point.

Even among the under-30 crowd—the disaffected Generation X'ers coveted by so many advertisers—it is not clear that glib ads are sure-fire winners. Though young people flocked to see *Men in Black*, for example, this summer's parody of a sci-fi blockbuster, they turned out in equal droves to see the earnest *Forrest Gump* in 1994.

Alan Cohen, the executive vice president of marketing at ABC, admits that the network worried that its campaign would be too hip. It even dropped two particularly snide lines ("Books are overrated" and "Let someone else save the whales").

In the end, of course, ABC's shows rather than its ads will determine whether the network spends another season in the ratings cellar. Mr. Cohen said the ads would begin to integrate ABC stars like Drew Carey while maintaining their irreverent tone.

Even Mr. Kuperman of Chiat/Day is hedging his bets. After years of vacuous network advertising, he says, it would be unfair to expect any single ad campaign to revive ABC's ratings. After all, he noted, "it's the product that succeeds or fails."

Questions for Critical Thinking and Discussion

1. According to Landler, how is ABC (and other companies) crossing the line from irony to cynicism? Do you think this approach is a good one? Why or why not?

2. Landler believes that "ABC's shows rather than its ads will determine whether the network spends another season in the ratings cellar." If this is true, how could the ad campaign backfire?

30

Saturday Morning Fever:
The Hardsell Takeover of Kids TV

TOM ENGLEHARDT

Tom Englehardt is the author of Beyond Our Control: America in the Mid-Seventies *(Riverrun Press, 1976) and has written for* Harper's, Mother Jones, New West, *and other magazines.*

Englehardt considers the conflict that occurs when you mix children with marketing-for-profit. He describes how programming for kids has been completely taken over by toy product tie-ins and what the ramifications of such marketing ploys might mean to the development of children's perceptions, their education, and their understanding of the world.

Children's television is filled with furry bears and fruit-scented little girls, robots and Smurfs, muscle-bound blond princes and antiterrorist teams, talking unicorns and shrill chipmunks elbowing each other off the screen every half hour or so to demonstrate their unique buyability while mouthing extracts from a random loop of recorded messages: be polite, be happy, be sure to hug, be a good student, consult with others, respect your elders, cheating doesn't pay, don't fight, follow the rules.

Few adults, of course, look at children's television carefully. For any adult who looked, however, it would be hard to avoid the impression that the plots repeat each other continually, no matter who produces them. Whether aimed at little girls and syrupy sweet, or at little boys and filled with "action" sequences in which the forces of Good triumph, however provisionally, over the forces of Evil, the plots involve an obsession with theft, capture, and kidnapping (emphasis on the "kid"), with escape, chase, and recapture, with deception and mechanical transformation from one shape or state of being to another—all strung together to make each show a series of predictable permutations. Lame homilies (what the industry calls "prosocial messages") are then tagged on and the shows are set into partial motion with crude animation techniques.

This essay was excerpted from Todd Gitlin's *Watching Television* (Pantheon, 1986). It also appeared as an article in *Mother Jones*, September 1986, pages 39–48, 54.

Our mythocultural past is ransacked to concoct a tiny, preset group of images: rainbows for happiness, red hearts for warmth, unicorns for magical regeneration, blondness to indicate superiority. A few worn-out characters and stories from a Disney childhood are thrown in. The Classic Comics version of *The Iliad* is recalled by a constant reuse of the Trojan horse as a plot device. Some frog princes, witches, and demons are introduced. . . .

Star Wars is stripped down for everything from Darth Vader–like voices to Death Stars and space-battle special effects. And that's it, kids TV: a simple set of almost interchangeable parts, authorless in any normal sense, even peopleless—living adults and children having been banished to PBS, cable programming, and an occasional network special.

One would pardon visiting aliens from the planet Eternia (*He-Man*), Arcadia (*Voltron*), or Thundera (*Thundercats*) if they mistook such crude, repetitious, and heavy-handed fare for badly done propaganda put together by some unseen, and certainly uninspired, hand. But our aliens might then wonder, as critics of kids TV sometimes do: If this is propaganda, what is it for? If it's meant to convince, why are these shows so lacking in conviction that even their most violent sequences are without resonance or emotional consequence? And finally, if these shows are so bad, why, as the industry constantly reminds us, do earthling young choose to watch them in such extraordinary numbers?

The fact is, there has probably never been a more creative moment in children's TV than the present one; more creative, that is, as long as what appears on the screen is seen as a listless by-product of an extraordinary explosion of entrepreneurial life force taking place elsewhere—in the business of creating and marketing toys. In fact, to answer any of our aliens' questions, we must first grasp that burgeoning business world behind the screen, whose story has all the elements critics claim are missing from children's TV. It is original, daring, and educational, filled with action as well as with breathtaking experimentation.

It's the story of how "authorship" as a business concept shifted from television studios to the toy industry as well as to greeting card companies, advertising agencies, and cereal makers—and how, in only a few years, a relatively small-scale business of licensing popular kids characters to appear on products has been transformed into a multi-billion-dollar industry. This neat trick has been accomplished by unleashing the corporately minted "licensed character" and with it, for television, the program-length commercial.

Character licensing itself goes back to 1904 when the Brown Shoe Company purchased the rights to use the name of Buster Brown, a popular comic strip character, to promote its children's shoes at the St. Louis World's Fair, and it's been connected to selling children's products—from Mickey Mouse watches to Shirley Temple dolls—ever since. Character licensing was made to order for children's television, which from the 1950s on spawned highly successful licensing ventures.

The process of old-time TV merchandising started with a successful show; a toy company then came along and paid for the right to make a doll of the show's main character; a clothes company came along and paid to make pajamas featuring the character; and so on. These toys and other products might or might not, in turn, be advertised on TV. The coordination was minimal, the sums of money involved relatively modest. As Joseph Barbera, cofounder of the Hanna-Barbera cartoon studios, television's largest producer of animated programs, put it in the late 1970s when his characters appeared on more than 4,500 different products: "When a program is on the air for more than one year, we stand the chance of selling merchandise. If it doesn't stay on the air, and the networks don't renew it, then merchandisers just aren't interested."

Then came the first of several breakthroughs that changed the face of children's television and the nature of child consumerism. A young director named George Lucas formed Lucasfilm, part of whose purpose was to license his own creations, the characters that were about to appear in a film called *Star Wars*. In 1977, as that movie blasted off into the war-film void of post-Vietnam America, the small plastic figurines of Luke Skywalker, Han Solo, Princess Leia, Obi-Wan Kenobe, Darth Vader, and their various minions (licensed out to and created by Kenner Products) took the toy world by storm, becoming the most coveted and most often acquired boys toys of that time.

Not long after, two employees of the American Greetings Corporation, Tom Wilson and Jack Chojnacki, set up under the American Greetings aegis a separate licensing branch whose task was to create new characters imbued with instant, strong public identification possibilities. Basing their first attempt on a specially commissioned survey of the qualities young girls supposedly found most appealing, Wilson and Chojnacki created a pinkishly garbed little girl with an oversized head and christened her Strawberry Shortcake. Introduced in 1980, she was soon given her own animated TV special (rejected in those innocent days by the networks, which saw the show for the ad it was.)

But Ms. Shortcake needed no network to make her way in the world. She quickly became America's number one baby doll, starring in special after special on over a hundred stations around the country and appearing on hundreds of products selling an astronomical aggregate of more than $1 billion worth of herself.

Naturally, it quickly dawned on the toy industry, card companies, and others that if they too were to create their own characters, each with his or her own "backstory," they could make all the licensing money previously taken in by the TV companies that created the shows. Where the first corporate explorers ventured at their peril, others soon rushed to their profit. Among the earliest entrants in the licensed-character sweepstakes, the Smurfs confirmed and extended the Shortcake strategy. Seven-plus cutely named dwarfs without Snow White, the Smurfs are little blue creatures that live in mushroom-shaped cottages, eat smurfberries, and avoid an ineffectually evil wizard named Gargamel. Although the Smurfs were spun from the imagination of a Belgian cartoonist named Peyo, their blandly sweet adventures might easily pass for a purely corporate creation. Adopted by the American licensing firm Wallace Berrie, the Smurfs were in any case quickly treated that way. A host of Smurfable products and a 1981 debut on NBC's Saturday morning cartoon lineup quickly garnered more than $1 billion in sales and turned *Smurfs* into America's most-watched children's TV program.

Despite such individual programming successes, the dominance of the program-length commercial still seemed by no means assured. By 1982 only two and a half hours a week of them had made it onto the screen, concentrated in the Saturday morning kids ghetto, plus a few odd specials in other time slots. It took the strongest man in the universe, an action figure named He-Man, to make the final breakthrough. To understand his impact, we must first explore the ways this wave of nascent entrepreneurial strategizing, fueled by Reagan-inspired deregulation, blasted the program-length commercial into orbit.

In the 1970s the Federal Communications Commission, under pressure by activist groups like Action for Children's Television, had taken a significantly more interventionist stance on children's issues. But in 1981, when newly elected President Ronald Reagan appointed Mark Fowler as head of the FCC, that position was quickly reversed. Under the banner of deregulation, Fowler announced that "it was time to move away from thinking about broadcasters as trustees. It was time to treat them the way almost everyone else in society does—that is, as businesses." For, as he said on a different occasion, "television is just another appliance. It's a toaster with pictures." At Christmastime 1983 the FCC finally lifted its children's policy guidelines from 1974, which had begun a process of pressuring the industry to curb some of the worst excesses of children's TV, and followed up in 1984 by allowing TV stations to air as many commercial minutes in a given time period as they chose to, a ruling that in effect sanctioned the program-length commercial.

As soon as the direction of Fowler's FCC became clear, the networks began to unload children's programs. In 1982 CBS fired 20 people doing alternative programming for children and dropped the children's news show *30 Minutes* and began phasing out the low-rated *Captain Kangaroo*. ABC and NBC heaved sighs of relief and followed suit. In fact, an FCC study showed that from 1979 to 1983 the average time commercial stations allotted to children's programming dropped from 11.3 to 4.4 hours a week, and the after-school time slot was left without a single regularly scheduled network children's series.

As the networks pulled out, Prince Adam, a.k.a. He-Man, moved in. Filmation Associates scripted a fantasy about He-Man, a plastic figurine developed in 1981 by Mattel.

Although turned down by ABC, Mattel and the Westinghouse-owned Filmation took a novel approach to distributing the TV show *He-Man and the Masters of the Universe*. They syndicated their first 65 half-hour daily shows to independent stations around the country for their after-school time slots.

He-Man made his debut in September 1983 at the very moment when late afternoon commercial TV was denuded of network kids programs and filled with reruns of defunct adult shows. And so was born the first daily cartoon tailor-made for afternoon syndication in which almost every object you see on screen can promptly be bought in a nearby store.

The show set instant ratings records. Within a year, it was being sold in 147 markets covering 87 percent of the nation, and in 32 other countries as well. Since 1984 these figures have risen, while Mattel has managed to license out He-Man to innumerable licensees, which now produce everything from lunch boxes to Halloween costumes. Mattel, by its own count, sold 70 million of the action figures in 1984 alone.

Certainly, it was fitting in the Age of Reagan that the strongest character in the universe—not some plush baby doll or namby-pamby low-rated educational show—should conquer new territory for the marketing strategy first pioneered by American Greetings. He-Man had, in short, smashed into the soft underbelly of television, where ad rates for adult shows sink to near insignificance, and he took it the way Reagan took Grenada. In He-Man's wake, a whole industry locked into place.

. . . .

. . . [T]he card companies have hit pay dirt; the giant toy companies are selling their dolls by the millions; the advertising agencies, as in radio of the '30s and '40s and adult TV of the '50s and '60s, are once again deeply, lucratively involved in overseeing the production of TV shows for their clients; the film production companies that used to make 13 animated episodes of a kids show each season to be played over and over again are now doing a booming business year-round, producing 65–90 episodes of all the action-adventure daily shows; second-level independent stations have gotten a giant afternoon boost from essentially free daily shows with a built-in, instant-recognition audience of children; and other businesses beyond enumeration are profiting from the situation. In fact, everybody's profiting except perhaps the kids watching the TV screens where a stream of licensed characters flicker by in programs so flaccid it's hard to believe they bear any relationship to the juiced-up world that generates them.

Yet for an adult viewer, the shows' very lack of inspiration, and their authorless, randomly repetitive, interchangeable quality give them a strange sort of fascination. Just as the industry has been deregulated economically, so in some sense what appears on screen has been deregulated emotionally to produce a sort of crude twilight zone of present-day American consciousness.

Several vivid urges and anxieties leap from the screen of the supershow to which children's commercial TV adds up: an explosive release of aggression as superheroes and robotic saviors solve all human problems while playing with fantasy versions of the Reagan military budget; unfettered acquisitionism as advertisers pull out all the stops to induce kids to really *want;* and managed emotion in which tiny humanoid beings intervene to correct our inability to feel, love, hug, and care. Along with these go a pervasive sense of nuclear anxiety, an uneasiness with science and technology bordering on paranoia, and a stance of passivity in which humans are shown to be totally resourceless and must rely on nonhuman creatures to help, nurture, and defend them. In sum, it leaves us with a TV-generated vision of Americans as a nation of overarmed, trigger-happy, grasping, anxious, and love-starved people who feel deeply sorry for themselves and beleaguered in the world—something, that is, of a self-portrait of the Reagan era.

Kids TV can be divided into four zones, each of which fills in parts of that self-portrait: action-figure superheroes syndicated in afternoon time slots, with some carryover to Saturday and Sunday mornings; specials aimed at little girls; the network Saturday morning schedule; and finally, the ads.

The Universe of the Action-Figure Superhero

Once upon a time, there was a series of soldier figures made by Hasbro and sold under the name of G.I. Joe to little boys. Then came the post–Vietnam War era, not a propitious selling atmosphere for "a real American hero," whereupon Joe and his ilk were quietly retired. Now G.I. Joe is back, this time with his own daily afternoon show. He is a bit smaller—perhaps, as Peggy Charren of Action for Children's Television says, because of inflation—but he comes equipped with a sort of animated A-Team pitted against a group of international terrorists (name: Cobra), that great Reagan-era bogeyman, and armed to the teeth.

In fact, this fall's toy and TV season is highlighting terrorism, with Rambo and his Force of Freedom bursting onto the afternoon screen locked in daily combat with General Terror and his S.A.V.A.G.E. terrorist group. Coleco Industries, creator of the Rambo action-figure line, even beat Reagan to the conceptual punch with a character named Mad Dog, conceived well before the raid on Libya. *Advertising Age* reports that this year more than $40 million may be spent on ads supporting terrorism-related toy lines.

Most action-adventure shows, however, have snubbed this somewhat more conventional sector of the defense budget, preferring the world of *Star Wars* first envisioned as a fantasy by George Lucas and only later promoted by Reagan's High Frontiersmen. Reagan himself clearly feels safest in space, and the producers of these shows still tend to agree that outer space, high tech, and faraway enemies in a distant future are a safer, tidier, less complicated way to turn after-school TV into a war zone.

Whether in space or on earth, the emphasis is on teamwork. Rugged individualism plays no part on kids TV. After all, no one wants to sell only one action figure. The whole point is to get the child to buy whole teams of good guys and bad guys—color-, price-, and weapon-coordinated to the ads that follow on other shows. No longer the masked man and his lone sidekick, but the M.A.S.K. team and its V.E.N.O.M. opposites. So the program writers must find not plots but strings of team-action sequences with their explosively animated displays of technoweaponry.

. . . .

In fact, in every way—vitality, size, power, ability, intelligence—humans cede center stage to their technology, or its slightly more human superhero relatives, who use superscience and unheard-of weaponry to solve all human problems. Lacking a giant robot or an advanced fighting missile-armed truck, humans are invariably helpless and passive in the face of crisis. Passivity is not a happy state, however, and underneath the miraculous curative interventions of good technology lies a half-hidden world of fear, suspicion, and anxiety about a science that dwarfs humanity; a world in which you can never trust what you see because it may instantly metamorphose; a world in which genetic experiments gone awry create frightening mutants and in which a scientist's well-meant formula in the wrong hands turns a house pet into a wild beast; a world alive with a pseudoscientific language as ominous in what it promises as it is perverse in its absurd inaccuracies.

On children's TV, a once dreamed-of, machine-produced life of leisure has somehow transformed itself into a perilous vision of imminent disaster. TV science, in its hydra-headed technological form, has completely taken over our on-screen lives—and the unspoken message is that it may turn on us at any second. The ultimate form of this scientific betrayal is, of course, nuclear cataclysm, perhaps particularly ascendant on kids TV right now, as in video games, because of the increased fears of nuclear war the Reagan presidency brought with it.

Nuclear menace has, in short, become a fixture of kids' television life — yet it has scarcely been remarked upon by the critics of these shows. On the face of it, this omission is curious, given academic, critical, parental, even official alarm about "violence" on television. However carefully tabulated and studied such TV acts of violence may be, the category of violence itself is almost meaningless, covering as it does anything from the total destruction of a planet to Miss Piggy's hitting Gonzo with a pillow. Such violence floats in an abstract space uncoupled from the real world. The category, by omitting distinctions, leaves no opening to explore: for instance, the parallels between the Reagan-era military budget and the increase in violent acts and baroque weaponry in these shows.

Perhaps most important, no one mentions that this on-screen violence is of a strangely ritualistic and utterly unconvincing nature. Nor does anyone seem to wonder whether such convictionless mayhem induces in children an indifference to suffering in the real world, some strange form of visual pleasure, or some utterly unexpected set of reactions. "Violence" is simply a catchall category that allows moral crusaders to vent their displeasure without either analyzing what's really going on in front of our kids' eyes or discussing why and how it gets there.

Were someone to come up with another formula guaranteed to attract boys aged 2 to 11 to licensed-character products, the mesh of toy companies, card companies, advertising agencies, and film production companies that make TV's violent shows would abandon them in a minute — and what would be the result? We already know part of the answer: Rainbow Brite, Strawberry Shortcake, the Care Bears, and all their "nonviolent" ilk, the sort of shows so sickly sweet, so poorly made, and so obviously false that a viewing adult almost yearns for the Incredible Hulk or Skeletor or the Monster Minds to land in their midst and tear the place to bits.

Managed Emotion

As superweapon-wielding specialists in aggression dominate center stage in boys TV, a group of bossy, demanding doll-like creatures dominate the relentlessly "happy" realm of girls TV. These psychotherapists of children's TV (and their accompanying voice-overs) are intent on teaching such evidently unknown skills as "the magic of hugging" or "caring" or "getting through the tough times in life." Without the special effects of the action-adventure shows to light up the screen several times each half-hour, what's left are shows so ritualized, so perfunctory that they hardly seem to happen at all. A review of five of these shows, recapped in the *Chicago Tribune,* found them remarkably alike. Each involved "very innocent, sweet, high-voiced creatures . . . that lived in a pleasant, happy land. They were threatened by bad people (giants, things from dark swamps, or creatures without good feelings). In each story, one member of the happy land was captured by a bad guy and the rest of the do-gooders got up enough courage to rescue their friend."

Of course, these shows are still driven by the teamwork imperative of boys TV, which in these shows shades over into the more emotion-laden areas of togetherness, cooperation, and sharing. (In fact, one of the worst emotion-crimes you can commit in any of these happy lands is to be alone.) Thus, these shows are intimately linked to the seasonal launching and selling of new lines of dolls and other licensed products—not singly, but in bonded groups: ten or more Care Bears; scads of My Little Ponies; eight Hugga Bunch plush dolls with their own baby Hugglets in their arms, each carefully linked to a single-valued emotional state or trait that the producers declare to be somehow lacking in the world of kids.

Such shows have one advantage over their action-adventure cousins. The gaping holes of inaction in them allow producers to do what critics have demanded and parents have asked for: throw out the "violence" (even the bad guys tend to be dopey rather than truly evil or frightening), and put in some *real* values in the form of prosocial messages. Take cooperation, for instance. Everyone realizes that kids should cooperate, while any fool (and TV producers are no fools) with child-development experts and extensive research departments to call on knows that if your show advocates co-operation you can't easily be faulted. And if it so happens that you'd prefer to sell groups of little bears/puppies/fairies/ponies, then how useful to have wholly admirable reasons for suggesting that a parent plunk down a couple of hundred dollars. What better than urging kids to get into sharing and to-getherness and cooperation by buying whole, integrated, cooperative, loving sets of huggable, snuggleable, nurturing dolls? ("Ten Care Bears are better than one," as one Care Bear special put it.)

One implication of all these shows surely is that you are alone, that you've got emotional problems you probably can't express, that you're not as happy, as loving, as caring as you certainly could be, that at the very least there's room for improvement; that, in short, we've all got at least one foot in that dismal swamp world with those dopey bad guys, and we could do a lot better *if* we got some help. But it's going to cost. About 20 bucks a doll. And one doll won't do. Not by a long shot, not unless you're a one-emotion girl.

The need to sell numerous little beings adds a special, unintended twist to the darker, more antisocial messages that underlie even the most relent-lessly positive of these shows. If we all have trouble with caring or hugging, if intervention is called for, and if you also have to sell lots of licensed char-acters, then you have to present the managing (or healing) process as a highly complicated one that needs lots of cooperation by lots of highly specialized dolls, so specialized that instead of being complex individual personalities, they are not more than carefully labeled fragments of a personality: Tender-heart Bear, Share Bear, Cheer Bear, Grumpy Bear. Together they must engage in a series of specialized interventions as complex as those of any real-life medical unit. If, in addition, you have to add new characters each year, then you must somehow create even more personality fragments.

All this personality fragmentation reflects familiar if less than pleasant feelings most people live with to one degree or another in our society: anxiety, helplessness, emotional flatness, a desperate need for self-improvement sustained by a lack of self-respect. Yet this is not simply us mirrored on the screen, but a version of us tailored to sell goods to kids. In such a TV world, the girls shows amount to training in becoming passive creatures awaiting the ministrations of our dolls.

Saturday Morning

Saturday morning is the networks' ghetto for kids; and even if viewership is falling year by year (just as on adult TV), huge hunks of advertising money still flow in as the kids in the millions hunker down to watch their favorite cartoons.

In the last couple of years, the sacred precinct of Saturday morning has been overrun by licensed characters. Still, hidden away in its crevices, sometimes updated in incongruous ways, one can find traces of kids TV history, even of that rarest of all elements, living human beings. For the relatively small audience of children watching between seven and eight o'clock, there are still a few programs with actual people, like *Kidsworld* on CBS. These, like the public service ads that surround them, are the most integrated shows on children's TV, blacks and Hispanics naturally tending to cluster in those hours that make no difference to advertisers.

Then too one can still find a few old cartoon favorites like Bugs Bunny and the Road Runner cavorting on the screen, and dolled-up versions of the oldest of our interventionist superheroes like Superman and Wonder Woman, as well as their post-1960s superneurotic superhero friends, not to speak of the Great Dane detective Scooby-Doo, the Pink Panther (and sons), and Alvin and the Chipmunks, still singing away.

Generally speaking, Saturday morning shows are more diffusely targeted than the boys afternoon shows or the girls specials, their goal being to pull in for their advertisers audiences of both sexes ranging from ages 2 to 11 (and possibly beyond, since some teenagers do watch). As a result, these shows try to offer a little of everything to everybody in the simplest, easiest, and usually cheapest ways possible. Any show may mix fake science with rainbows, or nuclear anxiety with unicorns.

With rare exceptions, production values are dreary at best. *Jim Henson's Muppets, Babies, and Monsters* (CBS) looks, in this barren landscape, like a work of near genius because it mixes striking juxtapositions (a cartoon door opens onto an old-movie Tyrannosaurus rex), odd angles (adults are seen as looming feet and ankles), crazy plot twists (the babies replay, with some humor, old movie and TV scenes), and messages that don't simply bash you over the head. But far more typical are the churning feet of characters chasing one another with stiffly immobile upper bodies, or the mouths that move in conversation while everything else stays still.

. . . .

The Ads

It's no news that ads are the life force of children's television. Only in them does the energy of the business itself break onto the screen in carefully constructed playlets, imaginative musical riffs, clever bits of animation with stunning production values, and fancy camera work. Perhaps the greatest compliment to their mesmerizing power was the decision of the creators of America's premier educational program for kids—*Sesame Street*—to base their program on the ad form, with the highly acclaimed but mixed results achieved to this day. Lots of glitz and fun, but also an implicit assumption that nothing can stay on the screen for long; that kids' attention spans just won't take it.

Of course, the variety of kid-oriented products that can support the price of an ad on television is extremely limited. A 30-second spot on Saturday morning in the autumn costs an average of $40,000; the same 30 seconds on the ever-popular *Smurfs*, $60,000. Cereals (mostly presweetened), toys, and candy are the dominant advertisers, followed in fast-sinking order by other food products, chewing gum, carbonated drinks, fast food, toothpaste, and the odd sneaker or piece of clothing. This pretty much boils down to sugar and brand name toys, which can't help but make its own contribution to the repetitious nature of much of children's TV.

With show production costs relatively low—no human actors left to pay residuals to, very partial animation farmed out to cut-rate shops in Asia, the contractual right to repeat shows many times over—and ad rates above what the networks could get for adult programming at these hours, kids TV is still considered profitable for the networks. Advertising money, however, is increasingly being siphoned off Saturday morning into the non-network afternoon hours, and there have been rumors that one of the networks may actually pull out of Saturday morning children's programming altogether.

Studies have shown that really young children cannot distinguish between ads and shows. By the time they reach seven or eight years old, however, they not only distinguish but often discount the ads, even watching them less carefully than the shows themselves. This is undoubtedly one reason why so much energy is expended to fill the ads with a throbbing life force. Such studies may be reassuring—don't worry, those 350,000 ads a typical child watches before high school graduation don't really fool the kids—but they are also somewhat beside the point for two reasons. First, with the coming of the program-length commercial, the barriers between ad and show have been so broken down that often little more than a formal distinction remains; and second, even if kids can be shown to discount the more obviously false claims and messages of individual ads, what they actually see are ads en masse, a flood of ads that have their own larger messages to offer, their own story to tell about what is desired and not, valued and not, important and not in our society. Ads en block are, in fact, a heightened, crystallized vision of just what the rest of children's TV is really saying.

Consider the flow of Saturday morning advertising, in which a particular tension exists between regular commercial advertising and public service ads. The public service ads cluster, for economically obvious reasons, in the unpalatable, low-viewer, early morning hours, slowly mixing with, and then being elbowed aside by, the paid ads as soon as larger masses of kiddie viewers come on board. So any Saturday, any network channel will begin with ads calling on viewers to eat well and build strong teeth, "give a hoot, don't pollute," cook your own food "to build your body and build your health," eat snacks that are good for you, help fight cancer, make sure teenagers don't drink and drive, and reject cigarettes or drugs because they are vicious destroyers.

Here, then, is a vision of life that involves these elements: problems (drugs, drunkenness, disease, accidental death, pollution); the dangers of the city; nonwhiteness, for problems and a dangerous urban landscape somehow go with blacks, Hispanics, and other minorities; drabness, partly because the world of old schools and tenements where these problems take place is dark and drab, partly because with rare exceptions the money to go into such spots is limited; and finally, in a more positive vein, the need for good eating, nutrition, and sound health.

By nine o'clock, however, this vision has been displaced by a contrasting one. Drabness has become Day-Glo brightness; the gray, ominous city has been replaced by a green, suburban countryside (the very paragon of those idyllic planets of action-adventure shows and the innocent cloud worlds of girls specials); brown and black skins have been whitened (with blacks pretty much left to *Fame*-like dance numbers in which kids rock through school corridors for fruit bars, chocolate, and the like); and dark hair has been transmuted into a blinkingly unreal silvery blondness.

In a typical ad, one sees an all-white porch with white settee or swing, just a hint of lush greenery, a flood of the yellowest sunlight, and two girls (at least one of them awesomely blond) hugging little dolls; or perhaps a glistening kitchen with glistening white children eating their cereal while cartoon animals hop around the table; or an all-white bedroom with little light-brown- and blond-haired children dressed in pastels romping with their toys on the bed—a window behind them letting in the same golden sun with the same hint of greenery beyond.

The unspoken message is overpowering. You want to be here, in an idyllic, almost rural suburb; not *there* in the dark, frightening city. These are the winners. *Those* are the losers, or why wouldn't they be associated with the good shows? And, of course, as this dream of the good life sells products, so it sells itself, unnoticed, unmentioned, unconsidered.

Apologists for the new order of children's things enjoy likening it to the traditional world of myths and fairy tales (or at least to an earlier world of children's cartoons and their subsequent licensing histories). And it is true, possibly because small children are so naturally vulnerable, that they always have needed to imagine a world of large protectors and greater-than-life-size threatening figures. Traditional fairy tales certainly have had their share of interventionist superheroes and dastardly, magic-wielding villains, not to speak of early technowizardry (capes that guarantee invisibility, seven-league boots, pumpkin coaches). Nonetheless, at the heart of the fairy tale and of classic children's literature in general is a human journey or struggle involving the exhibition of human courage, cleverness, trickery, or even betrayal. It's the human, often the human child, who makes the trip, who confronts, evades, or solves the problem; and it is that human, not the superhero or a magical instrument, who is transformed in the end. If a lesson is drawn from all this, often in rather unsocial terms by our contemporary standards, it does emerge in some fashion from the crosscurrents of the human tale itself.

None of this holds on kidvid. For the first time on such a massive scale, a "character" has been born free of its specific structure in a myth, fairy tale, story, or even cartoon, and instead embedded from the beginning in a consortium of busy manufacturers whose goals are purely and simply to profit by multiplying the image itself in any way that will conceivably make money.

By pulling the "character" out of its traditional environment, the kids consumer industry has also done a miraculous job of responding to loss of network viewership. In fact, if one were to include hours spent in front of VCRs watching licensed-character shows, or simply hours with licensed characters in other forms (whether in fantasy play with G.I. Joe action-figures, listening to Berenstain Bears tapes, reading Wuzzles books, cuddling a Rainbow Brite doll, or going to bed in Masters of the Universe pajamas), product "viewership" can only have risen dramatically in recent years. While TV has clearly remained a central prop in the kids consumer world, that world has covered its bets by spreading elsewhere. *Turn off the TV tomorrow, parents, do everything the critics want you to do, and your kids still can't avoid us, because the Image, our images, are everywhere, smashed into a million identical bits and scattered throughout the world your children inhabit* — so says the industry. Parents who try to duck this attack simply by denying the TV set to their children have missed the point

Nor are there sufficient alternatives, though the FCC chairman, Mark Fowler, thinks differently, arguing that children's programming on PBS and the growth of cable channels have made further guidelines of any sort beside the point. This is what Peggy Charren of Action for Children's Television calls the Reagan administration's Marie Antoinette attitude toward kids: "Let them eat cable." It is true that PBS and cable TV—the lands of exile into which humans have been banished from the cartoon universe of commercial TV—harbor some real variety as well as some age-specific programming.

But PBS, only a single stop on the TV dial, can hardly be a total children's channel—because if a given hour is programmed for preschoolers, then school-age kids have nowhere to turn. And these are, in any case, not exactly the best of times for PBS. The Reagan administration's budget cutting, the difficulty of getting corporate underwriting for kids programming, and the drying up of foundation subsidies as foundations pull back to deal with other desperate areas of Reagan-era funding shortages, have made it hard for PBS to hold the line on children's programming, much less to expand to fill the void left by commercial channels. And though cable reaches almost half of all American homes, Nickelodeon, with its 26 million households, reaches nowhere near all of them; and the expensive, upscale, "wholesome" Disney pay channel far fewer yet. In addition, Nickelodeon is suffering from a commercialization that is bound to lead it in expectable directions—starting in January 1984, it began taking ads.

In any case, the fact is that as far as kids are concerned (*Sesame Street* and HBO's *Fraggle Rock* aside), commercial TV is pretty much where it's at. The kids like it, and this is what critics have trouble explaining away; for if kidvid is really a flat, repetitious, utterly predictable backwater of some other far more energetic world, why do kids incorporate it into their fantasy life and fantasy play, into their desires and dreams?

As a strange sort of collective afterthought of the computer age, filled with interchangeable plots grabbed randomly from the junk heap of culture, kidvid may be as close to myth as we can get. Perhaps its robotic transformations are our bizarre *Metamorphoses*, and what's on the screen reflects us in a purer way than any other cultural form. This, then, would be the sense in which children's TV is propaganda—propaganda meant to sell our own lives to our children. It may, in the end, be our truest educational television—because, unlike TV's prosocial messages, it does teach our children what we most value.

This may be why, every few years, the media suddenly get in a frenzy about the effect of TV on kids. *Newsweek*, for instance, cries out in its headlines about KIDVID: A NATIONAL DISGRACE with a fervor it would never apply to the "disgrace" of American film or the "disgrace" of American culture. It's not that the critics are wrong; it's just that the periodic frenzy is cyclic enough to be suspect. However kids are actually treated in America, ideally we want to think of them as belonging to another race of beings, rather like the little denizens of Strawberryland, innocents open to the best we can possibly teach them. We want to see them as different, more sensitive, somehow more human than ourselves, and so children's TV offends in ways the usual critiques do not touch. It disturbs because we shudder to see our children attracted to balder versions of what we are attracted to.

Perhaps many of us also want to see ourselves as more immune to consumer dreams and Reagan-age fantasies than we are, so that it's like meeting yourself naked on a busy street in some hideously embarrassing dream to see your child love He-Man or Rainbow Brite with a possessing passion, or hunker down to watch a morning of kidvid. But why, after all, should the kids who live in our houses not be attracted to what, in only slightly more sophisticated form, is meant to attract us all: dreams of buying glitzy toys (promising more than they can ever deliver) with which to play out our fantasies. Why should children in our world appreciate shows that do not sell them anything?

The Reagan era has let loose dreams, fears, anxieties—of aggression and destruction, emotional deprivation, unfettered acquisitionism—let them loose with a passion. And who would claim, based on the results of recent elections, that Reagan's dreams, and fears, had no takers? No one could be untouched by them, least of all our children. For better or worse, childhood is not an immune age of life. If we want a different set of images on the screen, we'll have to produce not just better plots, but a different production system with different goals in a different world.

Questions for Critical Thinking and Discussion

1. Englehardt's essay first appeared in 1986. How much has children's television changed since then? Has it gotten better or worse? Explain.

2. Are any of the same concerns, controversies, or criticisms about television content for children applicable to contemporary programming? Provide specific examples.

3. What do you think should be done about children's television? Keep in mind that broadcasters have a business to run and they must make a profit in order to stay in business. Do you think kids should be treated as a special group (exempt from advertising, for example, because they are a valuable resource) or should they be treated as simply another market to be "targeted" by advertisers?

chapter 11

Theories of Mass Communication

31

Shifting Worlds of Strangers: Medium Theory and Changes in "Them" Versus "Us"

JOSHUA MEYROWITZ

Joshua Meyrowitz is a sociologist at the University of New Hampshire. He is interested in media influences and authored the groundbreaking book No Sense of Place *(Oxford University Press, 1985).*

This article uses a medium-theory perspective to address one variable related to "technological communities" — that changing boundary between "them" and "us." The ways in which oral, print, and electronic modes of communication each foster a different balance between strangers and "familiars" are outlined.

Shortly after Guglielmo Marconi perfected his invention of wireless communication in the late 1890s, the British Army became one of his first clients. The British believed that wireless would give them a great advantage on the battlefield. But only months after employing Marconi's invention in the Boer War, the British were distressed to discover that the Dutch settlers they were fighting in South Africa also had wireless equipment, apparently manufactured in Germany (Barnouw 1966, p. 16).

The story of wireless in the Boer War holds a lesson about technology and social change that has not yet been grasped fully by many of those studying media and society: Although it often appears that the impact of a new communication technology depends primarily on "who-communicates-what-through-it-for-what-purpose," the more significant effects are usually in the overall change in the nature of social (in this case, military) interaction. Rather than simply giving one side an advantage over another, wireless changed the nature of warfare.

Similarly, the spread of printing, radio, television, telephone, computer networks, and other technologies have altered the nature of social interaction in ways that cannot be reduced to the content of the messages communicated through them. Yet the overwhelming majority of studies about "media" have tended to focus primarily on message content and the social forces that shape the content.

This article first appeared in *Sociological Inquiry* (February 1997), Vol. 67(1), pages 59–71.

Beyond Content Analysis: Media as Social Contexts

The content approach to studying media offers many insights. But the limits of this method for understanding long-term change can be seen by considering another example from the past. A look only at the content of printing during its rapid spread through Europe in the sixteenth century would have suggested that this new medium was going to strengthen religion and enhance the power of monarchs. Most books, after all, were of a religious nature, and their content was regulated by the Church and crown. Yet it is now widely believed that printing ultimately helped foster the scientific revolution and the development of constitutional systems. By making possible new patterns of knowledge development, storage, and distribution, printing advanced the secularization of society and undermined the power of royalty (Eisenstein 1979). These consequences grew from those structural features of printing that made it different from oral communication and from handwritten manuscripts, not from the content per se. Thus, even the widespread distribution of traditional content, the Bible, had a revolutionary impact. As Martin Luther understood well, the printing of the Bible decreased the power of the Catholic Church as prime possessor and interpreter of God's words (Innis 1951).

Of course media content is important, especially in the short term. Political, economic, and religious elites have always attempted to maintain control by shaping the content of media. And the stakes in such struggles are often quite high. William Carter, for example, printed a pro-Catholic pamphlet in Protestant-dominated England in 1584 and was hanged. Our current information environment is also choked by the ways in which television and other media are controlled. But content questions alone, while important, do not foster sufficient understanding of the underlying *changes in social structures* encouraged or enabled by new forms of communication.

. . . .

Implicit in most media research to date is an image of media as relatively passive "vessels" or "conduits." Media, in this view, *hold* or *send* messages, and the messages are the subject of study. Implicit in the notion of "technologically structured communities," however, is a different metaphor for media: media as settings or environments for social interaction.[1]

Medium Theory

The image of media as environments involves what I have called "medium theory." I use the singular, *"medium* theory," because what makes this approach different from most other "media theory" is its focus on *the particular characteristics of each individual medium or of each general type of media.*

(All electronic media, for example, share some characteristics that make them different from all print media.) Medium theorists are interested in differentiating between media. Broadly speaking, medium theorists ask: How do the particular characteristics of a medium make it physically, psychologically, and socially different from other media and from face-to-face interaction, regardless of the particular messages that are communicated through it?

Although the issues explored by medium theorists would seem to rest within the natural terrain of sociology, most medium theorists have come from other disciplines, such as the classics, political economy, literature, history, anthropology, and communication. . . .

Medium questions are relevant to both micro-level (individual situation) and macro-level (cultural) changes. On the micro level, medium questions ask how the choice of one medium over another affects a particular situation or interaction (e.g., calling someone on the phone versus writing them a letter versus sending them an e-mail message). On the macro level, medium questions address the ways in which the addition of a new medium to an existing matrix of media may alter social interactions and social structure in general (e.g., how the widespread use of the telephone has changed the role of letter writing and influenced the nature of social interactions in general). The most interesting—and most controversial—medium theory deals with the macro level.

The macro-level analyses of the medium theorists are often more difficult to test and apply than the results of focused studies of particular media messages. Nevertheless, this perspective is of potentially great significance because it outlines how media, rather than functioning simply as channels for conveying information between two or more social environments, are themselves social contexts that foster certain forms of interaction and social identities.

I use a medium-theory perspective here to address very briefly one variable related to "technological communities"—the changing boundaries between "them" and "us."

Shifting Connections and Disconnections

Typically, analyses of live or mediated communities focus on closeness and connections. I would like to suggest that a more inclusive perspective also involves looking at changing patterns of distance and *dis*connection. Communities are defined by their boundaries. And with every change in boundaries comes a new form of inclusion and exclusion, a new pattern of sharing and lack of sharing of experience.

Some analysts of societal change have argued that the rise of modern urban centers following the Industrial Revolution created the new experience of a "world of strangers" (Sack 1988). This view certainly captures one explicit experiential component of the shift from rural agricultural communities to industrial cities, from Gemeinschaft to Gesellschaft. But this view also incorrectly suggests that "strangers" had no role in the structure of traditional societies. Further, it suggests that there was a one-time shift to a world of strangers rather than a more complex series of changes in the role of strangers.

In place of the dichotomy of traditional society versus modern world of strangers, I offer a trichotomy. I suggest that we are now living in the third major phase in conceptions of "strangers" and "familiars," a third manifestation of the balance of "them" versus "us." I argue that traditional, modern, and postmodern societies each could be referred to accurately as a "world of strangers," but the relative place, definition, and experience of strangers is different in each.

Each of the three phases—traditional, modern, and postmodern—is linked in many important ways to a dominant mode of communication: traditional to oral communication, modern to literate communication, and postmodern to electronic communication.[2] Each evolution in communication forms has involved a shift in social boundaries and hence a shift in the relationship between self and others.

Each shift in communication is accompanied by a shifting sense of place, by a change in our perception of what George Herbert Mead (1934) called the "generalized other," those others who seem significant enough for us to imagine how they may be imagining us. Each shift also is accompanied by a new sense of what I have called the "generalized elsewhere" (Meyrowitz 1989), that general imagining of how our locales may be viewed from the outside.

There is space here to sketch these three phases only in the broadest of strokes. I am not concerned here with giving definitive assessments of each of these phases. Rather, I wish to highlight the boundary issues worth exploring when looking at the changes in group identity that may occur with changes in forms of communication.

Traditional Oral Societies: Familiar Insiders and Distant Outsiders

In oral societies, the preservation of ideas and mores depends upon the living memory of people. This form of "living library" ties people closely to those who live around them.

In a traditional oral society, almost everyone one sees on a regular basis is familiar. Relative to other social forms at least, there is not a high degree of social differentiation in role and experience. "Strangers" are not an explicit part of everyday encounters. But in a sense, strangers play a more important role in traditional oral societies than in any other form of social organization. There is, after all, an underlying awareness of a vast, mysterious external world filled with faceless "others." In fact, the often subliminal awareness of a larger world of strangers is one of the nearly constant forces that keeps members from leaving the community physically and psychologically. The boundary that keeps strangers out also keeps insiders in and binds this form of society together.

Modern Print Societies: Homogenized Segregation

With the rise of the modern urban-oriented industrial society, however, there is increasing contact with, and more explicit awareness of, "strangers." That is, it is a common experience to see and have at least limited interaction with people from very different social worlds.

The rise of such a modern society is supported by, and further supports, the spread of literacy. Print factories serve as the prototypes of all mechanized production. Printed documents disseminate the plans and ideas of mass production. And print helps to establish distant markets by producing the advertisements and mail-order catalogues that reach rural as well as urban settings (Ewen and Ewen 1982).

In Western culture, the printing press and the relatively wide availability of printed materials further undermine the importance of the oral community. For the literate, there is a retreat from the web of community life and extended kinship ties and a move toward greater isolation of the nuclear family.

At the same time that printing creates smaller units of interaction at the expense of the oral community, it also bypasses the local community in the creation of larger political, spiritual, and intellectual units. The ability to *see* on a printed page what were once only spoken folk languages, for example, fosters a sense of unity among all those who use the same language (not just among those who speak it in the same time and place). Conceptions of "them" versus "us" change. Feudal societies based on face-to-face loyalties and oral oaths begin to give way to nation-states and to nationalism based in large part on a shared printed language. Printed constitutions literally help to "constitute" each nation, as do printed laws, printed national histories, and printed national myths (Meyrowitz and Maguire 1993). Similarly, religious cohesion no longer depends exclusively on shared rituals with those one can see, hear, and touch. The potential for religious unity across great distances (along with disunity among those in the same place) is fostered by the patterns of sharing of holy *texts*.

In terms of social roles, the spread of print supports compartmentalization and specialization. The new emphasis on reading as a source of wisdom and religious salvation widens the gap between those who can read and those who cannot. Further, distinctions in levels of reading ability come to be seen as tied to "natural" differences in rank and identity.

The young and the illiterate are excluded from all printed communication and are increasingly seen as different from literate adults. Modern conceptions of both "childhood" and "adulthood" are invented in Western culture in the sixteenth century, and their spread follows the spread of schooling (Ariès 1962; Stone 1977). Multiage roles, behaviors, and dress begin to splinter into separate spheres for people of different ages and reading abilities. In the literate classes, children are more frequently isolated from adults and from children a year or two younger or older. Many topics are deemed unfit for children's ears and eyes. Adults use books as a private context within which to discuss what topics and books are and are not appropriate for children. With the help of such books, children are shielded from much information—and from the adult conspiracy to control their knowledge.

As printing spreads, women are told by men that only men need to become fully literate, and men use restricted literacy to enhance their positions relative to women. The public male realm is increasingly isolated from the private female realm. Minimally literate women are given more of the responsibility of caring for the increasingly dependent illiterate children.

For men, identities splinter into a multitude of separate spheres based on distinct specialties and mastery of field-specific stages of literacy. The new grading of texts serves as a barrier to straying from one field into another.

Unlike oral societies with oral vows of allegiance, print societies develop a form of leadership organized from a distance and based on inaccessibility, delegated authority, and tight control over public image. Machiavelli's *The Prince*, written at the start of the print age, is an early "public-relations manual" for political leaders.

Separate training and etiquette manuals are published for people of each sex and for those of different ages. Indeed, every category of age, sex, and class begins to be increasingly isolated from the information and experiences of others.

Separate information systems foster distinct uses of separate places, with increasingly particular rules of access to them and distinctions in appropriate behavior within them. People pass from role to role many times a day and change status through various rites of physical and social passage many times in a lifetime.

Print leads to an emphasis on stages, levels, and ranks. The world comes to seem naturally layered and segmented. There is a place for everything, and everything is to be in its place.

Michel Foucault (1977) argued convincingly that the membranes around prisons, hospitals, military barracks, factories, and schools thickened over several hundred years leading up to the twentieth century. Birth, death, education, mental illness, and celebrations were increasingly removed from the home and put into isolated institutions. Foucault described how people were increasingly separated into distinct places in order to homogenize them into groups with single identities ("students," "workers," "prisoners," "mentally ill," etc.). The individuals within these bounded categories were, in a sense, interchangeable parts. And the groups themselves were elements of a hierarchically organized social machine.

But because Foucault did not see the relationship between these changes and the spreading influence of literate modes of thought and organization, he did not observe the current, postmodern counterprocess.

Postmodern Electronic Societies: Global Webs of Individual Idiosyncrasy

As the membranes around spatially segregated institutions have become more informationally permeable, through electronic media, the notion of special spheres for different types of people and activities has been diminishing. Rather than highlighting the modern society's notion of differences between groups and the interchangeability of people within social categories, the current postmodern trend is toward integration of members of all groups into a relatively common sphere of experiential options—with a new recognition of the special needs and idiosyncrasies of *individuals.*

As I have detailed elsewhere, electronic media differ from print media along a number of significant dimensions that interact with the structures of group identity, socialization, and hierarchy (Meyrowitz, 1985, 1986). While print tends to divide its audience into groups based on education, age, class, and gender, a great deal of electronic information and experience is shared across demographic categories.

In the postmodern electronic society, the social functions of physical locations become fuzzier. The family home, for example, is not a less bounded and unique environment, as family members have access to others and others have access to them. We can remain at home, yet travel via TV and VCR remote controls through dozens of psychological video spaces in the course of a few minutes, or interact through customized telephone and computer networks. We "travel" through, or "inhabit," electronic settings and landscapes that are no longer defined fully by walls of a house, neighborhood blocks, or other physical boundaries, barriers, and passageways.

Metaphors aside, of course, it is not possible to experience the whole world as one's neighborhood or village. Even apart from the numerous political, religious, economic, and cultural barriers that remain, there is a limit to the number of people with whom one can feel truly connected. Electronic media, therefore, foster a broader, but also a shallower, sense of "us."

The effect of these boundary changes is both unifying and fractionating. The forms of group identities and place-defined roles characteristic of modern societies are bypassed in both directions: Members of the whole society—and world—are growing more alike, but members of particular families, neighborhoods, and traditional groups are growing more diverse. On the macro level, the world is becoming more homogeneous. We see more adultlike children and more childlike adults, we see more career-oriented women and more family-oriented men, and our leaders try to act more like the person next door even as our real neighbors want to have more of a say in local, national, and international affairs. But on the micro level, individuals experience more choice, variety, and idiosyncrasy. *Just as there is now greater sharing of behaviors among people of different ages and different sexes and different levels of authority, there is also greater variation in the behaviors of people of the same age, same sex, and same level of authority.* It is now more difficult than ever to predict the activities and behavior and knowledge of a person based on his or her age and gender and physical location. And many of the daily social roles that were once unthinkingly enacted are now the subject of constant doubts and negotiations.

National sovereignty is also challenged by new forms of communication. Scientific exchanges, banking, product design, and courtship rituals now take place in no place, through international satellite links and computer networks. As a result, much importing and exporting no longer involve reaching borders or passing through customs, and governments have diminished control over their citizens' knowledge and experiences.

Just as modern European nations developed with the help of printing in the vernacular, which bypassed the face-to-face communication of the feudal system and its network of oral oaths of allegiance, new technologies are fostering the rise of a system of quickly changing neofeudal alliances on a global scale.

Increased *information* movement leads to increased *physical* movement, such as travel and trade across national boundaries. Fax machines, e-mail, and computer networks encourage visiting scientists, exchange students, tourists, and international romances. It is exciting to cross borders and discover differences. But ironically, the more that borders are crossed, the greater the similarity of once very different social arenas. As a result, the notion of "foreign" is becoming an increasingly foreign notion. (Ted Turner, for example, banned the word "foreign" from CNN's newscasts several years ago.)

Again, there is a dual process—a movement toward unification across boundaries but also a splintering within boundaries:

- Russia seeks a union with the West, as its own union begins to crumble.
- Europe moves toward economic unity, as Yugoslavia tears itself apart.

- English becomes an increasingly international language, but school-children in some U.S. cities speak dozens of different languages and cannot communicate with each other.

  · · · · · · · · · · · · · · · ·

- Computer networks link the world, but people in the same office often have trouble sharing files from different programs and computers.

- International and multidisciplinary academic exchanges and projects are spreading rapidly, even as communication between members of the same discipline or department breaks down over disagreements about method, perspective, and ideology.

  · · · · · · · · · · · · · · · ·

As ties are forged across national boundaries, average citizens are increasingly able to make new mental separations: between the people of a country and their government, between an individual and his or her geographic location, between the fate of a nation and the fate of its corporations.

Traditional boundaries blur; new alliances link former enemy nations and bridge incredibly large territories, as in the Gulf War alliance. But there is simultaneously a rise in factional and ethnic violence within areas that formerly seemed relatively peaceful, as in Sarajevo and Los Angeles. Most of the wars now being fought are *within* national boundaries, not across them.

As boundaries blur, we scholars also lose some of our academic footing. We lose our subjects when they seem to change too quickly for us to develop thoughtful and well-documented analyses of them. As we increasingly cross boundaries and shift perspectives, we become sufficiently distanced from our own work habits to gain a new subject: self-reflexive analyses of our own role as researchers. Such analyses are increasingly being included in research accounts. We also increasingly confront the uncomfortable thought that our disciplines, as organized bodies of knowledge and perception, are of necessity also organized bodies of ignorance. This view is at once liberating and exhausting. As we discover more and more commonalities across disciplinary boundaries, we find it more difficult to justify the line at which we stop reading and stop referencing.

Even in our homes, experience is splintered: A son may walk around the house with a Walkman, a daughter's eyes may dart between a parent's face and a computer screen, and a spouse may leave an intimate embrace to find out what just came in over the home fax machine. More than ever before, therefore, the postmodern, electronic era is one in which *everyone* else, foreigner or family member, seems somewhat familiar—and somewhat strange.

I believe that the recently much discussed strengthening of ethnic and cultural identities is merely the most *visible* level of fragmentation, and that the more significant consequence of globalization may be a heightened sense of individual psychological isolation. Ironically, then, the wider sense of global sharing may be leading us simultaneously to a retreat from traditional groupings to the boundaries of our own individual idiosyncrasies.

Glocalities

The rootlessness of the postmodern landscape is, of course, relative rather than absolute. Place and locality continue to be very important (e.g., Cox and Mair 1988), but their function and use have been radically transformed by new communication patterns (Calhoun 1986, 1988; Meyrowitz 1985, 1989). We continue to live in physical settings, but we increasingly share information with and about distant others.

In a sense, the world is becoming a collection of what I have called "glocalities" (Meyrowitz 1991)—places that are shaped both by their local uniqueness and by global trends and global consciousness. Localities everywhere now advertise their uniqueness through increasingly homogenized means. The locality is commodified from an external marketing perspective for "sale" to businesses, investors, and tourists; it is "sold" to locals as well.

Glocalities are characterized by permeable boundaries between the locality and the globality. So-called local news, as presented on television, for example, contains precious little in it that is truly local. Such programs convey satellite images of national and international news and weather. And even the supposedly "local events" on TV news are increasingly packaged the way local events are packaged elsewhere (often with the guidance of the same or similar television news consultants). Further, as Barkin (1987) argues, "community problems" on local news are typically presented as local manifestations of national problems.

On local media in general, one now tends to hear two types of "voices": (1) the "voice from nowhere" that has little or no hint of a local accent, and (2) the self-conscious "voice from here" that presents a version of how people elsewhere think locals from "here" speak.

Although we remain dependent in many ways on our spatial environment and on our fellow inhabitants of local space, electronic media expand our sense of the generalized elsewhere through increased awareness of other places and of nonlocal people. These media work against a strong feeling of the primacy of place by giving us a constant sense that people in other localities are having many similar, often simultaneous, experiences. There is now a wide range of current, and quickly changing, topics of conversation and humor that transcend localities. Further, access to nonlocal people is now, via the telephone and e-mail, often faster and simpler than access to physical neighbors. As mutual sharing and accessibility to those near us becomes less exclusive, many forms of locality-based mutual interdependence dissipate. We expect less from our neighbors and expect them to expect less of us.

Conclusion

In summary, I see three different "worlds of strangers": oral, print, and electronic:

1. Each traditional oral society has a relatively thick boundary separating it from every other oral community. Each oral society is a small world of "familiars" separated from a vast and mysterious world of strangers.

2. Modern print societies mix together formerly distinct oral communities. There is a new, larger boundary around the nation state, but there are also new internal boundaries around social categories (age, sex, class, ethnicity, etc.) within the society. Members of the modern nation-state move in and out of the internal boundaries on a regular basis, and the encountering of strangers within the boundaries of the nation is a frequent occurrence.

3. The postmodern, electronic matrix leads to more permeable boundaries between different nation states and more permeable boundaries around social categories within nations. There is a sense of global familiarity, as well as a greater sense of individual idiosyncrasy and strangeness of local others.

In this third, postmodern world of strangers, radio, TV, telephone, and computer "spaces" can provide senses of place and experience, but they are quickly shifting. Cybercommunications are exciting because they allow participants to define new contexts easily, but these contexts are often ones that also can be escaped from simply through the creation of other electronic contexts. Today, many members of society are hungering for a renewed sense of place, but also want to retain experiential mutability, informational mobility, and behavioral fluidity (Aufderheide 1987). Paradoxically, electronic communities help to bridge a gap created by the dilution of place-defined meaning and experience, yet they simultaneously dilute those remaining nonmediated meanings even further, hence increasing our dependence on mediated forms.

Endnotes

1. For an analysis of contrasting metaphors implicit in media research, see Meyrowitz (1993).
2. Of these stages, only orality has ever existed in pure form. Literate and electronic cultures are hybrids. Literate cultures continue to speak, and electronic

cultures continue to speak and read and write. To refer to a "literate culture," then, is to use a short-hand term analogous to "industrialized society." Such concepts do not suggest that speech or agriculture have disappeared, respectively, only that a new technology is playing a major role in reshaping society. For discussion of a fourth, transitional phase between orality and print-based literacy, scribal culture, see Meyrowitz (1994).

References

Ariès, P. 1962. *Centuries of Childhood: A Social History of Family Life in Early Modern France,* translated by Robert Baldick. New York: Vintage.

Aufderheide, P. 1987. "The Look of the Sound." Pp. 111–135 in *Watching Television,* edited by T. Gitlin. New York: Pantheon.

Barkin, S. M. 1987. "Local Television News." *Critical Studies in Mass Communication* 4:79–82.

Barnouw, E. A. 1966. *A Tower in Babel: A History of Broadcasting in the United States to 1933.* New York: Oxford University Press.

Calhoun, C. 1986. "Computer Technology, Large-Scale Social Integration, and the Local Community." *Urban Affairs Quarterly* 22:329–349.

(see Meyrowitz) 1988. "Populist politics, communications media and large scale societal integration." *Sociological Theory* 6:219–241.

Cerulo, K. A., J. M. Ruane, and M. Chayko. 1992. "Technological Ties That Bind: Media-Generated Primary Groups." *Communication Research* 19(1): 109–129.

Chayko, M. 1993. "What Is Real in the Age of Virtual Reality? 'Reframing' Frame Analysis for a Technological World." *Symbolic Interaction* 16(2): 171–181.

Cox, K. R., and A. Mair. 1988. "Locality and Community in the Politics of Local Economic Development." *Annals of the Association of American Geographers* 78:307–325.

Eisenstein, E. 1979. *The Printing Press as an Agent of Change: Communication and Cultural Transformations in Early Modern Europe.* 2 vols. New York: Cambridge University Press.

Ewen, S., and E. Ewen. 1982. *Channels of Desire: Mass Images and the Shaping of American Consciousness.* New York: McGraw-Hill.

Flayhan, D. 1993. "Orality, Literacy, Class, and the Oppression of Women: The Case of Ancient Greece." Paper presented at the Speech Communication Association annual conference.

Foucault, M. 1977. *Discipline and Punish: The Birth of the Prison,* translated by Alan Sheridan. New York: Pantheon.

Innis, H. A. 1951. *The Bias of Communication.* Toronto: University of Toronto Press.

Mead, G. H. 1934. *Mind, Self, and Society: From the Standpoint of a Social Behaviorist,* edited by Charles W. Morris. Chicago: University of Chicago Press.

Maguire, J. 1989. "Disinformation in the Era of Perestroika: TV Imagery and the Felt Insignificance of National Borders." Paper presented at the Conference on Deception in Economics and Politics, Stockholm, Sweden.

Meyrowitz, J. 1994. "Medium Theory." Pp. 50–77 in *Communication Theory Today,* edited by D. Crowley and D. Mitchell. Cambridge, England: Polity Press.

——. 1993. "Images of Media: Hidden Ferment—and Harmony—in the Field." *Journal of Communication* 43(3):55–66.

——. 1991. *The Changing Global Landscape.* Atlanta: Quest.

——. 1989. "The Generalized Elsewhere." *Critical Studies in Mass Communication* 6(3):326–334.

——. 1986. "Media as Social Contexts." Pp. 229–250 in *Contextualism and Understanding in Behavioral Science: Implications for Research and Theory,* edited by R. Rosnow and M. Georgoudi. New York: Praeger.

——. 1985. *No Sense of Place: The Impact of Electronic Media on Social Behavior.* New York: Oxford University Press.

Meyrowitz, J., and J. Maguire. 1993. "Media, Place, and Multiculturalism." *Society* 30(5): 41–48.

Sack, R. D. 1988. "The Consumer's World: Place as Context." *Annals of the Association of American Geographers* 78: 642–664.

Stone, L. 1977. *The Family, Sex, and Marriage in England, 1500–1800.* New York: Harper & Row.

Strate, L. 1994. Heroes: "A Communication Perspective." Pp. 15–23 in *American Heroes in a Media Age,* edited by S. J. Drucker and R. S. Cathcart. Cresskill, NJ: Hampton.

Questions for Critical Thinking and Discussion

1. What does it mean to be a member of Joshua Meyrowitz's "Postmodern Electronic Societies"? What are some of the shared behaviors among people of different ages, sexes, and levels of authority? What are some of the variations in behaviors among people of the same ages, sexes, and levels of authority?

2. Meyrowitz presents us with a conundrum. He tells us that today we are searching for a renewed "sense of place." While we want to obtain (or retain) some individuality, we also want to be "connected" to general society. Electronic communities help us do that by erasing location or "place" from our definitions of meaning and experience. But then we become more dependent on mediated forms. Do you think this ultimate dependence on mediated forms is necessarily a bad thing? Explain.

32

Postmodernism Defined, at Last!

TODD GITLIN

Todd Gitlin is a professor of culture, journalism, and sociology at New York University.
   You have heard the term postmodernism *thrown around the cultural conversation for years. It has been used to describe everything from an art movement to a theoretical perspective, to personality types or styles. Gitlin provides (at last!) an understandable explanation of what the term means and how it has been co-opted, used, or misused by many.*

Journals, conferences, galleries, and coffeehouses are spilling over with talk about postmodernism. What is this thing, where does it come from, and what is at stake? If it is nothing more than chat to keep the cocktail parties humming, why the volume, why the heat? True, in literature as in art, fashion, architecture, etc., style always attracts interest. On matters of style careers turn and cease to turn; commentators and consumers alike "position" themselves to be à la mode. But what is striking in recent years is that elements of a postmodern style have attracted such attention (and dismay) in field after field, genre after genre that it is reasonable to surmise that a general sensibility is among us.

   This phenomenon cannot be explained by the aesthetic problems and history of any particular art form. Postmodernism in the arts corresponds to postmodernism in life. French theorist Jean-Francois Lyotard describes the scenario: "One listens to reggae, watches a Western, eats McDonald's food for lunch and local cuisine for dinner, wears Paris perfume in Tokyo and 'retro' clothes in Hong Kong." To argue about postmodernism, therefore, is to argue about more than postmodernism. Postmodernism is more than a buzzword or even an aesthetic; it is a way of seeing, a view of the human spirit, and an attitude toward politics as well as culture. It has precedents, but in its reach it is the creature of our recent social and political moment. In style, more than style is at stake.

   To get beyond vague talk and knowing genuflection, it is never a bad idea to start by deciding what we are talking about. We can get a rough fix on postmodernism by contrasting it to its main predecessors, realism and modernism.

This article was excerpted from *Dissent* (Winter 1989) and appeared in *Utne Reader* (July/August 1989), pages 52–59.

The Three Eras of Civilization

	Production	Society
Pre Modern **1000 BC–1450**	*Neolithic Revolution* agriculture handwork dispersed	*Tribal/Feudal* ruling class of kings, priests & military peasants
Modern **1450–1960**	*Industrial Revolution* factory mass-production centralised	*Capitalist* owning class of bourgeoisie workers
Post Modern **1960**	*Information Revolution* Office segmented-production decentralised	*Global* para-class of cognitariat office workers

In the realism that rode high in the 19th century, a work of art was supposed to express unity and continuity. Realism mirrored reality, and criticized it. The individuals portrayed were clearly placed in society and history. High culture was just that — higher, more valuable, than popular culture.

In modernism, voices, perspectives, and materials were multiple. The unity of the work was assembled from fragments and juxtapositions. Art set out to remake life. Audacious individual style threw off the dead hand of the past. Continuity was disrupted, the individual subject dislocated. High culture quoted from popular culture.

Postmodernism, by contrast, is completely indifferent to the questions of consistency and continuity. It self-consciously splices genres, attitudes, styles. It relishes the blurring or juxtaposition of forms (fiction-non-fiction), stances (straight-ironic), moods (violent-comic), cultural levels (high-low). It disdains originality and fancies copies, repetition, the recombination of hand-me-down scraps. It neither embraces nor criticizes, but beholds the world blankly, with a knowingness that dissolves feeling and commitment into irony. It pulls the rug out from under itself, displaying an acute self-consciousness about the work's constructed nature. It takes pleasure in the play of surfaces, and derides the search for depth as mere nostalgia.

One postmodernist trope is the list, as if culture were a garage sale, so it is appropriate to evoke postmodernism by offering a list of examples, for better and for worse: Michael Graves' Portland Building, Philip Johnson's AT&T, and hundreds of more or less skillful derivatives; Robert Rauschenberg's silk screens, Warhol's multiple-image paintings, photo-realism. Larry Rivers' erasures and pseudo-pageantry, Sherrie Levine's photographs of "classic" photographs; Disneyland, Las Vegas, suburban strips, shopping malls, mirror-glass office building facades; William Burroughs, Tom Wolfe, Donald

Time	Orientation	Culture
slow-changing reversible	*Local/City* agrarian	*Aristocratic* integrated style
linear	*Nationalist* rationalization of business exclusive	*Bourgeois* mass-culture reigning styles
fast-changing cyclical	*World/Local* multinational pluralist eclectic inclusive	*Tastes-Cultures* many genres

Barthelme, Monty Python, Don DeLillo, Joe Isuzu "He's lying" commercials, Philip Glass, *Star Wars*, Spalding Gray, David Hockney ("Surface is illusion, but so is depth"), Max Headroom, David Byrne, Twyla Tharp (choreographing Beach Boys and Frank Sinatra songs), Italo Calvino, *The Gospel at Colonus*, Robert Wilson, the Flying Karamazov Brothers, George Coates, the Kronos Quartet, Frederick Barthelme, MTV, *Miami Vice*, David Letterman, Laurie Anderson, Anselm Kiefer, John Ashbery, Paul Auster, the Pompidou Centre, *The White Hotel*, E. L. Doctorow's *Book of Daniel*, *Less Than Zero*, Kathy Acker, Philip Roth's *Counterlife* (but not *Portnoy's Complaint*), the epilogue to Rainer Werner Fassbinder's *Berlin Alexanderplatz*, the "language poets"; the French theorists Michel Foucault, Jaques Lacan, Jacques Derrida, and Jean Baudrillard; television morning shows; news commentary clueing us in to the image-making and "positioning" strategies of candidates; remote-control-equipped viewers "grazing" around the television dial.

Consider also Australia's Circus Oz, whose jugglers comment on their juggling and crack political jokes in a program infused by (their list) "Aboriginal influences, vaudeville, Chinese acrobatics, Japanese martial arts, fireman's balances, Indonesian instruments and rhythms, video, Middle Eastern tunes, B-grade detective movies, modern dance, Irish jigs, and the ubiquitous present of corporate marketing." Consider the student who walks into my office at the University of California dressed in a green jersey, orange skirt, and black tights.

There are important differences among these. Donald Barthelme is wistful about the dignity of the pre-modernist tradition in literature ("In the Tolstoy Museum"); Kathy Acker ransacks and trashes it. But whether disassembling or dissembling, postmodernists know that they—and we—are living hip-deep in debris.

So what's new? It has been argued that postmodernism is nothing more—or less—than the current phase of a modernist tradition (nice oxymoron!) already nearly a century old. True enough, for all the fanfare, postmodernism is, by definition, known by the company it follows. It is too modest (or is that only a ploy?) to pretend to be more than a sequel—which may be nothing more than an aftermath or a hiatus. Still, postmodernism peels away from its predecessor in several respects: its blasé tone, its sense of exhaustion, its self-conscious bemusement with surfaces. The question remains—whether brand new or a "new improved" modernism—just what does postmodernism express (and repress) at this historical moment? Why should this spirit have surfaced recently, and why is it so anxiously debated?

A phenomenon this sweeping cannot be traced to a single beginning. Six theories have surfaced in recent debates. They are not mutually exclusive, but their emphases are different. Each contributes to an explanation; none alone is sufficient.

The Global Shopping Center

The Marxist critic Fredric Jameson, among others, has argued that postmodernism is an ideology well suited to express and expand the global economic system that capitalism has become. High consumption capitalism requires a ceaseless transformation in style, a connoisseurship of surface, an emphasis on packaging and reproducibility: Postmodernist art echoes the fact that the arts have become auxiliary to sales. In order to adapt, consumers are pried away from traditions, their selves become "decentered," and a well-formed interior life becomes an obsolete encumbrance. Even "life-styles" become commodities to be marketed.

In effect, postmodernism expresses the spiritless spirit of a new global class of customers linked via borderless mass media with mass culture, omnivorous consumption, and easy travel. Their experience denies the continuity of history; they live in a perpetual present garnished by nostalgia binges. Space is not real, only time. The postmodernist style makes sense to the new consumer. In the global shopping center (as Richard Barnet and Ronald Müller have called it), local traditions have been swamped by the workings of the market. Anything can be bought, and to speak of intrinsic value is mere sentimentality. Postmodernist literature cultivates place names in the same way consumers flock to the latest ethnic cuisine—in the spirit of a collector, because the uniqueness of real places is actually waning. It makes much of brand names (even ironically) because they have become the furnishings of our cultural "home." How else to represent this new world than through postmodernist flatness? The postmodernist motto is, "You can't beat trash culture, so join it."

The trouble with this sweeping, impressive argument is that it is too sweeping. Aiming to explain so much, it glides over actual artists and the relation between specific experience and artistic choices. Moreover, these particular economic changes have been at work for 50 or 75 years; then why are their artistic consequences showing up only now?

The Scientific Method

Perhaps, it has been argued, scientific reason is the corrosive force that has eroded the authority of longstanding artistic modes, especially the familiar narrative style in fiction. Quantum theory and microphysics have undermined certainty and continuity. Voilà, postmodernism, which enshrines the discontinuous and "reinforces our ability to tolerate the incommensurable." Something like this has been argued by the theorist Lyotard ("The Postmodern Condition"), whose slapdash style, in the French mode, is to insist rather than to argue. But the argument, if I understand it, is clumsy. The advance of science has been accelerating for centuries, yet the postmodernist style is no more than two decades old.

The Television Generation

More concretely and modestly, the critic Cecelia Tichi argues that postmodern fiction—at least the work of Ann Beattie, Bret Easton Ellis, Bobbie Ann Mason, and Tama Janowitz, among others—is "video fiction." Anesthetized writing re-creates the experience of watching television. Attention span shriveled, a new generation of authors writes in televisionese. They write in the present tense because that is television's only tense: Everything is always happening right now, in the middle; there are no beginnings or ends. Growing up on fragmented television, to which they gave their fragmented attention, these writers produce "short scenes juxtaposed almost at random." Their characters live inconclusively, "forever poised for action rather than engaged in it," because that is what television-watching feels like. To Ms. Tichi's speculation I would add that postmodernism echoes (or produces) the "couch potato" phenomenon, which renders ironic the slug-a-bed passivity that TV's critics deplore: You can mainline your television and mock it at the same time. But if fiction simply transcribes an impoverished experience, is it not impoverished fiction? Tichi's observation is acute, but television cannot explain all of postmodernism.

The American Grab Bag

It is also irresistible to conclude that postmodernism extrapolates the long-established eclectic logic of American culture. Postmodernism was born in the United States because juxtaposition was always the essence of our poly-ethnic culture, which is less melting pot than grab bag. "There is no dis-tinctively American culture," the essayist Randolph Bourne wrote in 1916. "It is apparently our lot rather to be a federation of cultures." Alexis de Tocqueville described American culture 150 years ago as a marketplace jam-boree with amazing diversity striving for recognition. This means that no style, no subject is intrinsically superior to any other. What could be more American than humbling the highbrow? In this sense, the essence of Amer-ican culture is the variety show, finding a place for everyone—postmod-ernism's prototype. The raucous, disrespectful side of postmodernism is explained by this theory. Unfortunately, so is the bland side. The cult of the least common denominator is also an American tradition; we keep cultural peace by forcing everyone to sheathe their swords.

The Post-'60s Syndrome

Postmodernism is, more than anything else, a reaction to the 1960s. It is post-Vietnam, post-New Left, post-hippie, post-Watergate. History was rup-tured, passions have been expended, belief has become difficult; heroes have died and been replaced by celebrities. The 1960s exploded our belief in progress, which underlay the classical faith in linear order and moral clar-ity. Old verities crumbled, but new ones have not settled in. Self-regarding irony and blankness are ways of staving off the anxieties, rages, terrors, and hungers that have been kicked up but cannot find resolution. The blank, I've-seen-it-all postmodernist tone, in this light, is self-imposed cultural anesthesia, a refusal to feel (except for punkish rage, in which only one thing can be felt: loathing). The fear is that what's underneath hurts too much; better to repress it.

The Yuppie Factor

Postmodern currents run especially deep among people born in the 1950s and 1960s. Postmodernism, in other words, has a demand-side as well as a supply-side. From this angle, postmod is, let's face it, a yuppie outlook. It re-flects an experience that takes for granted not only television but suburbs, shopping malls, recreational (not religious or transcendent) drugs, and the towering abstraction of money. To grow up post-1960s is to experience af-termath, privitization, weightlessness; everything has apparently been done. Therefore culture is a process of recycling; everything is juxtaposable to everything else because nothing matters. This generation is disabused of au-thority, except, perhaps, the authority of money; theirs is the bumper sticker, THE ONE WITH THE MOST TOYS WINS. (Perhaps the ultimate postmodern experience is to shift information bits and computer bytes around the world at will and high speed.) The culture this generation favors is a passive adaptation to the feeling of being historically stranded—after the 1960s but before what? Perhaps the Bomb, the void hanging over the horizon, threatening to pulverize everything of value. So be cool. In this light, postmodernism is anticipatory shell shock. It's as if the Bomb has already fallen.

Postmodernism, which fancies itself as ever so disdainful of history, turns out to be all too embedded in it. Because such a variety of forces have funneled together to nourish postmodernism it's likely that the tendency will be with us for some time.

How, then, can we develop a workable political point of view for the postmodern era? I think what we need is a politics of limits. Simply, there must be limits to what human beings can be permitted to do with their powers. Most of the atrocities to which our species is prone can be understood as violations of limits. The essence of a politics must be rooted in three protections: (1) The ecological: The earth and human life must be protected against the Bomb and other manmade perils; (2) The pluralist: The social group must be protected against domination by other social groups; (3) The libertarian: The individual must be protected against domination by larger groups. A politics of limits respects horizontal social relations—multiplicity over hierarchy, juxtaposition over usurpation, difference over deference: Finally, disorderly life in its flux against orderly death in its finality. The democratic, vital edge of the postmodern, the love of difference and flux and the exuberantly unfinished, deserves to infuse the spirit of politics. Needless to say, this still leaves many questions unsettled: What happens when there are conflicts and internal fissures among these objectives? What kind of authority, what kind of difference, is legitimate? Respect for uncertainties is of the essence of postmodernism. This is the properly postmodern note on which I suspend the discussion for now.

Alongside the blasé brand of postmodernism we see around us, I am trying to say there is another kind—one in which pluralist exuberance and critical intelligence reinforce each other. Here we find jubilant disrespect for the boundaries that are supposed to segregate cultural currents.

The postmodernist arts, in toto, express a spirit that comports well with American culture in the '80s. Alongside ostensible belief, actual disengagement. The standard ideological configurations of "liberal" and "conservative" belief are decomposing, although the decomposition is masked by the fact that the old political language is still in force. The patriotic words are mouthed while the performers signal, in the manner of *Moonlighting* (and Reagan at his self-deprecating best), that they don't really mean them (quite). In *Stranger Than Paradise* and David Letterman as well as in the

Republican party, there is a love for the common people and their kitsch tastes that is indistinguishable from contempt. In politics as in the arts distrust runs rampant while, beneath the surface, as David Byrne and Brian Eno have put it, "America is waiting for a message of some sort or another."

Postmodernism is an art of erosion. Make the most of stagnation, it says, and give up gracefully. That is perhaps what distinguishes it from modernism, which was, whatever its subversive practices, a series of declarations of faith. What is not clear is whether postmodernism, living off borrowed materials, has the resources for continuing self-renewal. A car with a dead battery can run off its generator only so long. Exhaustion is finally exhausting. But if it is true that deep social forces have been at work for a long time to produce the present cultural anesthesia, then postmodernism is not going to fade automatically. How does a culture renew itself? Not easily.

The deeply unsettling and inspiring project that artists and theorists and all of us face, is, more or less, the promise of something else—call it a hot postmodernism or a seriously global culture that would not be brought to us courtesy of McDonald's. Not by the imposition of the master culture over the minor, the elite culture over the popular. Rather, the rock-bottom value, the overriding principle of this global culture has to be the preservation of the *other*. The hallmark is coexistence: that in the preservation of the other is a condition for the preservation of the self; we are not *we* until they are *they*, for to whom else shall we speak, with whom else shall we think, if not those who are different from ourselves?

The ideal toward which politics strives is conversation—and conversation requires respect for the other. *The fundamental value is that the conversation continue toward the global culture.*

Questions for Critical Thinking and Discussion

1. Briefly describe the concepts of realism and modernism.
2. Some view postmodernism as a cop-out for noncreativity. For example, postmodernism's "living off of borrowed materials" and its shunning of history and historical context, make it seem like an excuse for people to simply produce whatever they like. It doesn't matter if it is original or important, or even if it is successful or long lasting.

   Others find the postmodern condition completely liberating because all of the modernist rules were simply meaningless political constructs to maintain the status quo.

   What do you think about postmodernism? What value does it have for our society? What negative influences could (does) it have on society?

chapter 12

Mass Communication
Research and Effects

All Quiet on the Feminist Front

bell hooks

bell hooks is a feminist theorist, cultural critic, and author of sixteen books. Most recently, she has produced two memoirs, Bone Black: Memories of Girlhood *(Henry Holt & Company, 1997) and* Wounds of Passion, *(Henry Holt & Company, 1997) as well as a collection of essays on writing called* Remembered Rapture *(Henry Holt & Company 1999).*

hooks uses strong language to communicate strong emotions about her frustration with the state of feminism in 1996. She illustrates how other cultural issues (e.g., racial equality, economics, politics) have been used to undermine feminist concerns such as sexual harassment and domestic violence. According to hooks, the most diabolical undermining of feminism emerges in the form of convincing "misguided women" that—at best—feminist work is being furthered and active feminists are out-of-touch manhaters or that—at worst—feminism isn't necessary anymore because all those old *"patriarchal" problems have already been solved.*

It used to be that feminism was a total woman thang. Outside of the nice white girls who filled women's-studies classes because they wanted to learn to be bad, everyone was content to think of us as just a bunch of bra-burning pussy-loving antimale morons who were never gonna have any impact on the rest of the world so no one really had to give a damn. In other words, back in the day when feminist politics had a serious radical edge it was not a movement that everyone was dying to join, but neither was it a movement that everyone wanted to trash. At the peak of the contemporary feminist movement, after all, the patriarchal boys used to tell the world that every single one of us unruly girls could be tamed by just "one good fuck."

Well, for many of us this life-transforming fuck never happened and we went right on telling the world that equal rights were for everybody, that gender roles had to be transformed, that folks who do the same work should get the same pay, that patriarchy was fucking up the family big-time, that practically all of us—female and male—had been violated by male domination, and that it really was life-transforming to JUST SAY NO. And fem-

This article first appeared in *Art Forum* (December 1996), Vol. 35(4), pages 39–40.

inism began to seep into the culture as a whole. Suddenly many of the issues first put on the table in all-female, confessional, consciousness-raising groups—domestic violence, child abuse, reproductive rights—were rocking the nation. So much changed that men could no longer simply ignore the movement or squash it with their ridicule. A lot of us women had had the wisdom to know that if men knew what they were really about, they would drop that dick-thing patriarchal madness and get in touch with liberation. And in fact, in the late '80s a lot of men started embracing feminism, dismissing crude biological determinism and living their lives on the equality tip. Feminism came to be the movement everybody could count on for a taste of freedom. That was when the backlash really began, and in this past year it reached an all-time peak.

Much of what Susan Faludi documented in *Backlash* in 1991 looks like child's play compared to the tactics deployed this past year to discredit feminism on every front. One of those tactics was to enlist as many women as possible who had previously benefited from the movement to give eyewitness accounts of it as both banal and corrupt. With Camille Paglia heading the crowd (after all, since girlfriend ain't been writing she'd have had no public play if not for all those times she could be found providing some antifeminist testimony or other), women themselves lined up. On the academic front, moving from a legacy of left politics to basic right-wing doublethink, Elizabeth Fox-Genovese offered her stellar tract *Feminism Is Not the Story of My Life.* In a more popular vein, Nancy Friday bashed feminism throughout *The Power of Beauty.* As the mass media applauded this move to rip feminism to shreds, a host of lesser-known white girls joined the antifeminist parade to get a day in the sun and a paycheck. Whether it was in *The New Republic, The Chronicle of Higher Education,* or *The Village Voice,* feminism was under attack.

Everywhere one turned, feminists were accusing other feminists of stealing their spot in the limelight. This was good old patriarchal competition at its best—blood sport. And no matter where or at whom the gun was aimed, feminism was the target. Hillary Rodham Clinton has never declared herself a feminist, but conservative media (which have always made it seem that every successful woman, no matter how reactionary, is a feminist in disguise) imposed the title on her to give the feminism they were attacking a concrete image. To discredit her was to discredit feminism proper.

Feminism was under attack generally, but a particular kind of feminism was particularly targeted—it was the radical dimensions that had to go. The revolutionary intervention that really transformed and renewed the contemporary feminist movement, giving it a broader base, was the recognition on the part of women and men engaged in feminist struggle that race mattered—

that it was impossible to fight against sexism without understanding the convergence of race and sex. This focus had emerged in the thinking of a broad spectrum of writers, such as media and film theorist Drucilla Cornell. Until the last year or so, though, the mainstream media showed little interest in the feminist theory that was really causing radical shifts in feminist thought and practice. But then, suddenly, the O. J. Simpson case and the Million Man March became the perfect patriarchal playing fields for challenging and undermining feminist insistence on the interlocking nature of systems of domination.

Audiences around the world were encouraged to see the Simpson trial apart from issues of sex and class — in other words, as primarily about the issue of race, or as yet another unfair attack on the disenfranchised black man. Simpson, actually a rich man with an expensive team of lawyers, was represented as the downtrodden black everyman who could not get a fair deal. Not only did this deflect people away from the issue of class power, it hid the fact that the real deal was the reinscription of patriarchal privilege, via a discounting of the issue of male violence as a relevant concern for everyone in a society that sustains such privilege by equating the ability to be violent with masculinity.

The trial did gain an even larger audience for already popularized feminist concerns like sexual harassment and domestic violence, but that only deluded many misguided women into seeing it as furthering feminist work. In fact, conservative mass media were creating the image of concerned feminist white women who care about male violence being attacked by ferocious antifeminist black women who only think about race and stand by their man at all costs. In a matter of months, the incredible body of work done by black women feminist thinkers to highlight the convergence of racism and sexism, the way the two systems sustain and perpetuate each other, was rendered suspect. (Reformist white feminists and conservative black cultural-nationalist "womanists" who had always frowned upon the linkage of sexism and racism actually welcomed this separation of the two issues.) And white women were sent the message that they'd better stay in the arms of benevolent white patriarchy or their lives would be at risk and they'd have no one to blame but themselves.

If the Simpson trial became a way to whip white girls into shape and remind them that father knows best (not to mention letting black men know they get a better deal if they side with the ruling patriarchy), the Million Man March in late 1995 definitely served notice on black women. It told the world that the major problems in black life were caused not by interlocking systems of domination based on race, sex, and class, but by uppity black women who just won't get to the back of the bus and let black men be the patriarchs they were born to be. The "atonement" that the march was all about was actually black men's atonement for their refusal to assume the role of benevolent patriarchs—but no more.

At the same time, black feminist thinkers who critiqued the march were written off as traitors to the race. No matter what our political history, no matter whether we'd spent years on the black liberation front, if we weren't down with the march we were anti–black male and therefore anti–black family. The fact that many of us opposed the march because of its reinscription of patriarchy, its support of militarism and imperialism, and its attack on single mothers and welfare went unnoticed. Astute feminist political critique was ignored in favor of that old misogynist terroristic strategy—just proclaim, "They hate black men." Meanwhile, black male leaders on the left showed that they had no difficulty supporting Minister Farrakhan and making plans for "the future of the race" without including the wisdom of feminist sisters.

Let's not think for a minute that the reason the march got so much play in the mass media was that white folks are so scared of black men gathering together. In fact white folks seemed to welcome black men climbing on the conservative bandwagon and calling for more homosocial bonding, more patriarchy, more men at the head of everything. Quiet as this was kept, much of the march's rhetoric echoed that of the white male Christian group the Promise Keepers: homophobia, male domination, women at home taking care of the children, kind fathers disciplining and punishing without abuse.

This was not just backlash, it was the demand for erasure: LET'S ALL JUST PRETEND THE FEMINIST MOVEMENT NEVER HAPPENED! Let's just act as though women have always had rights and the nation's most pressing problem was these uppity free women who are so busy harassing men (according to the movie *Disclosure*) that a boy doesn't stand a chance. Let's just act as though, when there's no welfare, men will work and provide for families. Let's just act as though there really were jobs for everybody, work was easy to find, and housing was cheap and available. Ultimately, let's just pretend that there's no racism—no sexism—that anybody who speaks out about oppression is just whining and should shut the fuck up, nobody's listening. That was the message of 1996.

Questions for Critical Thinking and Discussion

1. What is meant by the "backlash" of feminism?

2. The statistics certainly support the idea that inequality exists. But according to hooks, feminism has been politically disempowered and feminists who speak out are simply dismissed as whiners or manhaters. In fact, "liberated" women are portrayed as suspicious or even dangerous to men. If, so to speak, the troops have been "disarmed," how can equal rights for women continue to be advanced?

3. What response would you give to someone who is actively involved in the advancement of equality (racial, gender, etc.)? Why? If you are one of these actively involved people, what kinds of responses do you get from others?

34

African American Images on Television and Film

HERB BOYD

Herb Boyd is the national editor of The Black World Today. *An award-winning journalist, Boyd is the author of nine books, including* Brotherman: An Odyssey of the Black Man in America, *(Fawcett Books, 1996), an anthology that he co-edited with Robert Allen and which received the 1995 American Book Award. Boyd has taught Black Studies for almost thirty years at various universities and currently teaches African and African American history at the College of New Rochelle in Manhattan.*

Boyd begins his essay by providing a brief but succinct history of black images on television. In contemporary television, dramas are still devoid of serious black issues and personalities while the comedy format seems to be embracing more and more black characters (albeit, at times, still in stereotypical ways). Boyd argues that "the images of blacks in the media is a troubled condition. There has never been a decade that the media did not find a despicable image to assail the black American experience."

Racial tension, the image of blacks on television, and the dreaded N-word all converged recently during a highly controversial episode of *NYPD Blue* on ABC-TV. Detective Andy Sipowicz, portrayed by Emmy-winner Dennis Franz, is questioning a community activist, Brother Kwasi, played by Tom Wright, about a basketball game he helped to organize in which several people were shot, one of them fatally. At the end of their emotionally charged encounter Sipowicz asks Kwasi to accompany him to the station for further interrogation.

"I don't have to go anywhere with you," Kwasi explodes. "You dealing with the one nigger in a thousand who knows what you can and cannot do."

Even angrier, the detective snaps: "I'm dealing with the nigger whose big mouth is responsible for this massacre."

This confrontation and its results are suddenly the show's main theme, pushing the massacre to the margins. And Sipowicz is soon at odds with his partner and his superior, a black officer played by James McDaniel. There are several scenes where Sipowicz attempts to justify his use of the word by insisting that Kwasi said it first.

This article first appeared in *Crisis* (February/March 1996), Vol. 103(2), pages 22, 24–25.

Ironically, a black writer, David Mills, authored the script, and while it is cleverly wrought with an intense, double-barrelled complexity, there remain some troubling points. First of all, it is unlikely that such a hardcore black nationalist would ever refer to himself as a nigger, especially in an eyeball-to-eyeball confrontation with a white cop. The word is inconsistent with the character.

"And even if the word comes out of his mouth," says musician Eli Fountain, "the police officer has no right to repeat it. He is a public servant and not a private citizen. When he puts on that uniform or pinned on that badge and then uttered those words, he abdicated his authority."

Cut to another show and another scene. On a recent segment of *ER*, an ambulance driver brought to the hospital several black children who had been neglected by their crack addicted parents. The driver made a passing remark about "people like that" who don't look after their children. Two black characters chided him for what they felt was a racist remark. The driver, normally a sympathetic character, is not given a chance to explain himself. Maybe he will in future episodes.

Succeeding shows may also explain why the black doctor, Peter Benton, is always so angry. "This is very distressing," TV critic Donald Bogle notes, "but maybe they have a show that will get to the bottom of his anger."

Despite the shortcomings of these segments, Bogle admits, at least there are some black characters in strong, dramatic roles. "When it comes to blacks on TV we get a steady diet of comedy. For years now it has been sitcom after sitcom, a perpetual laugh fest."

"Even when there is a serious theme on one of these shows, it tends to be laughed away."

A cursory glance at weekly TV programming confirms Bogle's assertion. On any given night on cable or the networks, the nation's view of black America is glimpsed almost exclusively through a comic prism and such fare as *Martin, Roc, Fresh Prince of Bel-Air, Benson, Sanford & Son, Family Matters, Sister, Sister, Living Single,* or the *Wayans Brothers*. Many of them reruns, none of them drama—not even dramedy.

"We have made very little progress on TV," Bogle sighs. Which means that we have hardly evolved at all since the days when Ethel Waters brought *Beulah* the maid into America's living rooms. And memories of *Beulah* emerged again with the recent death of Butterfly McQueen, best remembered for her fawning role of "Prissy" in *Gone With the Wind*, but who starred for several seasons as Oriole, Beulah's sidekick and foil.

"The history of blacks on the prime time network series, like that of blacks in films," Bogle writes, "has been fraught with its own peculiar set of contradictions, its own array of internal frictions and frustrations, and its own tiny evolutionary steps."

If *Beulah* presented viewers with the same image of the obedient, hard-working servant, mired in a white world, *Amos 'n' Andy* offered a hilarious, but no less demeaning slice of black life where white folks rarely appeared. Still, it was a show that was conceived by white men and for all of its hi-jinks and lampooning—some of it rather subversive—the show was soon banished to the sidelines under the relentless protestations of the NAACP. Diahann Carroll's *Julia*, Clarence Williams III in *The Mod Squad*, Bill Cosby on *I Spy*, Hari Rhodes on *Mission: Impossible*, and Michelle Nichols as Uhuru on *Star Trek* were about as much as black viewers could expect until the *Roots* phenomenon in 1977.

For eight consecutive nights this twelve-hour miniseries had most of the nation riveted to their chairs. More than 130 million people reportedly watched this sprawling epic based on author Alex Haley's family and his best-selling book.

"*Birth of a Nation*," President Woodrow Wilson had extolled, was "history written with lightning." *Roots* was the thunder, and it still resonates as a reminder of the great potential of drama when it's artistically rendered and culturally relevant to all Americans.

"What it showed," said Fountain, who is an inveterate consumer of black culture, "is how vast our experiences are. And it is deeper than *Roots*, if they would be willing to investigate."

The next watershed for blacks on TV occurred in the mid 1980s when *The Cosby Show* collared our collective attention and revived hope again of serious dramas. That the show made it to prime time was quite surprising, given the thinking of most white executives that viewers (whites) would not follow the adventures of a black family—no matter how enchanting—from week to week. After ABC passed on the series, NBC took a chance and we all know what happened—the Cos became an icon again and NBC garnered top ratings among the networks.

"One of the criticisms I heard repeatedly," says Diane Williams, an emerging writer based in New York City, "is that folks like the Huxtables did not exist. But they were familiar to me; I knew many families like this."

Another thing Williams knows is the tendency on the part of blacks to accept negative images of themselves. "Sometimes we are so starved to see ourselves on television that we will accept almost any image, even the most demeaning ones," she says. "We have been conditioned this way."

Unfortunately, she continues, we have not been programmed to struggle to keep positive dramatic shows on the air when they do appear, though they air with less and less frequency.

"Unlike many dramas designed for white viewers," asserts Michael Din-widdie, a former staff writer with the sitcom *Hanging With Mr. Cooper*, "black serious programs are never allowed enough time to develop an audience."

He mentions *Palmers Town, U.S.A.* and *Harris and Company,* two shows from the early 1980s that featured all-black casts, as well as the more recently discontinued *Under One Roof.* And what about *Frank's Place?*" he asks. "That show had great potential, and then suddenly it was gone."

Frank's Place was about a restaurant, The Chez Louisiane, in New Orleans. While viewers gained no insight on the joint's legendary cuisine, they were offered a delectable course of episodes about black Americans, the incidents and slights that plagued their possibility.

"Just when *Frank's Place* was getting a toehold," George Hill and Spencer Moon conclude in their study of the medium, "CBS moved it several times, put it on hiatus, then canceled it. The black community was upset. Why did CBS cancel an excellent show? *Hill Street Blues* and *Cagney and Lacy* were both resurrected after poor ratings and went on to successful runs. Black-cast shows have not been given the same opportunity."

Tim Reid succinctly explains what happens: "It was purely political." But rather than ruminate on the past, Reid lashes out at the controversial *NYPD Blue* episode and the racist comments allegedly made by a CBS executive.

"He made a statement that blacks stay up late watching television because they have no jobs to go to in the morning," Reid fumes. "I want to know where is the NAACP? There was a time when they would have a picket line in place before dawn for such remarks. I would take the lead on this myself, but if I jump out there, there is no back up, and, believe me, I know where a lot of bones are buried."

The NAACP may be slow to react to the remark, but Leslie Moonves, president of CBS Entertainment, said the allegations were serious and would be promptly investigated. Many black listeners of talk radio would welcome a similar attitude from its executives. Hosts such as Bob Grant, Barry Grey, and Jay Diamond, who routinely refer to black women using the B-word, are among the leaders of conservative radio shows, where Rush Limbaugh reigns as the big cheese. Ridiculing and bashing blacks are part of their nightly fare and they get lots of support from white listeners.

"This conservative radio movement," says Todd Burroughs, a syndicated columnist and a Ph.D. student in journalism at the University of Maryland at College Park, "exists because of a group of whites who feel disempowered. They feel their life experiences have been subverted, and so this is their way of closing ranks, circling the wagons."

While these shows attract black listeners who seek to challenge the racist bile and nonsense, these blacks are but a small portion of an audience who spends most of its time tuned into black radio where they can get the kind of information and entertainment that are less confrontational and demanding.

"Black people have a direct relationship with radio," Burroughs says. "It is more immediate and more potentially liberating than any other media . . . Listening to their favorite disc-jockeys, they can interact with them, talk back to hosts who understand how to take care of their needs and wants.

"Radio is of particular importance to young African Americans. The first thing they do when they get up in the morning is turn on the radio. The jocks are there playing the music they can relate to, and often speaking to them directly in a language they understand. Over the years the radio has been a source of education and liberation for me."

Burroughs likes his radio listening mixed with enlightenment and he quotes Bob Law, whose syndicated talk show reaches thousands across the nation, insisting that the hosts of the shows find time "between the records to provide information and education for survival."

Whether on radio, television or in print, the image of blacks in the media is a troubled condition. There has never been a decade that the media did not find a despicable image to assail the black American experience. From Jim Crow to Uncle Tom to Aunt Jemima to Willie Horton to O. J. Simpson, black men and women—or some heinous caricature—have been used to comfort white America while African Americans struggle to reclaim their dignity and humanity.

"The image makers busy themselves with thinking of new ways of getting these (negative) images before the world," writes James Muhammad, editor of the *Final Call*. "Consider the new cop shows that have cropped up that showcase black men being arrested and thrown to the ground and the increased presence of silly black men and women on denigrating talk shows like *Jenny Jones, Jerry Springer,* and *Ricki Lake* et al. There was a time when black people couldn't pay to get on TV. Now the exploiters are cruising the community for anybody who'll buck-dance and grin."

These black Americans, so lacking in self-esteem and recognition, seem willing to do and say anything to get their fifteen minutes of air time. In this respect, author Stanley Crouch contends, blacks are merely conforming to the American desire for the vulgar and the forbidden.

· · · · · · · · · · · · · · · · ·

There is nothing wrong with the quest for recognition and self-esteem. What matters are the means to these ends. The million or more black men who gathered in Washington, D.C. this past October were obviously seeking similar goals, but they did it with dignity, though the white media did all it could to nullify the impact of the event.

Why is [it] that the Million Man March was among the top stories in the black media, while the white media ignored it? Was the image too powerful and threatening? Did the sight of black men bonding and conducting themselves in a civil manner contradict their notion of us as a menace to society?

"The media," Muhammad concludes, "continues to fuel public disdain for black people by highlighting the negative and burying the positive images of our community. It is perpetuating the call for more prisons and a police state in the black community. There needs to be a more balanced view presented of the black community in the white media. And we need a stronger black media."

Questions for Critical Thinking and Discussion

1. What are some ways that blacks have been negatively stereotyped by the media? What could be the effect of such content within the black community and society at large?

2. List three things that must change in order to improve images of blacks presented by the media. What role can you assume in this process of improvement?

35

If Liberals Go Marching Back In

JAMES K. GLASSMAN

*James K. Glassman holds the DeWitt Wallace–Readers Digest Chair in Communica-
tions in a Free Society at the American Enterprise Institute. He is also a regular
columnist for* U.S. News and World Report *and for* Intellectual Capital, *an
electronic magazine distributed on the Internet, and a regular commentator for the*
Nightly Business Report *on PBS. Read his editorial, "The Liberals Go Marching
Back In" before you read the response by Stanley Baran, Professor of Radio-
Television-Film at San Jose State University. Do you see anything wrong with the
way in which the editorial was written? Racist content in the editorial piece makes
it past the newspaper's editors but not past the activist eyes of media scholar and
author Dr. Stanley Baran. He challenges the San Jose* Mercury News *with a letter
of his own, which is awarded the newspaper's prestigious Silver Pen Award.*

Part of Bill Clinton's appeal is that if he's re-elected, he'll prevent the Republicans from controlling the White House and Congress at the same
time. Polls show that Americans prefer divided government. In only six of
the past 28 years has the president's party held a majority in both the House
and Senate.

But with less than two months to go, Clinton's effective campaign may
be making one-party government more likely, not less. The surprise is that
the one party is Democratic, not Republican.

Recent surveys give Democrats a solid lead — six percentage points — in
what's called the "congressional generic ballot test" (do you prefer a Democrat or Republican as your congressman?). "These numbers," writes analyst
Charles E. Cook in *Roll Call,* "are not that different from the GOP advantage
in the days leading up to the 1994 election." In that year, Republicans won
by seven points nationwide and gained control of the House and Senate.

The race for Congress (as for president) is far from over, but if the vote
were tomorrow, Democrats could win back control of both houses. What
would such a one-party government be like?

The editorial first appeared in the San Jose *Mercury News* (September 11, 1996), page 7B.
Baran's response letter appeared in the San Jose *Mercury News* (September 21, 1996), page 7B.

The most striking characteristic is that the new House leadership would be further left than it's been in decades. Ironically, voters who reject freshman Republicans because they're "extremists" would be replacing them with senior Democrats even farther from the center.

Richard Gephardt, the next speaker, has transformed himself from a New Democrat into a populist bent on class warfare. The day-to-day operations of the House would be managed by Majority leader David Bonior, an intense and driven admirer of liberation theology.

The Appropriations Committee would be run by Rep. David Obey, who, in the words of the *Almanac of American Politics*, is "a true believer in traditional liberalism, Keynesian economics and economic redistribution." Like Gephardt and Bonior, he detests free trade.

The Ways and Means Committee—in charge of taxes, welfare and Medicare—would be chaired by Harlem's Charles Rangel, who enjoys near-perfect legislative ratings from liberal groups.

Rangel would be one of four black, liberal, urban congressmen to head important committees. Rep. Ron Dellums would chair the panel in charge of defense; John Conyers, judiciary; and William Clay, education and labor.

Also back with a vengeance at the helm of what's now called the Commerce Committee (with jurisdiction over telecommunications, securities, energy, health and much more) would be John Dingell. Two other liberal activists—George Miller and Henry Gonzalez—would chair the panels that oversee the environment and banking.

While Clinton today gets most of the attention, it's Congress that originates the laws. If Clinton decides in his second term that he's still a centrist (who knows?), he can expect opposition from these House leaders. It would be nearly impossible, for example, to continue to pare the deficit without significant tax increases.

But even with a majority, liberal Democrats can't work their will in the Senate, where 60 votes are required to get things done. For that reason, I suspect that one-party government would find its greatest successes along a path—a very dangerous one—that some Republicans seem ready to follow as well.

Its prime advocate is Labor Secretary Robert Reich, who expressed the theme in a speech Feb. 6 at George Washington University. "If the government is to do less," he said, "then the private sector will have to do more."

Reich did not mean that America's corporations would have to become more profitable and competitive, thus boosting economic growth and living standards, holding down the prices consumers pay and generating more tax revenues. He meant that, since the government doesn't have the money, the private sector would have to take more responsibility for general social-welfare chores.

Earlier this year a series of bills and proposals, largely ignored by the press, laid out the details. For instance, in February Sen. Jeff Bingaman, a moderate Democrat from New Mexico, presented a plan to create, for tax purposes—two corporate classes. "A-corps," the good citizens blessed by Washington, would pay lower taxes than other firms—as long as they contribute a government-mandated percentage of their payrolls to pensions and training, offer a health plan meeting the model "drafted by the National Association of Insurance Commissioners," etc., etc.

As someone who ran his own business, I appreciate the value of paid leave, pensions, health care, training and the rest. But in a free economy, decisions on these matters should be private—between managers and workers, uncoerced by Washington. Some workers, for instance, prefer higher pay to better health benefits. They should have that choice.

The unintended consequences of a Reichian system are dire. If every new worker comes loaded with onerous new costs, a business simply will cut back its work force, move production offshore, use third-party suppliers and buy more machines.

Freedom and flexibility are the main reasons the United States outperforms other mature economies. But Reich risks destroying the great capitalist jobs machine. And the leftists who may soon rule Congress will be only too glad to help.

Why Race Still Divides America

A Response to "If Liberals Go Marching Back In"

STANLEY J. BARAN, Ph.D.

James Glassman attempts to frighten readers with his dire prognostications about a liberal takeover of Congress (Opinion, Sept. 11). How does he do it? As usual for conservatives, he plays race in a most despicable fashion.

In the House of Representatives, Richard Gephardt is a "populist bent on class warfare." David Bonior is "an intense and driven admirer of liberation theology." David Obey is "a true believer in traditional liberalism." These men "detest free trade." But that's not enough. Whereas none of these scary liberals is identified by race, Glassman not only chooses to designate the race of his next group of liberals, but he turns them into a gang:

"(Rep. Charles) Rangel would be one of four black, liberal, urban congressmen to head important committees."

Apparently liberal and urban weren't enough. Being black and among a group of black men is the real threat to America. White America (including newspaper editors) accepts such characterization without question, as if these legislators' race (and only theirs) is a reason for concern. Then white America professes shock at African-American reaction to the O. J. Simpson verdict.

This is why race remains a central dividing factor in American society.

Questions for Critical Thinking and Discussion

1. Can you recall any other examples of content that seemed naively (or unintentionally) racist, sexist, or prejudiced in general?

2. Has anyone ever "called you" on something you said or wrote because it was (or could have been) construed as prejudiced? What are some strategies we can adopt to be sure we are being fair to others?

chapter 13

Media Regulation,
Freedom, and Ethics

36

Telecon

ROBERT W. McCHESNEY

Robert McChesney teaches journalism at the University of Wisconsin, Madison.
Corporations controlled the battle over the landmark Communications Law
of 1934. After 62 years and many new technological innovations (e.g., television,
satellites, personal computers), Congress has rewritten that law, and according to
McChesney and others, the public interest is again being ignored.

On June 15, the U.S. Senate overwhelmingly passed a new telecommunications bill that would deregulate the telephone, cable TV and broadcasting industries. The House is expected to pass a similar bill this summer, and the President has indicated that he will sign it.

The new legislation addresses the digital revolution in communications technology—which has blurred the distinctions between old industries such as telephone and cable, and led to the creation of entirely new industries like online computer services. Since this bill will shape what the *New York Times* calls "the $700 billion data highway," it may well be the most important piece of communications legislation since the Federal Communications Act of 1934, and it is probably one of the most important laws passed by Congress in decades.

You might think, therefore, that this legislation would have been carefully debated during lengthy hearings in which public interest groups were represented. But the brief hearings on the bill were dominated by business lobbyists, who actually wrote whole sections of the Senate measure behind the scenes. Organized consumer groups—who never challenged the corporate control of communications, but merely wanted certain regulations retained—were shut out of the process entirely. As Brad Stillman, a representative of the Consumer Federation of America, put it, "if you look at this legislation, there is something for absolutely everybody—except the consumer."

Communications policymaking has been largely impervious to public influence since the passage of the 1934 Federal Communications Act, which ensured that private corporations would dominate American telecommuni-

---

This article first appeared in *In These Times* (July 10, 1995), pages 14–17.

cations. Supporters of the 1934 law insisted that the public interest could best be served by companies primarily interested in making a profit. But by relegating noncommercial broadcasters to the margins of the U.S. airwaves, the legislation of 1934 seriously distorted America's media and tragically affected the quality of our political culture.

Today, however, spectacular new technologies hold the promise of revitalizing communications in the United States. Perhaps the most dramatic development has been the rise of the Internet and online computer services. The Internet has permitted mass interactive communication and has given millions of users relatively cheap access to information at lightning speed. Undoubtedly, much of the hype surrounding the information superhighway is just that—hype. Nevertheless, a democratically designed communications network—one that attempted to make a wide variety of information available to the largest number of citizens—could have an enormous and positive impact on politics, education and culture. A revitalized public debate concerning how best to establish a viable communications system in the public interest is long overdue. If this is an issue unworthy of public participation, then one must wonder what the purpose of democracy is.

But the debate in Congress over the future of telecommunications policy has disregarded issues of democracy and fairness. Lawmakers have focused instead on gutting regulations that impede the profitability of companies seeking to develop new communications technologies. And so, the current legislative process has been guided by the same assumption that led to the disastrous Communications Act of 1934: namely, that competition among corporations in the marketplace will provide the most efficient and democratic communications system.

The tightening oligarchy of telecommunications companies that arose in the wake of the 1934 law shows how misguided that assumption was. And there is no reason to believe that a new law based on the same logic will be any more viable as a guide to opening up the digital frontier. As one former Microsoft executive warned, "The information highway is too important to be left to the private companies." Our society must determine who will control the new technologies and for what purpose. Of course, in determining this question, we also dictate who will *not* control this technology and what purposes will *not* be privileged. Consider the history of the Communications Act of 1934—a case study in how the public interest can be sacrificed in badly managed debates over cynically conceived communications laws.

The current communications revolution closely parallels that of the 1920s, when the emergence of radio broadcasting forced society to address the same political questions. Radio broadcasting was then radically new, and there was great confusion throughout the '20s concerning who should control this powerful new technology and for what purposes. Much of the impetus for radio broadcasting came first from early ham radio operators and then from nonprofit and noncommercial groups that immediately grasped the public service potential of the new technology. It was only in the late '20s that capitalists began to sense that, by selling advertising and building national chains of stations, commercial radio could generate substantial profits. The capitalists moved quickly, however.

In the wake of a 1926 Supreme Court ruling that revoked all broadcast licenses, Congress hastily drafted a bill creating a new regulatory authority known as the Federal Radio Commission (the predecessor to today's Federal Communications Commission). Through their immense power in Washington, D.C., the commercial broadcasters were able to dominate the Federal Radio Commission so that the scarce number of channels were turned over to them with no public and little Congressional deliberation.

As the commercial networks began growing rapidly in the late '20s, a diverse broadcast reform movement attempted to establish a dominant role for the nonprofit and noncommercial sector in U.S. broadcasting. These opponents of commercialism—including religious groups, labor unions, educational organizations and women's groups—appealed to the public by tapping into the widespread disgust with the early advertisements on radio. "If [advertisers] are allowed to continue for another ten years," writer Upton Sinclair warned in 1931, "we shall have the most debased and vulgarized people in the world." The reformers maintained that if private interests controlled the medium, no amount of regulation or self-regulation could overcome the profit bias built into the system. Commercial broadcasting, the reformers argued, would downplay controversial and provocative public affairs programming and emphasize whatever fare would sell the most products for advertisers. They looked to Canada and Britain for workable models of public-service broadcasting.

But the reform movement disintegrated after the passage of the Communications Act of 1934, which established the FCC and remains the reigning statute for telecommunications in the United States. The radio lobby—with a sophisticated public relations campaign and support from other news media—won because it was able to keep most Americans ignorant or confused about communications policy. In addition, commercial broadcasters became a force that few politicians wished to antagonize; almost all of the congressional leaders who pushed for broadcast reform in 1931–32 were defeated in the 1932 elections, a lesson not lost on those who replaced them. With the defeat of the reformers, the industry argument that commercial broadcasting was inherently democratic and American went unchallenged.

In the case of television, Congress and the FCC determined in the 1934 law and in later decisions that a few enormous corporations would control the medium for the purpose of maximizing profits. This decision put the development of television on a path far different from that followed in many European countries, where noncommercial broadcasters have been able to pursue interests beyond profit. The effects of this choice have been ruinous for public debate in America. Today, the idea that private, for-profit broadcasting is synonymous with democracy is an unexamined tenet of our political culture.

Since 1934, the only politically acceptable criticism of U.S. broadcasting—and, more broadly, American telecommunications—has been to assert that it is uncompetitive and therefore needs more aggressive regulation. Liberals have argued that a scarce number of channels mandates aggressive regulation—not that the capitalist basis of the industry is fundamentally flawed. This is a far cry from the criticism of the broadcast reformers of the 1930s.

Now, with the current communications revolution vastly expanding the number of channels, the scarcity argument has lost its power. Liberals thus find themselves unable to challenge the deregulatory juggernaut. Contemporary public-service advocates would be wise to study the 1930s reformers to find a critique of commercial communication based not on the lack of competition, but on the very workings of the market, regardless of the amount of competition or the number of channels that technology may provide. This is the only type of public-service criticism that can hold any water in the digital era.

Because our society takes it for granted that private corporations rightfully dominate American communications, there has been little discussion questioning whether the information highway should be turned over to for-profit companies. Consequently, the mainstream press—accepting the primacy of corporate control and the profit motive—considers only which firms will dominate the communications revolution, and which firms will fall by the wayside.

The current range of legitimate debate is distressingly narrow. It starts with Senate Commerce Committee Chairman Larry Pressler, author of the Senate's deregulatory bill, who argues that profits are synonymous with public service. And it extends to Vice-President Al Gore, the proponent of 1993's tougher cable TV regulations, who accepts that there are some public interest concerns the marketplace cannot resolve, but insists that those concerns can be addressed only after the profitability of the dominant corporate sector has been assured. The Gore position can be dressed up to sound high and mighty, but the historical record is clear: If the needs of corporations are given primacy, the public interest will invariably be pushed to the margins.

Politicians may favor one sector over another in the battle to cash in on the information superhighway, but they cannot oppose the cashing-in process, except at the risk of their political careers. In the 1993–94 election cycle, political action committees linked to the telecommunications industry gave almost $7 million to politicians from both parties, according to figures compiled by the Center for Responsive Politics. The only grounds for political courage in this case would be if there were an informed and mobilized citizenry ready to do battle for alternative policies. Of course, citizens get their information from the corporate news media, which stands to benefit from the pending legislation. That is why telecommunications reform has been covered as a business story, not as a public policy story, and that is why the critical congressional hearings have passed virtually without public notice. In short, this is a debate restricted to those with serious financial stakes in the outcome.

In place of this non-debate, we need to challenge the entire theory of market-ruled communications. Free enterprise advocates argue that the market provides the only truly democratic policymaking mechanism because it rewards capitalists who "give the people what they want" and penalizes those who do not. But the market is not predicated upon the idea of one-person, one-vote as in democratic theory, but rather is predicated upon the rule of one-dollar, one-vote. The prosperous have many votes and the poor have none. And the market does not "give the people what they want" as much as it "gives the people what they want within the range of what is most profitable to produce." This is often a far narrower range than what people might enjoy choosing from. Thus, when Congress drafted broadcast legislation in the '30s, many Americans may well have been willing to pay for an advertising-free system, but this choice was not profitable for the dominant commercial interests, so it was not offered on the marketplace.

Is the current legislative situation therefore hopeless? Unfortunately, the immediate answer is an unequivocal yes. Some public-interest advocates have made thoughtful arguments for noncommercial interests to prevail on the communications highway. After all, it seems downright irrational to turn over control of society's central nervous system to a handful of transnational corporations guided strictly by profit. But this argument is now more marginal than ever.

At the same time, the sheer magnitude of the possibilities brought on by the new technologies will allow nonprofit niches to survive and perhaps even prosper in a regime of corporate domination. As long as the communications corporations continue to battle for control over the new markets, nonprofits may be able to exploit opportunities that will not exist once the industry has stabilized. In the late '20s and early '30s, for example—before the radio networks had consolidated legal control over the airwaves—civic groups were able to establish quite a bit of educational programming on the commercial stations. The networks, sensitive to charges that they cared only for profit, hoped to convince lawmakers of their benevolence by giving away airtime. Of course, soon after the 1934 law was passed, the commercial stations slashed their educational programming. Perhaps today, as TCI or Bell Atlantic attempts to convince America of its good intentions, some noncommercial group may be given free access to the information superhighway. Unfortunately, there is every reason to believe that today's nonprofits will fare just as poorly as yesterday's educators once the digital frontier has been tamed.

In some ways, the emergence of the new technologies could not have come at a more inopportune moment. In the 1930s an impressive array of civic organizations was willing to argue that it was inappropriate for communications media to be directed by the profit motive—back when even blue-blood Republicans questioned whether for-profit firms should dominate communications. Today, few Democrats would question the natural right of the private sector to dominate the information superhighway. We live in an era in which the very notion of public service has become discredited unless as a function of noblesse oblige. It thus should be no surprise that the private sector, with its immense resources, has seized the initiative and is commercializing cyberspace at a spectacular rate—effectively transforming it into a giant shopping mall.

The contours of the emerging communications battle are still unclear, but most business observers expect a flurry of competition followed by the establishment of a stable oligopoly dominated by a handful of enormous firms. What is clear is that the communications highway will not be devoted to reducing inequality or misery in our society. In fact, without any policies to counteract the market, the new technologies will probably create a world of information haves and have-nots, thereby exacerbating our society's already considerable social and economic inequality.

Nowhere is the absurdity of a profit-driven society more clear than in the case of communications, where technologies with the capacity to liberate are being constrained by the need to generate profit for corporate masters. In this sense, the battle to create a nonprofit and noncommercial communications system will be—and must be—part and parcel of progressive efforts to create a more just society.

Questions for Critical Thinking and Discussion

1. According to McChesney, how has the public interest been sacrificed during the many years the Communication Act of 1934 was in effect? Why were the 1934 laws written the way they were?

2. McChesney claims that "our society takes it for granted that private corporations rightfully dominate American communications." What do you think our system would look like if this wasn't true? Come up with a scenario for our media system that would not allow private ownership by commercial companies.

The Big Telecom Rip-Off Glides Through Congress

MOLLY IVINS

Molly Ivins is a columnist for the Fort Worth, Texas, Star-Telegram.

Many people saw the 1996 Telecommunications Act as an opportunity to return control of the broadcast spectrum to those who legally own the airwaves: the public — the people. While passed in Congress by overwhelming margins, the legislation was seen by some as a negative regulatory step. As Molly Ivins writes, "The people who own the media are the ones who are going to make all of the money from this legislation. They bought the politicians for $40 million."

Let's snuggle up for a few moments with the telecommunications bill that our only Congress just saw fit to pass by overwhelming margins.

Item No. 1 The most dread words in the English language are: "It has the support of everyone in the industry." Translation: We've just been screwed again.

Item No. 2 When you hear a right-wing Republican like Rep. Thomas Bliley Jr. of Virginia, the tool of the tobacco industry, claim, "Today, we have broken up two of the biggest government monopolies left, local television service and cable television," you should run screaming from the hall in terror. You know this is not a man given to breaking up monopolies.

Item No. 3 The story so far: In anticipation of the great free-for-all of market competition Bliley and others promise this bill will bring, the following has already happened: Disney bought Cap Cities/ABC; Westinghouse bought CBS; AT&T split itself into three parts and is laying off 40,000 workers (Bliley says the bill will "create thousands of new jobs"); merger talks are already under way between two of the giant Bell companies, Nynex and Bell Atlantic; the major players, including cable and software companies, have already formed numerous partnerships, with cross-ownership deals so complex that it looks like a spider's web when you make a chart of it.

This article first appeared in the San Jose *Mercury News* (July 7, 1996), page 6B.

Item No. 4 Senate Majority Leader Bob Dole is a craven tower of Jell-O; if you want to see a spineless politician, watch Dole on this bill. Less than two weeks ago, he said it was a "big, big corporate welfare project" to give away $70 billion worth of "digital broadcasting spectrum." Hell, it's the biggest rip-off in the history of the Earth.

The digital broadcasting spectrum is the public airwaves, folks; that's our property. We could make a hole in the national debt with that money; we could set aside zillions for educational programming for children; we could wire every school in the country for computer access. But what we're likely to get out of this is zip. Although the digital broadcast spectrum section of the bill is "in abeyance" for now, if you look at the voting—414 to 16 in the House and 91 (including Dole) to 5 in the Senate—you can see how much appetite our politicians have for taking on the broadcasters.

Six months ago, Dole was attacking Time-Warner for putting out tacky rap music. Time-Warner just snuck out of this bill with a pile of blue chips so big you can't even measure it.

Item No. 5 The telecommunications industry just got itself the finest bill that money can buy. Telecom companies have given $40 million to Congress during the last 10 years—$1.2 million in political action committee money during the last six months of '95 alone. Politicians in key positions to affect the bill got the most.

Item No. 6 This is the most important piece of legislation since health care reform was on the table; it will affect our lives in more ways and longer and cost us more money than anything short of health care reform. So how come your faithful news media have told you squat about it?

Look at who owns us, bubba. I'm a professional anti-conspiracy theorist, and I think there's too much paranoia in this country already. But I'm telling you, it's right there in front of all of us. The reason you know jack about this bill is because the people who own the media are the ones who are going to make all the money from it. They bought the politicians for $40 million. This bill is not going to "increase competition," for God's sake. It's going to lead to a merger frenzy that will make last summer look like kindergarten.

When I first started doing one-minute editorials for a local television station, I wondered how I could possibly say anything useful about anything in 60 seconds. Then I realized that it doesn't take that long to say, "Hang the bastards." Let's.

Questions for Critical Thinking and Discussion

1. What are some reasons why politicians would not want to "take on" broadcasters or vote to strictly regulate them? What do politicians have to gain from a good relationship with broadcasters?

2. Molly Ivins provides strong criticism of those who would take advantage of our communication system for personal gain (lots of money). Why does she consider mass media such an important, valuable resource?

38

Di Dies; We Follow the Money

JON CARROLL

Jon Carroll has been a columnist for the San Francisco Chronicle *for over fifteen years. He has also written for publications such as* Rolling Stone, Rags, Oui, *and the* Village Voice.

In this article, Carroll discusses the culpability of press and *audience in supporting intrusive reporting of celebrities' personal lives.*

The media seem to have had just a tiny psychotic break. They seem to have had a collective episode of dissociative behavior.

It's easy to make the diagnosis from hearing the patient describe the event. Many hours were logged by the media distancing itself from the media. "The death of Princess Diana raises questions about the role of the media," say the media. "Can the media be blamed?" wonder the media.

The media are apparently every news-gathering organization other than the one employing the commentator. The *Enquirer* announced that it would not buy any photographs of the actual bleeding body of the princess, and then congratulated itself for its restraint.

Other editors made a distinction between the paparazzi (bad) and everyone else (good). Never was the word "we" used, as in: What role did we play in the death of Princess Diana?

Television documentaries illustrated the evils of the paparazzi by showing many pictures of Diana taken by these same paparazzi. "Wasn't this invasion of privacy terrible?" they clucked, invading it again.

Let's eliminate the word "paparazzi" because it clouds the discussion. What we had here were free-lance photographers. Many of these photographers had working relationships with prominent wire services and newspapers.

And mostly, they took ordinary pictures. These ordinary pictures were purchased by major media outlets—the Associated Press, say, or *Time* magazine, or (if they were videos rather than still photos) CNN or Fox News.

This article first appeared in the San Francisco *Chronicle* (September 2, 1997), page E8.

No media company has the resources to hire 5,000 photographers to be at every place a newsworthy human might appear. Everyone uses free-lancers. And the ordinary photographs and videos—a celebrity enters a building, leaves a building, holds hands with a friend, plays with a child—are the bread and butter of free-lance celebrity photography.

The occasional fuzzy picture of an illicit embrace or a topless sunbath may be lucrative, but that's not where the steady money is. It's in the respectable photographs of fully dressed people in non-compromising positions.

And the photographers get those shots by staking out known haunts, or by using tips from restaurant employees, or by following limousines.

The *Chronicle* has often used the work of free-lance photographers, usually provided by Associated Press or Reuters. The picture of Dodi Faved and Princess Diana vacationing in San Tropez on Page A9 of yesterday's news-paper was undoubtedly taken by a free-lance photographer.

It is certain that Diana did not authorize, welcome or encourage this photograph. It was morally an invasion of privacy, even if it was technically legal. So when the media talk about the media as though they meant the tabloids only, or the paparazzi only, or whatever other convenient fiction is being used, it's nonsense.

We are it. We are doing it.

It is often pointed out by editors that they are only selling what the public is buying. It is often pointed out by people who deal in a morally questionable product that they are only selling what the public is buying. Drug dealers, prostitutes, pornographers, cigarette makers—they are only selling what the public is buying.

None of this is new. Media have had a chance to help regulate the prob-lem, and media have done nothing. There are no enforced standards for the behavior of free-lance photographers. There are no guidelines. If it's legal, it's OK. Don't ask, don't tell.

The proprietors of major media outlets control the money; they could control the behavior. They could not end the problem, but they could lessen it. They could decide (for instance) that celebrities on vacation should be al-lowed to recreate in peace.

They could decide that weddings and funerals are private affairs and agree to pool coverage of same. They could develop guidelines for behavior and attempt to enforce them. They could finally acknowledge that the cre-ation of a more civil society—so often called for in the editorial pages—starts right here.

Questions for Critical Thinking and Discussion

1. Jon Carroll points out that there are no enforced standards for behavior of freelance photographers. Compose a few behavioral guidelines that media producers should follow.

2. Based on the guidelines you proposed in question 1, consider how these rules could be enforced; that is, what rewards or penalties would be applied to your enforcement system?

chapter 14

The Internet and the World Wide Web: Changing the Paradigm

Technocracy R.I.P.

The Rise of Technology Signals the Fall of Technocracy

VIRGINIA POSTREL

Virginia Postrel is the editor of Reason, *a monthly magazine that covers politics, culture, and ideas from a dynamic libertarian perspective. She is a columnist for* Forbes ASAP, *a bimonthly technology magazine. She is also a frequent contributor to the op-ed pages of major newspapers and magazines and appears regularly on television and radio news and talk programs.*

Some people think advancing technology is a good thing; some people don't. Some think access to information should be controlled; others believe "information wants to be free." The importance placed upon human values such as freedom, simplicity of life, the environment, politics, employment, and economics (to name a few) are all connected to how one sees the future. Virginia Postrel explains the two "camps" that have emerged in the arena of "forging the future." She illuminates what these two groups have to gain (and lose) as a result of their struggle for the future and against one another.

Running for re-election in 1996, Bill Clinton and Al Gore promised again and again to build a bridge to the 21st century. Their slogan cast them as the candidates of the future, youthful builders and doers, the sort of people with whom forward-looking voters would identify. It was a comfortable cliché, ideology-free.

Or was it?

A century ago, "bridge to the future" was not a bland cliché, but a potent political metaphor—a conceit representing an entire philosophy of governing. Building bridges is an engineering feat requiring big budgets and teams of experts, not to mention careful planning and blueprints. Once complete, the result is a quintessentially static structure, going from known point A to known point B, changeless and unmoving. Fall off—let alone jump— and you're doomed.

Like an earlier Clinton/Gore plan to overlay the Net with a centrally planned and federally funded information superhighway, their bridge to the

---

This article first appeared in *Wired* magazine (January 1998), Issue 6.01, pages 52, 54, 56.

future isn't as neutral as it appears. It carries important ideas: The future must be brought under control, managed, and planned—preferably by "experts." It cannot simply evolve. The future must be predictable and uniform: We will go from point A to point B with no deviations. A bridge to the future is not an empty cliché. It represents technocracy, the rule of experts.

And it is technocracy, not liberalism or conservatism, that has been the dominant ideology of US politics for most of this century. That's why the metaphor of the bridge has withered into a cliché. Our political discussions simply assume that every new development—cultural, technological, or economic—requires some sort of program to make it turn out "right." Harvard historian John M. Jordan calls it "the peculiar American paradox of kinetic change made stable." It is the ideology of the best way—the one best way.

Most political arguments still center on competing technocratic schemes: Should there be a mandatory family-viewing hour on TV, or a V-chip? Should the tax code favor families with children, or people attending college? Should a national health insurance program enroll everyone in managed care, or should we regulate HMOs? The fight isn't over whether the future should be molded to fit someone's ideal. It's simply over what that ideal should be.

In 1995, about a year into the Republican takeover of the US Congress, one Capitol Hill insider explained what had gone wrong with Newt Gingrich's "revolution." The problem, he said, was that most members of Congress—"revolutionary" Republicans included—couldn't imagine life without central, generally governmental, direction. "They're good conservatives, so they want to reduce government," he said. "But they think of that as getting as close to the abyss as possible without falling off." It's a bipartisan consensus that the future is too important to be left alone—that the marketplace can't evolve privacy standards, that Washington must protect kids from popular culture, that cloning must be banned.

Clinton's bridge to the future thus represents the same governing vision as the bridge to the past Bob Dole offered in his own acceptance speech. Below both lies the abyss.

The Cold War long obscured the technocratic entente in US politics, dividing the landscape right and left. If you worried about containing the Soviets, you were on the right. If you feared US militarism, you were on the left. People who didn't comfortably fit—who, say liked entrepreneurship but were suspicious of the military, or who distrusted corporations but opposed godless communism—were pigeonholed anyway according to their Cold War views.

The 1990s changed all that. The Cold War evaporated, allowing new (and some very old) issues to come to the fore. Free markets are no longer simply what the communists don't have. They are powerful forces for social, cultural, and technological change, together shaping an unknown, and unknowable, future. Some people look at this and rejoice. Others recoil.

So, today's defining question is: What to do about the future? Do we search for stasis—a constrained, regulated, engineered future? Or embrace dynamism—the open-ended, evolving future? Do we demand rules to govern each new situation and keep things under control? Or do we limit rule making to broad and rarely changed principles, within which people can craft an unpredictable future? These two poles—stasis and dynamism—will increasingly define our political, intellectual, and cultural landscape.

The most powerful supporters of stasis are technocrats—people, often in position of power, who believe that the future can and should be engineered. Their central value is control, and they greet every new idea with "yes, but," followed by legislation, regulation, and litigation. People like Clinton, Gore, and Gingrich are "for the future," but they expect someone to be in charge. They get nervous at suggestions that the future might develop spontaneously.

So it is that Arthur Schlesinger Jr., who defined technocracy as "the vital center," looks at today's technological dynamism and sees chaos. "The computer," he wrote in *Foreign Affairs* last fall, "turns the untrammeled market into a global juggernaut, crashing across frontiers, enfeebling national powers of taxation and regulation, undercutting national management of interest rates and exchange rates, widening disparities of wealth between and within nations, dragging down labor standards, degrading the environment, denying nations the shaping of their own economic destiny, creating a world economy without a world polity."

Schlesinger is not exactly a technophobe. But he is horrified by the thought of forces beyond the control of technocratic wise men. He wants someone in charge. And by blaming the impersonal computer, he carefully omits the decentralized, individual choices that actually create the out-of-control world he finds so frightening.

Nearly a century later, technocracy remains the default assumption of American politics: "Got a problem, get a program." But from urban renewal to the "wars" on poverty and drugs, technocracy has not delivered on its grand promises. Rather than a smooth-running engine, technocracy has produced a Rube Goldberg device that grinds gears, shoots sparks, and periodically breaks down entirely.

As government has grown and special interests have multiplied, bureaucracies that once functioned reasonably well have become decadent, rigid, and insulated: The United States Postal Service is both high-handed and frequently incompetent. NASA is sluggish. Public schools are dedicated to mediocrity, when they are not outright failures. Power corrupts, and monopoly power corrupts absolutely.

It is almost impossible to eliminate or significantly reform any technocratic program, so strong are the interest groups—"veto players," in political-science jargon—who nourish and protect it. Journalist Jonathan Rauch calls the problem "demosclerosis," noting in his book by that name: "No one starting anew today would think to subsidize peanut farmers, banish banks from the mutual-fund business, forbid the United Parcel Service to deliver letters, grant massive tax breaks for borrowing. Countless policies are on the books not because they make sense today, but merely because they cannot be gotten rid of." Technocracy not only hampers private experiments. Over time, it has lost its own ability to adapt.

The technocrats who today still dominate both major parties have considerable power and minimal intellectual oomph. But they also have tacit allies in a second static camp: reactionaries, who want explicitly to go back to a real or imagined past. Ranging from Pat Buchanan to the followers of such influential green theorists as *Small Is Beautiful* author E. F. Schumacher, reactionaries have plenty of vitality but minimal power. Their central value is not control, but stability. Their ideal world is one of peasant virtues—limited ambition and, hence, limited change.

United by a hostility to innovation, reactionaries create seemingly odd alliances. In January 1995 Pat Buchanan and environmentalist Jeremy Rifkin upset CNN's *Crossfire* by agreeing—ostensibly across the ideological table—that the future is bleak, economic restructuring is bad, technology is too disruptive. Buchanan was reduced to telling Rifkin, "You sound like a Pat Buchanan column," while Rifkin could only counter, "I find myself in a position of agreeing with Pat once again, which gives me alarm." Surprised they may have been, but nationalist conservatism and technophobic environmentalism are two sides of the same stasist coin. A similar left-right coalition is pushing drastic cuts in immigration; this spring Sierra Club members will vote on whether to join. And then there is technology itself: environmentalist author Kirkpatrick Sale defends the Unabomber and ends speeches by smashing computers, while the conservative *Weekly Standard* echoes him in a cover headline, "Smash the Internet."

The great strength of the static coalition is its numbers: plenty of people have some specific vision of society they'd like to impose. The problem is agreeing on what that vision is. Buchanan wants to restore the blue-collar world of industrial work, while Sale condemns industrialism. Rifkin calls for special taxes on computers and telecommunications; Buchanan is a cable-television host.

Stasists know they want the world to hold still. But they cannot agree on which particular order—which one static, finite society—should replace the open-ended future. Ultimately, they are undone by the totalitarian quality of their position: stasism cannot triumph unless everyone's future is the same.

The dynamic side of the new landscape is far less self-aware but increasingly influential. Dynamists have the opposite problem from stasists, and the opposite strength. Though fewer in number, dynamists permit many visions and accept competing dreams. To work together, they do not have to agree on what the future should look like. They seek "simple rules for a complex world," in University of Chicago legal scholar Richard Epstein's phrase, not complicated regulations aimed at making the world simple.

Dynamists typically are drawn toward organic metaphors, symbols of unpredictable growth and change. "I like building things," says Esther Dyson, discussing her work with entrepreneurs in postcommunist Europe. "But I'd rather be a gardener than in construction. I'd rather go out and water the plants, and clear the path for the sun to shine, and have them grow themselves." Dynamism is, in the words of its most important theorist, the late economist and social philosopher Friedrich Hayek, "the party of life, the party that favors free growth and spontaneous evolution."

But dynamists so far are a party in name only. You can find them in Silicon Valley and on Wall Street, but most will call themselves apolitical because they aren't interested in fighting over technocratic schemes. Cultural studies, an academic field associated with the left, harbors some dynamists. They even crop up in such technocratic citadels as the World Bank and the occasional urban-planning school (notably USC's).

Although most libertarians are dynamists, dynamism shouldn't be confused with simple libertarianism. And dynamists may disagree—about the extent and nature of public goods, the limits of paternalism, and the justice of redistribution. Like stasists, they are often drawn into positions that don't make left-right sense.

What dynamists do agree on is protecting processes rather than trying to engineer outcomes. Consider the quintessentially technocratic—and predictably "bipartisan"—Communications Decency Act. Instead of rushing to impose a single standard, Representatives Christopher Cox (R-California) and Ron Wyden (now a Democratic senator from Oregon) saw the issue of Internet standards as a question of helping parents enforce their own norms—an interest Internet service providers trying to attract families obviously share. So Cox and Wyden came up with language protecting ISPs from the relatively strict libel standards applied to edited publications— merely selling a "family friendly," filtered service wouldn't make a company responsible for monitoring everything it carried. Eventually subsumed into the larger bill, Cox and Wyden's provisions were upheld when the US

Supreme Court struck down the rest of the CDA as unconstitutional. And today the Net still offers pornography—but people who don't want themselves or their children to see it have an easier time avoiding it.

Dynamists understand the limits of their own knowledge—and of everyone else's. They seek markets not as conspiracies, but as discovery processes, coordinating dispersed knowledge. And they worry about the way technocrats blithely trample individual efforts and override local knowledge. Says Representative Rick White (R-Washington), a critic of attempts to regulate cyberspace: "When Congress focuses on an issue, Congress sees the big, big, big, big, big, big, big, big picture. They're the ultimate big-picture people. And they really don't understand the details."

Working without details—let alone intimate knowledge—is the technocrat's hallmark. "We have governments by the clueless, over a place they've never been, using means they don't possess," says EFF cofounder John Perry Barlow. He's right, but the problem is hardly unique to the regulation of cyberspace. The creators of Post-it notes and plastics, TV shows and trucks, plus anyone who has ever hired an employee, built a building, or educated a child—all understand what it means to be governed by the clueless. Cyberspace is not the first dynamic culture that technocrats have tried to control; it is only the most recent.

Opposition to global trade, immigration, and new technologies has rallied stasist coalitions. Dynamists, on the other hand, barely know their "coalition" exists. They share beliefs in spontaneous order, in evolved solutions, in the limits of centralized knowledge, in the possibility of progress. They may see themselves as libertarian or progressive, liberal or conservative, playful postmodernists or hard-headed technologists. But they don't share an identity.

The Net is changing that. A symbol of dynamic, spontaneous evolution, it produces plenitude—anthropologist Grant McCracken's apt term for the way a dynamic society fills every available cultural and economic niche. You can find just about anything on the Net. And that drives stasists crazy.

Protecting cyberspace could become the catalyzing issue for a broader dynamist coalition, but only if the kind of people who read this magazine begin to see their situation as typical, rather than unique, part of a world of many evolving social and economic webs, their causes all bound up with others. Dynamists who bend metal, build houses, or distribute detergent will not rally to join cybersnobs who sneer at factories and think of themselves as the first people ever to turn ideas into wealth. If netizens become merely another interest group, they will miss a chance to fundamentally change American politics.

For technologists, especially, technocracy is an eternal temptation. When Al Gore's Silicon Valley fan club complained about lousy public schools, he

flatteringly asked club members to come up with alternatives. Instead of focusing on incentives and feedback, they immediately started designing new
technocratic gimmicks. The result was Dashboard, a push technology that
sends information to parents. But if parents don't like what they see, they
still have no recourse except to opt out entirely. The public schools' monopoly remains unchallenged.

Silicon Valley's infatuation with the vice president is itself peculiar. From
computer encryption to rock lyrics to energy use to biotechnology, Gore has
met dynamism and diversity with consistently technocratic, often reactionary rhetoric. His 1992 best-seller *Earth in the Balance* demands that we
adopt a "central organizing principle for civilization," a one-best-way moral
equivalent of war that subordinates all other goals. Few people in American
politics so perfectly combine both sides of the static coin.

The fabled date 2000, long the symbol of the future, will soon be upon
us—just another election year. But our politics will remain uneasy. As Cox
notes, "there are these schisms in both the Democratic and Republican Parties," and they are not going away anytime soon. Technological change does
not resolve political issues; it merely raises new ones.

To preserve the future as an ongoing process, dynamists will have to find
each other—across party lines, academic disciplines, and professional affiliations. To do that, they need to drop misleading Cold War labels. And they
have to find what they are for: not just the Internet, or free trade, or the
"new economy," but a world of richness and variety where people are free to
experiment and learn, to challenge themselves and each other, to cherish the
wisdom of the past and create the wisdom of the future.

Questions for Critical Thinking and Discussion

1. When considering the future, where do you place yourself on the "stasis vs. dynamism" debate? That is, do you think the future should develop in an open-ended, evolving way, or do you think we should
   construct the future cautiously with regulation and constraint? Can
   you recall any personal experiences that might have influenced your
   answer?

2. Virginia Postrel writes, "If netizens become merely another group, they
   will miss a chance to fundamentally change American politics." What
   is a netizen? And how does Postrel propose they can change American
   politics (through dynamism)?

40

How the Decency Fight Was Won

HOWARD BRYANT AND DAVID PLOTNIKOFF

Howard Bryant and David Plotnikoff are staff writers for the San Jose Mercury News.
Bryant and Plotnikoff claim that "The Internet's free speech supporters lost their historic battle over cyberspace decency standards because they were outgunned, outflanked, outconnected and out-thought" by savvy political veterans. This article provides an accounting of the battle over the Communications Decency Act and why it was ultimately passed in spite of censorship arguments.

The Internet's free speech supporters lost their historic battle over cyberspace decency standards because they were outgunned, outflanked, outconnected and out-thought in the most crucial battle of the on-line community's brief history.

Historically, the Internet's motley core of entrepreneurs and free spirits had avoided the inside-the-beltway machinations of Washington. But emergence of the Communications Decency Act, a part of the sprawling telecommunications overhaul law enacted recently, forced a hastily assembled coalition of on-line industry groups and civil libertarians to play the politics of engagement with lawmakers and conservative and family groups.

Not only were they ill-equipped for the bruising, hardball environment of Capitol Hill, but perhaps most importantly, they failed to make a critical realization: that the fight over standards had moved from legal and technical grounds to more emotional and moral grounds. To many in Congress, the issue was protecting children from pornography—not niceties of the technology or constitutional speech protections, and certainly not the sovereignty of the Internet.

"It was almost like a gunfight," says Brian Ek, the Washington pointman for the Prodigy on-line service. "We went in outgunned with the very real belief reinforcements were going to arrive, and they did not."

The decency act President Clinton signed recently provides six-figure fines and federal prison for people who make available indecent material— words or images—in on-line areas that may be accessible to minors.

Whatever the perspective on the law—that it's free-speech sabotage or vital protection of vulnerable youths—it's a historic move by the federal

This article first appeared in the San Jose *Mercury News* (March 3, 1996), pages D1–D2, D4.

government to regulate private and public communication in a medium that's reshaping personal and business life almost daily.

The yearlong battle over the act actually culminated shortly before Christmas, when a group of members of the House broke away from a meeting in an overheated, standing-room-only Capitol hearing room. They headed behind closed doors to settle on which of two competing Internet content provisions would survive and make it into what would become the behemoth Telecommunications Act of 1996.

When the deal was done, the Internet interests were dazed and uncomprehending. Outmaneuvered at the last second, their fight was lost by a single vote—cast by the most unlikely of players.

Here's how it all happened.

Filled with Confidence

Coalition Began in Spring to Shift Focus to Children

As the lawmakers retreated to their private meeting that Wednesday morning, the coalition pushing for government restrictions was confident.

Led by the National Law Center for Children and Families, the Family Research Council and a group called Enough is Enough, the coalition last spring began to leaflet, negotiate and jawbone with key political leaders, steering them toward the idea that controls were essential.

The group's core appeal was based on a passionate calculus: Children had access to some of the most hardcore pornography available; the kids should come first.

Removing technology as a base issue proved to be a remarkable feat, considering the fundamental issue *was* technology. To do that, the coalition used the vision of America's living rooms. Members were convinced: When lawmakers learned what their children, and the children of their constituents, could see on-line, children and adults engaging in sex acts with animals and each other, they would have no choice but to react accordingly.

That's where the famous Exon "blue book" came in. Sen. James Exon, a Nebraska Democrat who sponsored the decency provisions, compiled a collection of brutal images of pornography that can be found on the Internet, and he showed his book around the capital to vividly underscore his call for controls.

By contrast, "the other side would send their people to these senators, literally with laptops, to show them how the technology worked," said Donna Rice-Hughes of Enough is Enough.

With that—with laptop computers fighting a losing battle of perception against kiddie porn—Rice-Hughes and others knew the advantage was already beginning to shift their way.

"What we showed was that there was an evil being transmitted directly into the house, with no controls, with no way of stopping it," Rice-Hughes said. "We wanted to know what they were going to do about it."

Even more critically, the coalition forces were tightly connected to key players in Washington. For instance, Enough is Enough Executive Director Dee Jepsen is the wife of former Iowa senator Roger Jepsen, and that provided after-hours access to Washington's power brokers working on the telecom bill.

"There were a lot of calls at midnight to the senators and their staffs," Rice-Hughes said.

Smut-Buster Joins In

Former Prosecutor Helped Write Decency Standards

Perhaps the most crucial insider connection was a former top obscenity prosecutor in the Justice Department, and a former smut-buster in Cleveland, named Bruce Taylor. Over 20 years, Taylor had gained a reputation for having a strong First Amendment background, but while maintaining a hard enforcement edge.

It was late March when Sen. Dan Coats, R-Ind., approached Taylor and asked him to write decency standards for the telecommunications bill. Taylor was honored and took pride in the fact he was being called upon to win a battle, but knew he was in for the fight of his life. On-line services, cable TV companies and telecommunications firms had millions of dollars at their disposal, while his firm, the National Law Center for Families and Children, was only two years old and almost too tiny to notice.

Before the bill passed Congress, Taylor ended up meeting or conducting exclusive discussions with numerous insiders, including Sens. Exon, Charles Grassley, R-Iowa, and Jesse Helms, R.-N.C.

"They asked us: What was effective? What was constitutional? Would this fly? Would that fly?" Taylor said. "We had access to the Senate because they trusted us. They knew we wouldn't lie to them. They didn't know that about the others."

Another key Washington connection was Cathy Cleaver, director of legal studies for the Family Research Council, a Washington, D.C.–based advocacy group. Cleaver, like Taylor, was asked by Coats to assist in writing decency provisions.

"We had to change the status quo, which is always difficult to do," she said. "We had to forge new ground. The truth was that everybody wanted this bill, but not everybody wanted all of its provisions."

Beyond the emotions and the access, the winning coalition also benefited from missteps and miscalculations by Internet supporters. Most importantly, the Internet community failed to understand the historic tidal wave they faced—that the political climate made some form of law regarding the Internet inevitable.

Had the Internet community relinquished a no-law-at-all position, Taylor said, some compromise could have been reached.

"The difference between the law and the no-law people was that we knew Congress was going to do *something*," he said.

Own Worst Enemy

Arrogance Diminished Hope of Credibility

As the legislative process rumbled along, some in the Internet community also became their own worst enemies by insulting lawmakers who opposed them—hardly a way to influence people.

Example: In late February, Exon offered the first draft of his indecency bill to the Electronic Frontier Foundation, one of the key Internet community players, for critique and feedback. Sources say the EFF added five provisions that, in essence, would have gutted it by calling for a study and not providing the power to prosecute offenders.

Exon was infuriated.

"Exon was looking for input from both sides to forge something honest and reasonably constructed," Taylor said. "Instead, EFF hoodwinked him. They lied to him, and for that reason, no one listened seriously to anything they said."

Later, the EFF "would call everyone names," Taylor said. "(EFF lawyer Mike) Goodwin would call us Nazi censors if we didn't agree with him. Talk about a way to get doors slammed in your face."

Compared with the well-marshaled, well-connected team of veteran lobbyists allied with Cleaver and Taylor, the group lined up on the other side of the debate resembled a community-college football squad facing the San Francisco 49ers.

This junior college team was something called the Interactive Working Group, an ad-hoc coalition that included all the commercial on-line services, the Center for Democracy and Technology, the American Civil Liberties Union, the EFF and others. The working group had formed in 1994 to explore general First Amendment issues, digital privacy regulations and other legislation that would impact the Net.

Exon's indecency provisions were the first threat to galvanize them into plying the halls of Congress as a united front.

Of the large corporations behind consumer on-line services, only Microsoft, Apple and America Online had full-time legislative specialists in Washington last spring. The big consumer on-line services—Prodigy, CompuServe,

AOL, Microsoft, MCI and Apple—met for the first time ever as a group on Jan. 30, 1995, just one week before Exon's bill was introduced in the Senate.

"We were thrown into the biggest legislative battle in the history of our industry, literally one week after we organized," said Bill Burrington, America Online's assistant general counsel and director of public policy.

Because both their members and their technology were so unfamiliar on Capitol Hill, the working group faced a doubly daunting task: schooling themselves in the ways of Congress while simultaneously schooling legislators on the complex technical concepts behind Internet controls.

"We were starting from absolute scratch with the majority of the lawmakers," Burrington says. "Exon had his blue notebook, and we had our gray notebook computers loaded with parental control software demos."

The Internet was such unfamiliar turf for lawmakers that even after a year of tutorials, perhaps 10 percent of them understood the details of what they were voting on when Congress finally passed the telecommunications act, Burrington estimates.

Worse still, the working group's efforts weren't helped by the fact the Internet community was an unknown, faceless constituency in Washington. Actually, the Net denizens were worse than unknown: Given techno-myopia common inside the beltway, many were thought to be hackers, crypto-anarchists and porn entrepreneurs. While conservatives and members of the religious right could claim a large and well-organized base in almost any congressional district, the Net community always appeared to be from somewhere else.

Although the Net community tried to make its opposition to decency standards heard in Washington, anger and dismay festering on-line was never focused into a form that appealed to Congress. Indeed, some even say efforts such as e-mail campaigns and Net-based petitions may actually have backfired with members of Congress.

"The tone and language of the e-mail they were bombarded with was not the way they were used to being addressed," said Prodigy's Ek. "The perception they have in Washington of the typical Internet user is the guy with the broken glasses and the plastic pocket protector—and the angry e-mail helped cement that perception."

Counter Proposal

Free Speech Advocates Find Allies in Congress

In mid-June, shortly after an overwhelming Senate vote to pass Exon's decency act, the working group seemed to be finding a way to turn the tide, when it found two House members willing to sponsor a bipartisan counter-attack—Ron Wyden, D-Ore., and Chris Cox, R.-Newport Beach. Their bill focused on software that would put parents in control, sidestepping the main censorship question. It specifically barred Federal Communications Commission from Internet regulation.

When Cox/Wyden sailed through the House by an overwhelming vote of 421-4, the on-line interests were elated. After months of just reacting to Exon, they finally had a ball of their own in play.

And things just got better from there. As support for Cox/Wyden gathered, the working group was able to demonstrate specifics, such as an Internet content-labeling system, on the floors of the House and Senate.

"It was looking pretty good for us," Ek recalls. "We had more filtering software for parents coming out all the time—and (it) worked."

In the fall, lawmakers from both chambers assembled in a conference committee to morph together the different versions of the telecommunications bill passed in each house. Ek sensed from conversations with key players that the more middle-of-the-road family groups, such as Enough is Enough, could be brought around to see parental control software as an acceptable answer.

"It looked like the more radical elements of the religious right seemed to be becoming more isolated," he said.

Finally, at the end of November, after three months of inaction while Congress was embroiled in the federal budget dispute with Clinton, lawmakers returned their attention to the telecommunications bill and the question of objectionable material on the Internet.

During the layoff, it appeared the on-line community had begun to embrace the idea that a bill would be approved, and that any bill without criminal sanctions against smut-peddlers was not politically viable.

Toward that end, one Republican House member, Rick White, of Washington, tried to broker a compromise that used Cox/Wyden as a base and incorporated the criminal teeth of the Exon decency act. Instead of the broad decency language of Exon, it offered a more restrained "harmful-to-minors" standard thought to be more enforceable.

Thus the stage was set for a showdown Dec. 6. As House members of the conference committee met, White's compromise was approved, much to the delight of Internet industry advocates.

Over in a Flash

With a One-Word Change Compromise Hopes End

But delight turned to horror a few minutes later as Rep. Bob Goodlatte, R-Va., offered a one-word amendment substituting the "indecency" standard for White's "harmful to minors." Said one Net lobbyist in the Capitol that day: "This was the ghoul of Exon coming out of the closet right in front of us."

Two liberal Democrats, Pat Schroeder of Colorado and John Conyers of Michigan, voted for the indecency language, and in a flash it was over. Almost a year's worth of lobbying died in a surprise vote of 17-16. The decency standard was a done deal; there was no chance it would be reconsidered before the final bill was assembled.

"The members said they were with us, yet it fell apart right there," said Jerry Berman, director of the Center for Democracy and Technology and leader of the working group.

It was Conyers who was perhaps the biggest surprise. Why did one of the most liberal Democrats in the House provide one of the crucial votes to put decency standards over the top?

"The congressman is opposed to virtually all limits on freedom of speech," said his spokesman, Rodney Walker. "As far as why he voted for (the decency standard), I'm afraid there just isn't a short answer. I'm sorry."

With the votes tallied, it became clear the strategy set in motion months before by the pro-control coalition had worked marvelously. Once the debate moved from technology to child-porn and family safety, the on-line community found itself unable to fight on those terms.

"Everybody on the Net who followed this assumed we were able to go in and talk about this as a free-speech platform," said Ek.

Questions for Critical Thinking and Discussion

1. According to the Decency Act, any person who makes available indecent material—words or images—in on-line areas that may be accessible to minors are subject to fines and federal prison sentences. What kind of material is "indecent"? Who gets to decide the definition of "indecent"? Who *should* decide?

2. How will one determine whether minors will have access to various on-line areas? Come up with a couple of strategies that might be used to keep children out of inappropriate areas.

41

Cable TV: A Crisis Looms

An Array of New Rivals Has the Industry on the Defensive

ELIZABETH LESLY, RONALD GROVER, AND NEIL GROSS

Elizabeth Lesley and Neil Gross are Business Week *correspondents in New York. Ronald Grover works out of Los Angeles.*

Cable is in financial trouble. The authors present the economic and technological issues and possible strategies cable can take (and already is taking) to survive this era of new media competition.

James L. Dolan, chief executive of Cablevision Systems Corp., professes not to have a care in the world. The head of the country's sixth-largest cable operator, based in Woodbury, N.Y., on Long Island, says he's not worried about satellites, telephone companies, debt, or any of the ominous forces that he and other industry executives are battling.

. . . .

Starting to Deliver

. . . Cablevision['s] . . . stock has slipped 29% in the past year, and 1995 operating cash flow didn't cover even a third of its debt-service payments and capital expenditures. Worse, just to have a chance of surviving in the nasty competitive environment for cable, Dolan says he'll spend $460 million this year to upgrade his systems. Nonetheless, he says: "We're on the offense."

If it is true that the best defense is a good offense, then cable certainly needs the best offense it can muster. To be sure, cable companies have always faced high debt levels and tough fights with regulators. But now, regulations are being rolled back, and cable's monopoly-like hold on 67% of U.S. households is being seriously threatened by an array of new competitors. And the worst may be yet to come, as fearsome rivals such as Rupert Murdoch's News Corp. and MCI Communications Corp. work to launch American Sky Broadcasting, yet another direct-broadcast satellite service, in late 1997 or early 1998.

At the same time, many cable operators are suffering weaknesses in their operating results, which harms their ability to roll out quickly new tech-

This article first appeared in *Business Week* (October 14, 1996), pages 101–106.

nologies that require hugely expensive upgrades to their existing wires. How expensive? Schroder Wertheim & Co. cable specialist Philip Sirlin estimates that together they have to spend about $25 billion just to install hybrid fiber-coaxial cable and interactive capabilities. That is roughly equal to the industry's entire annual revenue. To date, he estimates, only about 25% of this work has been done.

That huge cost helps explain the string of delayed or never-delivered new services, such as interactive TV, cable modems, digital set-top boxes, and telephone service, that has left the industry with little credibility on Wall Street. A three-year index of the stock of large cable operators trails the Standard & Poor's 500-stock index by 60%.

The only way cable moguls such as Dolan, Tele-Communications' John C. Malone, and Time Warner's Gerald M. Levin can wriggle clear of their current predicament is to roll out their long-promised new services—fast. The two most viable are cable modems, which deliver high-speed Internet access to PCs, and digital set-top boxes which transmit better sound and pictures and allow cable operators to offer many more channels than in the past. Those new revenue streams are "there for us to take," says Continental Cablevision President William T. Schleyer. Those who can't move quickly "will have blown it," he says. "As an industry, we'd just hand over our business to the telephone companies."

This fall, most major cable operators are finally beginning to deliver the goods—though with limited offerings in only a handful of markets. Time Warner Inc. launched its Road Runner cable-modem service in Akron, Ohio, in early September, and Tele-Communications Inc. began offering cable-modem service to customers in Fremont, Calif., that same month. TCI will launch the first digital cable service on Oct. 21 in Hartford, Conn. Cablevision already provides telephone service to 350 commercial customers on Long Island. Also this month, Philadelphia-based Comcast Corp. will begin offering cable modems to nonpaying customers in a Baltimore test, with actual commercial service planned by yearend.

With new products coming to market, most in the cable industry don't accept forecasts of their decline. Even if new revenue streams are slow to emerge, there is still growth potential from traditional cable subscribers, they say. Currently, only two-thirds of the 95 million cable-ready homes subscribe, and Time Warner, especially, thinks it can find new customers as young people, more accustomed to paying for TV than their parents, increasingly head their own households. "This industry has been pretty scrappy, pretty nimble," says Time Warner Cable Ventures CEO Glenn A. Britt—the most senior executive at that company willing to speak about cable's prospects. "We are going to do a lot better than people think."

After all, the upgraded cable systems, with their huge capacity, offer many advantages over the wires owned by the telephone companies. "Cable operators have a distinct advantage because they are the ones with the fat pipe," says Motorola Inc.'s James M. Phillips, a vice-president with the company's Multimedia Group, which supplies cable modems to Time Warner. "In the digital world, speed defines everything. The more you [can] flow, the better your multimedia, video, graphics." Unencumbered by financial constraints, cable as a technology is a winner. And major banks appear comfortable with the industry's prospects. Says James B. Lee, head of global investment banking at Chase Manhattan Corp., the largest commercial lender to the cable industry: "Cable companies have always run very comfortably at these debt levels. They have almost infinite liquidity in the bank market."

But access to more debt capital certainly isn't the answer to the cable guys' troubles. They have plenty of other worries. Consider the two largest— Tele-Communications Inc. and Time Warner. TCI's Malone energized the industry in 1992 by predicting a world of 500 channels by 1994. That never came to pass, and a $35-a-share acquisition offer from Bell Atlantic Corp. fizzled as well. TCI now trades at about 14½, and the wily cable mogul is finding himself uncharacteristically boxed in. He has to spend billions to upgrade TCI's network—$1.9 billion in just the past year—even though continuing such spending will likely depress the stock price further.

Given this, TCI has no plans to rush forward with new services in most of its markets until there is proven customer demand. "The market will tell us when it is ready for the service it wants," says Brendan R. Clouston, CEO of TCI's cable systems unit. Over the past few years, TCI has quietly scaled back its once ambitious expansion and now will spend only in areas where it can expect a quick payoff. "We have all the money we need [for our plans]. We're not running around in any kind of a panic," says Clouston.

But some in the industry believe Malone is looking for a way out, most likely by spinning off TCI's sexier divisions, such as satellites and programming, and selling the core cable systems—if he can find a buyer. Malone "has made the decision that the cable business is not where he wants to be," notes Schroder Wertheim media analyst David J. Londoner. TCI declines to talk about its plans.

Phone-Company Incursions

Time Warner is perhaps in worse shape. CEO Levin gambled in 1995 by expanding Time Warner's cable holdings by paying $5 billion to acquire cable systems with about 4 million subscribers. In late 1994, he spent an estimated $100 million in a splashy debut of a trial interactive-TV service, called the Full Service Network, in Orlando. The network has never been rolled out elsewhere.

Now, the anchor of the cable systems is dragging down the entire media conglomerate. Time Warner's 1995 operating cash flow from cable was $3.3 billion, but it spent about $1.5 billion in debt payments and $1.4 billion in cable-related capital expenditures. Its operating margin has slipped from 10.3% in 1992 to 8.6% in 1995—to just 4.4% in the first quarter of 1996, says Moody's Investors Service. Analysts, shareholders, and some company executives have been pushing Levin to sell off cable assets to lessen the company's huge debt load and lift its laggard stock. It now appears that Levin may finally be giving in.

Surely no one could be blamed for wanting to avoid the coming crunch of competition. Direct-broadcast satellite, or DBS, is growing increasingly popular as providers such as DirecTV Inc. slash prices for a service of 175 or so digital channels that far outstrips what is now offered by cable. Rapidly growing DBS already lays claim to some 5 million U.S. TV sets. As the price of the equipment plummets and a customer's local TV stations are eventually included in the service, Donaldson, Lufkin & Jenrette Securities Corp. media analyst Dennis H. Leibowitz expects DBS will have 19 million subscribers by 2000. By comparison, growth of cable subscribers has flattened out at about 64 million—rising only 1.1% in the first six months of 1996.

Even TCI is trying to make a big push into DBS. In May, it allied with Canada's Telesat to launch two new services to beam programming to homes in the U.S. and Canada. But the Federal Communications Commission has objected, and the venture is now in question.

At the same time, incursions from telephone companies are under way across the country. The phone companies have a reputation for being slow and bureaucratic, but their healthy cash flows and blue-chip debt ratings make them a real threat to pinched cable operators. This year, Chicago-based Ameritech Corp. began offering cable service in 12 different cities in Illinois, Ohio, and Michigan. In Toms River, N.J., Bell Atlantic claims its cable operator has more than 75% of the 6,400 Adelphia Communications Corp. customers to whom it has offered cheaper cable service since February. Southern New England Telephone Co. delivered a nasty shock to the cable industry on Sept. 25 when it was awarded the right to offer cable service to the entire state of Connecticut. SNET is spending $4.5 billion on the wiring that allows it to offer cable, and it plans to roll out its new service in the first quarter of 1997.

The phone companies' stodgy reputation won't spill over into programming—they'll be providing much the same fare that cable operators offer. The 1992 Cable Act made it illegal for most networks, such as CNN and

Discovery Channel, to refuse to sell their programming to competing services. That's why DirecTV, for example, offers what many viewers think of as cable fare, such as HBO and CNN.

Also becoming a threat is wireless cable, a technology that several telephone companies are using to quickly and cheaply offer a service competitive with cable. Since it avoids costly wire installation, telephone companies can undercut existing cable rates and in turn force that market's cable companies to cut prices. That will hurt cable's cash flow and hinder its efforts to offer telephone services.

How will it all shake out? The likelihood is that the financially weaker cable operators will be gobbled up by other cable companies or by larger, better-financed communications giants. Glenn R. Jones, CEO of Jones Inter-cable Inc., based in Englewood, Colo., thinks that U.S. utilities and foreign buyers could begin buying up cable assets now that stock prices have fallen so low. For those players that cannot withstand huge operating losses as they battle for market share, it may come down to finding a buyer — or else. "There's going to be roadkill all over," says Robyn G. Nietert, a telecommunications lawyer at Brown Nietert & Kaufman in Washington, D.C. "There are no niches. There's no place to hide."

Deep Pockets

Continental's Schleyer says that it was the fear of thin resources in such an unforgiving environment that prompted the company to accept a $10.8 billion takeover offer last April from U S West Media Group, a separately traded division of Baby Bell U S West Inc. The deal is scheduled to close in November. Schleyer says his new parent's deep pockets will allow him to complete in two years the capital improvements that would have taken the company six years had it remained independent. And Jones made a deal with Bell Canada's holding company, BCE Inc., in late 1994. For $349 million, BCE got 30% of Jones and an option to acquire the entire company by 2002. Those Canadian resources enabled Jones to launch earlier this year a state-of-the-art system in Alexandria, Va., that offers cable, data, and phone service.

Jones's effort has taken a huge upfront investment. So far, it hasn't snared many customers, but it is being closely watched as other cable operators gauge the near-term consumer demand for these new services. Although faced with long periods before they can hope to see a return, the cable operators have to proceed. "The only way for cable companies to go forward is for them to spend what they have to spend. It's like they're stuck in a tunnel. [The competition] closes in around them to the point where they

---

Cablespeak

- **Bundling** A marketing effort to increase revenues from a single customer by offering a combination of services, like cable and telephone service

- **Cable modems** High-speed modems that use cable's thick coaxial wires to handle more data faster than thinner telephone wires

- **Digital compression** Crunches data to allow more information and TV programming to be transmitted over wires or through the air

- **Digital set-top box** Device that hooks up to a TV and can collect, store, and display digitally compressed TV signals

- **DBS** Direct-broadcast satellite beams TV content or data from a satellite to any TV hooked up to a compatible dish

- **Interactive TV** Two-way communications for information and entertainment on the TV screen

- **Wireless cable** A lower-cost version of DBS, in which signals are collected and transmitted to towers for retransmission to homes outfitted with special antennas

---

can't go backwards," says Lazard Frères & Co. media investment banker Steven Rattner. "If they don't [proceed], then they will perish."

Cable can blame Washington for a portion of its current troubles. Reregulation in 1992 cut into cash flows and may have slowed investments and new services. And for years, the big cable operators dithered by not demanding standardized cable modems and digital set-top boxes from outside manufacturers. Their indecision cost them their technological lead—of at least two years—over the telephone companies, acknowledges one longtime cable-industry executive.

Losing their lead was unfortunate. Had they been early to market with broadband technology and upgraded their systems to offer integrated digital-TV, data, and telephone service, the outlook for cable could have been quite bright. Yet even where cable operators started out ahead in the market, as with DBS, they lacked focus and speed. TCI, Time Warner, Cox Communications, Continental, Comcast, and General Electric started Primestar Partners, a DBS service, in 1990—four years before industry leader DirecTV was launched. But Primestar relies on a medium-powered satellite that requires a much larger dish and delivers fewer channels than the high-powered services offered by DirecTV, EchoStar Communications

Corp., and others. Long hobbled by the lack of a focused, unified marketing campaign, Primestar has dishes in 1.3 million homes, compared with DirectTV's 2.1 million, according to *Satellite Business News.*

Now, cable is ahead again—in high-speed Internet access—and many leading cable executives acknowledge that the lead is theirs to lose. "We're competing with ourselves to get it launched," says Brian L. Roberts, president of Comcast, the country's fourth-largest cable system. The cable pipe is already capable of handling huge amounts of data that skinny telephone wires can't now offer, despite ongoing experiments with data compression. Yet not even 5% of cable households have had the wiring upgrades necessary to support the cable modems, estimates Schroder Wertheim's Sirlin.

Still, the race for cable modems is only part of the game. More important for cable operators is their gambit to head off the growth of DBS by offering digital set-top boxes to a significant number of subscribers. Although cable operators have signed contracts for two million boxes, manufacturer General Instruments Corp. has actually made only 20,000.

Another battleground for cable: winning customer trust. Cable has long been derided for poor customer relations and irritating service interruptions. Now, a recent study by consultants Yankee Group Inc. shows that most consumers are eager for one company to provide combined TV, Internet access, and telephone service. But for more than 55% of the consumers surveyed, the winning choice would be long-distance or local telephone companies. Only 4.4% of the consumers would choose their cable company.

The industry has worked recently to guarantee more responsive service, but consumers' memories of those shortcomings haven't faded. Few consumers are apparently willing to risk unreliable phone service. Even worse for customer relations, most cable operators have hiked prices in the past year. On average, the industry has jacked up prices by 10% or more this year, so desperate are they for increased cash flow.

Although they don't say so, the rocky road ahead leaves many cable operators eyeing the exits. Like Continental and Jones Intercable, some sell out. But that may be less of an option now, with cable companies needing billions more to stay viable. Says Lazard's Rattner, who represented Continental in its sale to U S West this spring: "It's clear that the number of [interested] buyers is limited. And it may at the moment be fairly close to zero."

The biggest, and oftentimes most troubled, cable operators are left with few attractive options. At Time Warner, the bulk of its 11.8 million cable subscribers is held by a partnership 25% owned by U S West Media. The two companies have long been at odds, and negotiations to reorganize the partnership have been stalled for months because Levin has been loath to hand over control of the systems to U S West. But with cable in deep disfavor with investors, jettisoning the cable systems could goose Time Warner's long-depressed stock price.

TCI is in a similarly tough spot, since there is no clear buyer for its 14.5 million-subscriber cable system. Malone isn't betting his personal fortune on the future of cable systems. He has trimmed his stake in TCI to less than 1%, while he holds 30% of Liberty Media Corp., TCI's separately traded programming arm. And three years after his failed attempt to sell out to Bell Atlantic, an industry source says he is talking to AT&T about a deal. Neither company will comment on the rumor. But recently AT&T CEO Robert E. Allen said: "You can be assured we are not in an acquisition mode."

The only person who knows the endgame for TCI is, of course, Malone himself. But the much-feared cable mogul has been almost invisible for nearly a year, and he declined to be interviewed for this story. According to the company, he has suffered from prolonged bouts of the flu, in addition to spending months at a time at his vacation compound in Maine.

Malone did make a rare, brief appearance on Sept. 25 at a glitzy annual industry dinner in Manhattan informally known as the "Cable Prom." But he ducked out early, hustled into an elevator by cable-unit head Clouston as a reporter said hello. The rest of the cable moguls—Glenn Jones, Brian Roberts, Jim Dolan, Ted Turner—remained behind in the hotel ballroom, along with about 1,800 other industry executives, sticking with the party until the end.

Questions for Critical Thinking and Discussion

1. Typically, emerging technology is allotted great latitude when it comes to government regulation in order to foster competition and allow new companies to get established. However, this can often lead to trouble for existing industries. Should cable be protected by government regulation of new technologies? Or should the government simply back off and let the marketplace decide? Explain your answer.

2. Does it matter to you where you get your media service? Do you care whether it is the broadcasters, cablecasters, telephone company, or other technology entities? In terms of regulating media industries, what is at risk for the individual consumer?

chapter 15

The Changing Global Village

At 75, Voice of Britain Has a New Accent

KEVIN CULLEN

Kevin Cullen is a staff writer for the Boston Globe.

Now that the British Broadcasting Company (BBC) must compete with other media worldwide, it has changed its strategy in terms of producing and marketing content. Cullen describes how these changes are affecting various components of the BBC (e.g., news reporting, entertainment programming, economic) both inside and outside the organization.

LONDON—The initials "BBC" carry indelible sounds and images: international news delivered from exotic places by men with "Oxbridge" accents and more than one last name, 19th-century period dramas on *Masterpiece Theater*, and erudite monologues from tweedy Alistair Cooke.

But the British Broadcasting Corp. has moved well beyond those American stereotypes. The best-known characters of today's BBC are not appropriated from the works of Shakespeare, Dickens, or Jane Austen. The most important, or at least the most telling, BBC characters today are Tinky Winky, Laa Laa, Dipsy and Po, collectively known as the Teletubbies, stars of a preschooler's show that is to Britain what Barney the Dinosaur is to America.

The Teletubbies, and especially the aggressive international marketing of the show and the characters, reflect a new BBC that, like Britain itself, is gradually shedding tradition, balancing the pompous with the popular, and ready to fend for itself at the dawn of the digital age.

Because of its broadcasting monopoly through much of its 76-year history, the Beeb, as Britons call it, has produced quality programming. Across the globe, the BBC World Service has been a respected source of information, especially for those living under repressive regimes.

But the advent of digital broadcasting has brought hundreds of new viewing and listening options. The end of the Cold War has reduced that audience compelled to fiddle with a shortwave radio dial to find an announcer beginning the news with Greenwich Mean Time. So the BBC has had to reinvent itself. It is marketing its reputation for quality honed, ironically, by years of not having to worry about the bottom line.

This article first appeared in the Boston *Globe* (February 22, 1998), pages A1, A22–23.

For starters, the Beeb is selling its product internationally as never before. Its prime asset is its vaunted news-gathering operation, which with some 2,000 journalists in 42 foreign bureaus, is the largest in the world. The BBC's first international partnership, with WGBH in Boston, where *The World* radio program is produced, has grown from nine stations to more than 100 in the United States in less than two years. The concept will be duplicated soon in South Africa.

Sam Younger, managing director of the World Service, said his challenge is to cultivate more international partnerships. "We've moved from being product-led to being market-focused," he explains. "We've found we have niche audiences around the world, even where the media is developed, as in Boston."

In effect, the BBC has become a subcontractor in markets hungry for international news but lacking in media outlets capable or willing to send their own people abroad.

While Britain's independent stations sell commercials, the BBC is funded by a license fee of $160 a household charged annually to everyone with a television across the United Kingdom. That fee will bring in over $3 billion this year. The BBC also sells programs internationally, which produced another $130 million in profits last year.

While its period dramas of Masterpiece Theater are still popular, the BBC displays a hipper side today. Lifting from Prime Minister Tony Blair's "New Britain," the BBC has become a leading proponent of Cool Britannia, the ideology bent on replacing the stiff upper lip with a smile, or, in Louis Theroux's case, a smirk.

Theroux, who is the English equivalent of Michael Moore, the wiseacre documentary maker who loves to tweak the establishment, recently made one of his "Weird Weekend" programs about the American pornography industry. Shown in prime time, the program was more explicit than anything seen on American television.

Still, most people consider the BBC a bastion of good taste. Its reporters remain a study in restraint in an era when journalists often become celebrities. Some snickering critics point out that the BBC's chairman is named Christopher Bland. But the Beeb's defenders say it continues to produce quality TV and radio while becoming less snobby and more reflective of an increasingly diverse Britain.

Its most recent self-promotion is an eclectic mix of highbrow and popular culture. One of the ads that celebrate the BBC's 75th anniversary shows the Nobel laureate Seamus Heaney reading a poem on a desolate beach. Another is a rendition of Lou Reed's *Perfect Day*, in which dozens of pop stars from David Bowie to Bono and Tom Jones take turns singing a line or two. The recording has been a chart-topper for months. Still other ads offer testimonials from Sir John Gielgud, Sting, Shimon Peres, and Whoopi Goldberg.

Such marketing is a long way from the BBC that was founded in 1922 by a group of radio manufacturers primarily interested in creating an audience for their product. The BBC's first director, a Scotsman named John Reith, was determined to run a monopoly. He got his wish, thanks to a Conservative Party that saw it as a way to control a powerful new medium and a Labor Party that favored public ownership over capitalism. The Beeb maintained its monopoly of television until 1955, of local radio monopoly until 1973, and of national radio until a few years ago.

As BBC director general John Birt noted in his 75th anniversary address, "It was that privileged position that made the BBC powerful: It gave the institution confidence, influence, and a commanding lead." This is in part why almost half of TV and radio audiences in Britain remain tuned to the BBC.

But Birt conceded the monopoly "made the BBC, through much of its life, arrogant. And, protected from competition, the BBC felt no need to provide a service of wide appeal."

All of this changed with World War II, dramatic social shifts in British society, and the advent of competition. The elites who shaped a lofty BBC went off to war, creating openings for people closer to the ordinary listener. Pirate radio stations in the 1950s and 1960s forced BBC Radio to play more rock and pop music. And when independent TV went on the air in the late 1950s with shows like "Sunday Night at the London Palladium," the BBC felt obliged to show more popular programming.

Today's BBC television is a mix of highbrow drama, popular American shows like *The X-Files*, and obligatory doses of cricket. Many American journalists working here consider its news and current affairs programming consistently better than anything on American television.

There is an ongoing debate whether the news should still be broadcast in the traditional King's English or in what Birt calls "the rich tapestry of dialect and accent." The traditionalists are losing ground in this fight. Last summer, an American anchor began broadcasting for the BBC from London for the first time.

"I don't have an Oxbridge accent," Vicki Barker, a New Jersey native who presents World Update to more than 30 US stations, including WGBH, said with a laugh. "Our show is breezier, more colloquial. We don't have to enunciate in the King's English because we're on FM, not crackling over the shortwave. Technology is freeing us up."

Michael Foley, the media correspondent for the *Irish Times,* has studied the BBC's increasing commercialism. He notes that critics fail to appreciate that this commercialism allows the BBC to maintain quality programming while competing against better-financed media moguls such as Rupert Murdoch and Ted Turner.

"Under the Thatcher regime, the BBC's whole future was questioned by a government that couldn't stand the BBC," explained Foley. "The Tories saw the BBC as a bunch of pinkos. To protect its future, the BBC looked to its commercial side. Now you can see the BBC in hotel rooms all over the world. They are selling more and more to PBS. They've done a deal with the Discovery Channel. They have the world's most valuable broadcast archives. If you say BBC to any educated American, they think 'educated and civilized.' With that image, you can sell anything."

Some chafe at this ambition. Martin Bell, who was a BBC reporter for 35 years before being elected to Parliament last year, says the Beeb increasingly is practicing "rooftop journalism." He complains that the demands of myriad BBC radio and TV programs, especially its new 24-hour TV service, place compromising burdens on correspondents. Many are forced to deliver brief radio or TV reports, often from rooftops, instead of gathering more in-depth news in the field.

Bell, who covered the war in Bosnia, is also critical of what he says is the "mendacious" control of BBC mandarins who censored the gore that he and other reporters saw. Yet even while criticizing his former employer, Bell acknowledges the BBC is "a force for truth" that "holds other networks to certain standards."

Jackie Smith, a retired pub owner, fumes over how the Beeb spends its money. He recalls that a decade ago, a BBC producer appeared at his London pub and asked if they could use it for a TV show in exchange for a fee. Smith readily agreed but was stunned at the amount of time and money spent.

"They fed the entire neighborhood," he recalls. "It was like a party. Food everywhere. Lots of people standing around. It didn't look to me like anyone was working particularly hard."

Smith's complaint about alleged wastefulness is common. The BBC counters that other European countries have higher license fees.

Still, the perception that the Beeb wastes money led Birt to declare a jihad on spending when he took over six years ago. Under his tenure, the BBC has trimmed staff and bid work out to less costly independent producers.

One veteran BBC correspondent, speaking anonymously, concludes, "Birt's . . . hurt people I'm close to. But I think 50 years from now we'll put a statue up for him. The BBC couldn't survive if not for people like him."

Questions for Critical Thinking and Discussion

1. According to Cullen, what are some of the circumstances that have led the BBC to reinvent itself?

2. How does the BBC system differ from the American system in terms of the following?

   a. Ownership

   b. Economics (how are the systems funded?)

   c. Regulation (what role does the government have?)

   d. Audience

What do these differences mean in terms of content (programming fare) and audience input?

43

Europe's Technology Gap Is Getting Scary

DAVID KIRKPATRICK
REPORTER ASSOCIATE LENORE SCHIFF

David Kirkpatrick is a staff writer and on the board of editors for Fortune *magazine.*
   Europe has fallen far behind us in terms of technological advancements.
Kirkpatrick describes how this might affect European countries as well as world
communication and commerce.

To American eyes, European information technology, much like a European village, seems quaint. The Continent has never developed a computer industry to rival that of the U.S. But technologically backward as Europe is now, it's getting even more so: Not only doesn't Europe produce much infotech, its businesses aren't using much infotech either—and that has grim implications for European industry as a whole. Executives from American high-tech companies are acutely aware of this trend and have been issuing dire warnings of late about the risks to Europe's industrial competitiveness if the Continent doesn't keep up in computing. "Competitiveness today means speed," says Intel's general manager for Europe, the Middle East, and Africa, Hans Geyer, "and speed comes from PCs, E-mail, and using the Internet." In a recent speech in Europe, Geyer's boss, Intel CEO Andy Grove, warned of a growing "technology deficit," noting that even some less developed Asian countries are moving past Europe in their use of networked personal computers. Europe's companies "operate like old-line U.S. companies did ten years ago," he said at one stop. Microsoft's Bill Gates, also in a recent speech, spoke urgently about Europe's radically lower rates of business Internet usage compared with those of the U.S.

   Gates, Grove, and Geyer may sound self-serving—Intel and Microsoft stand to make enormous amounts of money if or when Europeans decide to bring their technology up to date—and American companies do tend to overstate the benefits of computers. They are not overstating the danger facing Europe, however, and other people who follow the industry tend to agree with them. "Europe is horribly behind the U.S. on new technology," says one expert, Michael Gale, a Briton who researches the European mar-

This article first appeared in *Fortune On-Line* (March 17, 1997),
www.mouth.pathfinder.com/fortune/1997/970317/fst.html

ket for Austin, Texas–based IntelliQuest. "It's scary. There's significant trouble ahead for these guys," agrees Aaron Goldberg of Computer Intelligence (CI), which surveys computer use at companies around the world.

The numbers are shocking, especially for the larger countries such as Germany, France, Italy, and Britain. IntelliQuest figures that 54% of the adult population of the U.S. uses a PC either at home or at work; the figure for France is 33%. Among white-collar workers, Microsoft data show that in the U.S. more than 90% use a PC, whereas in Western Europe only 55% do. CI finds that for a typical large business site with more than 1,000 employees, there are 75% more PCs and five times as many local area networks installed in the U.S. as there are in Europe. Moreover, since technology adoption is growing more slowly in Europe than in either the U.S. or Asia, Europe is falling ever further behind. The U.S. market for PCs grew 15% in units during 1996, but in Western Europe it grew only 7.1%, according to International Data Corp.

There are a lot of reasons for Europe's technological lag, including ongoing economic weakness and an aversion to tools considered overly "American," notably in France. There also appears to remain a continent-wide cultural resistance to the information sharing that goes with widespread personal computing. Intel's Geyer has observed that, amazingly, CEOs of several European PC companies don't have computers in their offices. "Let's not even talk about other industries," he says, "where in most cases the chair the CEO sits on costs more than a good PC." Explains CI's Aaron Goldberg: "In many European companies the goal is to rise to a high enough position where you don't have to use a PC. It's a status symbol not to use one." Though most American business people find such Luddism hard to believe, some of Europe's foremost technologists shrug it off. Francois Fillon, France's minister of postal service, telecommunications, and space, is surprisingly upbeat for someone known as an aggressive campaigner for greater use of technology. Fillon says that to assess France's progress, you must count not only PCs but also France's seven million terminals for Minitel, the aging government-sponsored online system. Most experts outside the French government, however, argue that while Minitel was revolutionary when introduced in the early 1980s, it's been obviated by the Internet. Nonetheless, says Fillon, France has "extremely ambitious plans to bring about the total integration of France into the information society, using French means and French methods."

Europe does have some successes, technologically speaking. A few of Europe's smaller nations, including Sweden, Finland, and the Netherlands, are among the world's most technologized. CI also finds that the computing gap with the U.S. is much narrower among smaller firms. Europe is actually ahead of the U.S. in the use of digital cellular phones, as well as in the use of electronic smart cards instead of cash for consumer purchases. On the Internet, too, there are some signs of European progress: Netscape, the Internet software powerhouse, says sales of its Net server software are booming in Europe.

But these are only a few bright spots in an otherwise bleak European tech picture. "I'm scared for European industries today," says Intel's Geyer, who then adds melodramatically, "and I'm scared for the future of my children." He's also scared for the future of his company's sales, of course, but his fears about Europe's future are justified.

Questions for Critical Thinking and Discussion

1. What does it matter if Europe does not keep up-to-date on technology? Beyond creating new markets for established American technology companies to tap into, what could be the effect of Europe's technology gap?

2. What are some of the reasons for Europe's technological lag? How could these "problems" be solved?

3. Technology advocates take for granted that everyone believes (or they try to convince you to believe) that technological progress means societal and cultural progress. Can you think of any reasons why Europe should *not* scurry to catch up in the technological race? Are there circumstances where technology has not provided a positive experience for you?

Antidotes 1–5

DAVID SHENK

David Shenk provides commentaries for NPR's All Things Considered *in addition to writing columns for a variety of periodicals such as* Hotwired, Wired, *the* New York Times, *the* Washington Post, Harper's, *the* New Republic, Spy, Salon, Feed, *and the* New Yorker.

Instead of simply asking all of the difficult questions about media influence or effects and audience literacy, Shenk ends his book-long media analysis with specific strategies for becoming more media literate or at least becoming more actively involved in the mass communication process.

Antidote 1

Be Your Own Filter

The first remedy is simply to identify the clutter and start sweeping it away. Most of us have excess information in our lives, distracting us, pulling us away from our priorities and from a much-desired tranquility. If we stop just for a moment to look (and listen) around us, we will begin to notice a series of data streams that we'd be better off without, including some distractions we pay handsomely for.

Turn the television off. There is no quicker way to regain control of the pace of your life, the peace of your home, and the content of your thinking than to turn off the appliance that supplies for all-too-many of us the ambiance of our lives. . . .

It is not enough to simply turn the TV off; one must also make it somewhat difficult to turn it on again. . . .

Giving up the television, or even reducing the weekly allotment, isn't nearly as easy as it sounds. There is a reason we watch so much of it. Television is physically hypnotic, an extremely comfortable way to forget about our troubles and tensions in the real world. One key to its enormous success is that even stupid television is mesmerizing. The more channels we have to

This article is excerpted from Shenk's book *Data Smog* (New York: Harper Edge, 1997), chapters 18–22, pages 185–213.

choose from, the greater the temptation to surf around from one unsatisfying offering to another.

. . . .

Avoid news-nuggets. All-news channels, wire services, and top-of-the-hour headlines may be the only fabric we have left holding us together as a nation, but that isn't reason enough to sacrifice your attention span to the incessant drone of traffic updates, murder trial play-by-play, postures of outrage from the president and the mayor, composites from the NYSE and NASDAQ, and a dozen sports scores you don't much care about. But we all pay attention anyway, because of the drama. An hour later, we will get an update on the new composite and the latest political soundbite. . . .

Skip them. Spend those five minutes each hour doing something more productive, like conducting one meaningful conversation. To be a well-informed citizen, spend some quality time each day reading more thorough news and news analysis.

Leave the pager and cell-phone behind. It is thrilling to be in touch with the world at all times, but it's also draining and interfering. Are wireless communications instruments of liberation, freeing people to be more mobile with their lives—or are they more like electronic leashes, keeping people more plugged-in to their work and their info-glutted lives than is necessary and healthy? For sanity's sake, people ought to be allowed to roam free away from the information superhighway for at least some portion of each week.

Limit your e-mail. As one spends more and more time online, e-mail quickly changes from being a stimulating novelty to a time-consuming burden, with dozens of messages to read and answer every day from colleagues, friends, family, newsgroup posts, and unsolicited sales pitches. The biggest problem with e-mail is also its greatest virtue: It's cheap. The transaction cost is so low in terms of both money and effort that people find it all too easy to transmit messages and contact you. . . .

. . . For those of us who spend a fair amount of time working on a computer, maintaining control over our e-mail in-boxes is critically important. If we're spending too much time each day reading and answering e-mail that has virtually no value, we must take steps to control it. . . .

Say no to dataveillance. With some determination and a small amount of effort, one can also greatly reduce the amount of junk mail and unsolicited sales phone calls. It involves writing just a few letters, requesting to have your name put on "do-not-disturb" lists, which some 75 percent of direct marketers honor. . . .

Resist advertising. We read, watch, and listen to advertisements all day. Must we also wear them on our clothes?

Resist upgrade mania. Remember: Upgrades are designed to be sales tools, not to give customers what they've been clamoring for.

Be your own "smart agent." A new class of robotic "smart agent" software is becoming available to help consumers automate their information-filtering needs—software such as IBM's InfoSage, . . . which delivers a customized set of news stories according to programmed preferences. Other programs weed out e-mail not written by a select list of people.

But for reasons we've already discussed, smart agents are not the answer to the information glut. Regardless of how efficient they become, they will never be adequate substitutes for our own manual filtering. Instead, we must become our own smart agents.

As your own smart agent, you are responsible for managing your own personal signal-to-noise ratio, enhancing the signal—information that is accurate, relevant, economical, articulate, and evocative—and eliminating anything that blocks out or distracts meaning. . . .

Ultimately, determining what qualifies as signal and what is merely noise is a subjective experience. Each individual must judge what is noise, and devise personal filtering mechanisms. But the person who does not even inquire—this is the person who will surely continue contributing to the smog and choking on it with the rest of us.

Cleanse your system with "data-fasts." As your own smart agent, you are also your own data dietitian. Take some time to examine your daily intake and consider whether or not your info diet needs some fine-tuning. . . . You could also consider limiting yourself to no more than a certain number of hours on the Internet each week, or at least balancing the amount of time spent online with an equal amount of time reading books.

In addition to the daily regimen, many victims of glut . . . have found that periodic data-fasts of a week or month have a remarkably rejuvenating effect. One sure way to gauge the value of something, after all, is to go without it for a while.

Antidote 2

Be Your Own Editor

After learning how to filter input, one must shift concern to the equally important task of limiting output. Here, we also have a new creed to adopt, and a new slogan:

Give a hoot, don't info-pollute.

Introducing the concept of the information litterbug. Amidst the data smog, a new kind of social responsibility has emerged—an obligation to be succinct. Just as we've had to curtail our toxic emissions in the physical world, the information glut demands that we all be more economical about what we say, write, publish, broadcast, and post online. . . .

. . . Everything from voice-mail messages to office memos to book reports to speeches to Web pages should be crisp, clear, and to the point. This is our new obligation to one another. By reducing the amount of needless information, we will also reduce the amount of vulgarity, as people feel less need to be sensational to attract attention. Our tone will become more civil. Our social signal-to-noise ratio will begin to improve.

. . . .

In the information society, this challenge applies to every one of us. Is that word/image absolutely necessary? Technology has given us the power to gather lifetimes of information and to broadcast the data at almost no effort or cost. With that opportunity comes the awesome responsibility of self-editing, of information restraint.

The good news is, the payoff for this restraint is high. As we severely limit content, we learn to savor it more. . . .

Antidote 3

Simplify

Between input and output, there is life itself. How does one live a meaningful life in an ever-more complex and distracting world? One helpful ingredient, I've found, is to embrace a new paradigm of simplicity.

. . . .

This enthusiasm for minimalism has spread in our household. My wife and I have made a habit out of using a Polaroid camera to document our lives, savoring the severe limitation. We take one picture at a time. We patiently wait for it to develop. We examine the picture and compare it to our life experience.

It costs more, but in our glutted environment that can be a very good thing, encouraging us to limit our use of the camera to one print per "event." Its expense means that I will take just one picture and I will cherish it. In a universe of speedy possibilities, it is a speedbump, a boundary for which I am grateful. We have in our kitchen a stack of Polaroids taken over the last several years, of house and dinner guests. One per. It is a compact and satisfying historical record. Each one captures one brief moment of an entire evening, and somehow seems just the right size record to help us conjure up the rest of the evening in our minds. It is a memory trigger, an aid, a point of reference.

. . . .

. . . [T]here is a growing movement in this country called "voluntary simplicity" (inspired by a book of that name by Duane Elgin), which is dedicated to the pursuit of a more sustainable, balanced life. "To live more simply is to live more purposefully and with a minimum of needless distraction," writes Elgin. Sympathetic magazines and radio shows have been cropping up, endorsing the notion that, without forsaking technology, we should make an effort to use the most basic technologies available that can get the job done—preferably tools whose function anyone can plainly understand.

Antidote 4

De-nichify

How to change our electronic Tower of Babel into a modern Agora? The answer is easy, though the solution is not: We need to talk to one another. Recall Bill Bradley's challenge: "When was the last time you talked about race with someone of a different race? If the answer is never, you're part of the problem."

Radio talk show host Brian Lehrer has found a way to fuse some of our social fragments back together. Lehrer, host of WNYC's *On the Line* in New York City, is bucking the national trend toward specialization and nichification. He is a generalist, covering as wide a range of social and political issues as he possibly can, reaching out to different cultures and niches. Lehrer justifiably advertises his show as "dialogue, not diatribe."

One highlight of this effort is Lehrer's annual multicultural outreach on Martin Luther King Day, when he invites listeners to call in and read one-minute excerpts from works about an ethnic group different from their own. The purpose is to force people to consider different life perspectives. It works.

. . . Generalists are working for a less-fragmented world of isolated experts, toward a world of common understanding.

. . . Theirs is exactly the kind of regular effort that establishes a foundation of understanding and tolerance. As the information society fosters niches, all of us, whether we are media professionals or not, should make some effort to avoid letting our lives become completely segmented. Specialization is empowering and rejuvenating, but also inherently limiting. We can't all have our own radio show, but we can tune into such shows and read general interest magazines and newspapers; we can make a point to reach across niche boundaries; we can avoid specialized, exclusive jargon whenever possible; we can introduce ourselves to our neighbors regardless of whether they share our skin color, and we can attend more formal inter-ethnic forums. And, of course, we must take every opportunity [to] speak out against ethnic intolerance.

As we reach across cultural boundaries and pursue interdisciplinary studies, we are pursuing the best kind of education—not just learning how to become more efficient at a specialized task, but how to interact with the rest of humanity. These sorts of pursuits enable us to embrace the joys of education as the best possible antidote to data smog. Education . . . is anti-glut. It is the harnessing of information, organizing it into knowledge and memory. Education also breeds a healthy skepticism, and will help consumers fend off manipulative marketing tactics. Education is the one thing we can't get overloaded with. The more of it, the better.

Antidote 5

Don't Forsake Government; Help Improve It

Finally, for collective fixes more appropriately enacted on behalf of all society, we must call on that awkward but thoroughly necessary beast, government.

Yes, *government*. Federal initiatives are badly needed, mostly because technology policy is too important to be surrendered to chance or to the wealthiest corporations. The cyber-libertarian community has made anti-government rhetoric a fashionable part of the information revolution, mostly in response to a lot of very thoughtless federal legislation. After a particularly stupid law was signed by President Clinton in 1996—the Communications Decency Act, which aimed to excessively curb speech online—leading cyber thinker John Perry Barlow issued a "Declaration of the Independence of Cyberspace," which rashly proclaimed the Net to be its own world, not a functioning part of conventional society:

> Governments of the Industrial World, you weary giants of flesh and steel, I come from Cyberspace, the new home of Mind. On behalf of the future, I ask you of the past to leave us alone. You are not welcome among us. You have no sovereignty where we gather. . . . I declare the global social space we are building to be naturally independent of the tyrannies you seek to impose on us. You have no moral right to rule us . . .

Respectfully, I dissent. The Net is not literally a new world vested with its own sovereignty; it is a new and exciting facet of society, created and subsidized by a democratic government that, for all of its well-publicized bungling and wastefulness, actually works pretty well. Barlow is absolutely correct in describing cyberspace as a very different organism from our physical world. Ultimately, though, the former must fall under the jurisdiction of the latter. Physical space is where we are born, where we require food and shelter and protection, and where we must govern ourselves as human beings.

So, as many people wittingly and unwittingly lend their enthusiasm for technology to political movements that enfeeble government, it is critical that we stand up for what is right. To get the good that technology has to offer without choking on the bad will take strong collective effort. We should redouble our efforts to root out bad government—Gingrich and friends can certainly help in this regard—and realize that protecting basic freedoms and values often means that government needs to be stronger, not weaker.

Tempting though it often is, we must resist the urge to snidely dismiss the relevance and utility of government. In fact, we must embrace our democratic government and what it stands for—a body created by the citizens in order to serve the interests of their collective society. Government is cumbersome and often frustrating, but it is also essential in the effort to protect a democratic nation, to maintain civility and to help its citizens prosper. In finance, labor, commerce, law, energy, communications, housing, and the environment, we have relied on government to help establish rules and standards for progress, safety, and fairness. I say this not as a reflexive supporter of bureaucracy, but because our public sector has endured an unwarranted bashing in recent years. Good government has helped to make the United States an unparalleled success story in the history of humankind.

There is a special wrinkle, though, in promulgating regulations for the information society. That wrinkle is the First Amendment to the U.S. Constitution: "Congress shall make no law respecting an establishment of religion, or prohibiting the free exercise thereof; or abridging the freedom of speech, or of the press; or the right of the people peaceably to assemble, and to petition the Government for a redress of grievances."

This is perhaps the most important distinction between conventional pollution and data smog. No one has an inalienable right to pour dioxin into the ground; legislating against it, therefore, is fairly straightforward. But the right to say and publish virtually anything is a sacred one in a free society. We can't—and wouldn't want to—infringe on personal or political expression. So, instead, we should seek to control some of its unsavory consequences, and rein in some of those who would use technology to abuse or exploit us. Here's some of what government can specifically do in this regard:

David Shenk's Pie-in-the-Sky Legislative Agenda

The government should help citizens defend themselves against data spam. Our quality of life is seriously hampered by unsolicited phone calls, faxes, mail, and e-mail. We have a right not to be harassed, and there is a very simple solution. The Telephone Consumer Protection Act of 1991 made it illegal to use an auto-dialing phone machine or to make calls with a pre-recorded voice. This law should now be amended to address the problem of junk e-mail by barring, among other things, software that automatically plucks e-mail addresses from all over cyberspace and indiscriminately includes them in marketing solicitations.

Furthermore, this new legislation should establish on behalf of all consumers a national, mandatory "do-not-disturb" registry of names, phone numbers, addresses, and e-mail addresses by which all mass-marketers would be legally obliged to abide. Current do-not-disturb lists . . . are voluntary. . . .

Cities and states should guarantee refuge from data smog. Excessive stimulus takes its social toll, and we must begin to compensate for this loss by severely restricting advertising and other noisy intrusions into our common spaces. Libraries and parks will not suffice as the only havens from the noise and commercial glut. As people begin to recognize the importance of glut-free rooms and roads, local governments will respond by designating "Zones of Quiet."

. . . .

Prohibit government agencies and companies from using information for unauthorized purposes. To combat dataveillance, we need a sweeping new privacy law, an upgrade of The Federal Privacy Act of 1974. The new legislation should live up to the core principle of the previous law (subsequently gutted by other laws): *Information collected for one purpose should not be used for another purpose, unless and until specific permission is granted by the individual involved.* . . .

. . . The new law should remove the inequity by extending real privacy to *all* transactions. Whether you are subscribing to a magazine, buying a modem, signing a petition, renewing your driver's license, taking a random drug test, enrolling your child in school, or paying your taxes, you should be assured that the personal data you turn over will go no further than that particular institution. All information should be presumed confidential unless permission to the contrary is granted.

The FTC should root out consumer fraud and improve efforts at consumer education. It is time for the government to become a full-fledged consumer advocate. The vast majority of Americans are concerned with deception in ads, and favor more regulation. But the government has never been very responsive to this concern. Because political campaigns in this country are financed largely by corporations, politicians frequently forget that they are supposed to be working on behalf of consumers.

Now, because of increased distraction, the consumer is more vulnerable than ever to manipulative advertising. A new Consumer Education Act should remedy this by beefing up the Federal Trade Commission, the agency in charge of overseeing advertising claims. The FTC's current policy is that consumers must match their wits against advertisers. . . . Considering the resources and sophistication of marketers, this hardly seems a fair fight. . . .

A . . . proactive FTC would criticize questionable marketing practices and would impose fines and embarrassing press coverage on the offenders.

. . . .

All government documents should not only be accessible, but approachable. In our glutted society, government has a special responsibility to communicate with its citizens concisely and articulately. Tax forms are not the only documents that should be able to fit on a postcard. The essence of legislation, regulations, and court rulings should also be something that any literate person can understand. A new Government Information Act should ensure that citizens have not just online access, but actual understanding of the workings of the government.

Reformulate the issue of "information have-nots." Much political hay has been made of late about the danger of the widening gap between the "information haves and have-nots." "If we allow the information superhighway to bypass the less fortunate sectors of our society, even for an interim period," Al Gore has warned, "we will find that the information rich will get richer while the information poor get poorer with no guarantee that everyone will be on the network at some future date."

Gore and other politicians are sadly missing the point. The disenfranchised citizens of our country are not in need of faster access to bottomless wells of information. They are in need of *education*. There is an important difference, and government must recognize this distinction soon. Jonathan Kozol has written eloquently of the inequities that underlie the crisis in our educational system. The so-called information poor don't need Internet access; they need basic classroom materials, building infrastructure, and highly qualified teachers.

. . . .

Consensus conferences on technology policy. Finally, and most important, we need to overhaul the way we develop all technology policy. This would be a formidable challenge if it were not for the fact that a wonderful working model already exists right across the ocean.

In 1987 the Danish parliament came upon a fix for the perennially antidemocratic nature of technology policy. Traditionally, because of technology's inherent complexity, only technologists from the military, businesses, and universities have been invited into the policy-making process. For democracies like Denmark and the United States, this has frequently led to needless confusion and unrest. Nuclear power, bovine growth hormone, and food irradiation are just three of many instances where closed-door policy formulations have backfired after they were put into place. Not letting ordinary people confront the implications of policies until they are implemented is like deciding to bake an apple pie in order to find out if your friend is allergic to apples.

There is a better way, and Denmark has found it: consensus conferences. Consensus conferences establish a natural bridge between technologists, policy-makers, and ordinary citizens. The Danish Board of Technology recruits a diverse group of citizens, who are promptly immersed in one particular issue facing the parliament (genetic testing, for example). As a rule, the citizen panel contains no technical experts and no representatives from relevant interest groups. Panelists are supplied with necessary background material and asked to make specific policy recommendations on a pending matter of biotechnology or information technology. After two weekends of deliberation, the panel is convened for a four-day public forum in which the citizens hear testimony of experts and interest groups, cross-examine the experts, deliberate, and finally issue a report and conduct a press conference.

. . . .

Now the Loka Institute, an Amherst, Massachusetts–based think tank specializing in technology policy, is spearheading a worthwhile effort to persuade the U.S. to adopt such a system. With respect both to policy and public awareness, the idea makes a lot of sense. The consensus conference represents precisely the kind of paradigm this nation must embrace in our new age of electronic democracy, in order to make citizen knowledge commensurate with the power of their opinions (as registered in polls). Above all else, it is imperative that in the coming years we strive to keep the quality of our thinking as great as the quantity of our information.

Questions for Critical Thinking and Discussion

1. Have you ever felt like a slave to technology? If your answer is yes, cite specific examples. If you answer no, consider how long a period of time (i.e., how many days in a row) in your life that you've gone without any television or radio consumption. Or how often do you simply let the phone ring without letting your answering machine pick up or screen for you?

2. David Shenk lists nine strategies you can use to "Be Your Own Filter." What are they? Do they seem easy or difficult to attempt?

3. When Shenk urges you to "Be Your Own Editor," he brings up an interesting point: People can be the producers of their own media content. What interesting content have you produced for yourself or to share with others?

4. In what ways can you simplify and de-nichify? Do you think these strategies would add more meaning or satisfaction to your life? If so, in what ways? If not, then what will?

5. Sit quietly alone in a room (no music or other background distractions) for 30 minutes. Did the time seem to go by quickly or slowly? What were you able to hear or to think about without the usual immersion in "data smog"? Do you think that the government should protect our right to be "guilt free" as Shenk suggests?

Acknowledgments

Jonathan Alter, "Let's Stop Crying Wolf on Censorship." From *Newsweek*, November 29, 1993. Copyright © 1993 Newsweek, Inc. All rights reserved. Reprinted by permission.

Stanley J. Baran, "Why Race Still Divides America," *San Jose Mercury News,* September 21, 1996. Reprinted with permission.

Beyond The Ratings Staff, "Move Over Boomers, The 'Xers' Are Here, Or Are They?" *BTR, Beyond The Ratings Television: A Magazine for the Television Industry,* Spring 1993. Copyright © 1993 The Arbitron Company. Reprinted with permission of Arbitron.

Herb Boyd, "African American Images on Television and Film," *The Crisis*, February/March 1996, Vol. 103, No. 2. Kimberly Massey wishes to thank The Crisis Publishing Co., Inc., the magazine of the National Association for the Advancement of Colored People, for authorizing the use of this work.

Howard Bryant and David Plotnikoff, "How the Decency Fight Was Won," *San Jose Mercury News,* March 3, 1996. Copyright © 1996 San Jose Mercury News. All rights reserved. Reproduced with permission.

Warren Buffett, "Smokers' Hacks," from *Toxic Sludge is Good for You,* John Stauber and Sheldon Rampton, editors, Common Courage Press, 1995. Reprinted with permission from Common Courage Press.

Don L. Buroughs, Dan McGraw and Kevin Whitelaw, "Disney's All Smiles," *U.S. News and World Report*, August 14, 1995. Copyright © 1995 U.S. News and World Report. Reprinted with permission.

Lorraine Calvacca, "The Color of Money, Part I," *Folio,* November 1996, Vol. 25, No. 16, originally appeared in *Folio: The Magazine for Magazine Management,* November 1996. Reprinted with permission.

Jon Carroll, "Di Dies; We Follow the Money," *San Francisco Chronicle,* September 2, 1997. Copyright © 1997 San Francisco Chronicle. Reprinted by permission.

Neva Chonin, "The Girl Wide Web," *The San Francisco Bay Guardian* on-line edition, February 11, 1998, www.sfbg.com, A&E. Reprinted by permission of the author.

Kevin Cullen, "At 75, Voice of Britain Has a New Accent," *Boston Globe,* February 22, 1998. Reprinted courtesy of The Boston Globe.

The Cultural Environment Movement, "The People's Communication Charter," *The Cultural Environment Monitor,* Fall 1996, Vol. 1, No. 1. Reprinted with permission from The Cultural Environment Movement.

Tom Englehardt, "The Shortcake Strategy," from *Watching Television,* Todd Gitlin, editor. Copyright © 1986 by Tom Englehardt. Reprinted by permission of Pantheon Books, a division of Random House, Inc.

Paul Espinosa, "The Rich Tapestry of Hispanic America Is Virtually Invisible on Commercial Television," *The Chronicle of Higher Education*, October 3, 1997, Vol. 44, No. 6. Reprinted with permission from the author.

Stuart Ewen, from *PR! A Social History of Spin!* Copyright © 1996 by Basic Books, Inc. Reprinted by permission of BasicBooks, a subsidiary of Perseus Books Group, LLC.

Katherine Fulton, "A Tour of Our Uncertain Future," *Columbia Journalism Review*, March/April 1996. Copyright © 1996 by Columbia Journalism Review. Reprinted with permission.

George Gerbner, "The Stories We Tell," *Media Development*, April 1996. Reprinted with permission from the author and The Cultural Environment Movement.

Todd Gitlin, "Postmodernism Defined At Last!," *Dissent*, Winter 1989. Reprinted with permission from the publisher.

Todd Gitlin, "The Dumb-Down," *The Nation*, March 17, 1997. Reprinted with permission from the March 17, 1997 issue of *The Nation* magazine.

James K. Glassman, "If Liberals Go Marching Back In," *San Jose Mercury News*, September 11, 1996. Reprinted by permission of the author.

Carey B. Goldberg, "'Buy Nothings' Discover A Cure for Affluenza," *The New York Times*, November 29, 1997. Copyright © 1997 by The New York Times Co. Reprinted by permission.

bell hooks, "Slant: All Quiet on the Feminist Front," *Art Forum*, December 1996, Vol. 35, No. 4. Copyright © 1996 Artforum. Reprinted with permission from the publisher and the author.

Molly Ivins, "The Big Television Rip-Off Glides Through Congress," *San Jose Mercury News*, July 7, 1996. Copyright © 1996 Molly Ivins.

Pico Iyer, "History? Education? Zap! Pow! Cut!, *Time Magazine*, May 14, 1990. Copyright © 1990 Time, Inc. Reprinted by permission.

Charisse Jones, "Radio Activity," *Vibe*, October 1996. Reprinted with permission from *Vibe* Magazine.

Ellwood Kieser, "TV Could Nourish Minds and Hearts," *Time Magazine*, September 14, 1992. Copyright © 1992 Time, Inc. Reprinted with permission.

Bridget Kinsella, "The Oprah Effect: How TV's Premier Talk Show Host Puts Books Over the Top Is Oprah Bringing in New Readers?" *Publishers Weekly*, January 20, 1997. Reprinted with permission. Copyright © 1997 by *Publisher's Weekly*.

David Kirkpatrick, "Europe's Technology Gap is Getting Scary," *Fortune On-Line*, March 17, 1997, www.mouth.pathfinder.com/fortune/1997. Copyright © 1997 Time, Inc. All rights reserved.

Stanley Klein, "Hollywood Guilds Put the Moves on Multimedia," *New Media*, March 1994. Copyright © 1994 New Media Magazine. Reprinted with permission from *New Media* Magazine.

Mark Landler, "Now Worse Than Ever! Cynicism in Advertising," *The New York Times*, August 17, 1997. Copyright © 1997 by The New York Times Co. Reprinted by permission.

Joann Lee, "Shop Talk at Thirty: A Look at Asians as Portrayed in the News," *Editor and Publisher*, April 30, 1994, Vol. 127, No. 18. Reprinted with permission from the author.

Elizabeth Lesly, Ronald Grover and Neil Gross, "Cable TV: A Crisis Looms," *Business Week*, October 14, 1996. Copyright © 1996 by The McGraw-Hill Companies, Inc. Reprinted by special permission.

James Martin, "Holiness, Royalty, and Fame," *America*, October 4, 1997, Vol. 177, No. 9. Reprinted with permission of James Martin, S. J. and American Press, Inc., 106 West 56th Street, New York, NY 10019. © 1998 American Press, Inc. All Rights Reserved.

Robert W. McChesney, "Telecon," *In These Times*, July 10, 1995. Reprinted by permission of the publisher.

Joshua Meyrowitz, "Shifting Worlds of Strangers: Medium Theory and Changes in 'Them' Versus 'Us'" *Sociological Inquiry*, Vol. 67, No. 1. Reprinted by permission of the author and the University of Texas Press. All rights retained by the University of Texas Press.

Mark Crispin Miller, "The Crushing Power of Big Publishing," *The Nation*, March 17, 1997. Reprinted with permission from the March 17, 1997 issue of *The Nation* magazine.

Lance Morrow, "Folklore in a Box," *Time Magazine*, September 21, 1992. Copyright © 1992 Time, Inc. Reprinted with permission.

Linda P. Morton, "Targeting Minority Publics," *Public Relations Quarterly*, Summer 1997, Vol. 42, No. 2. Reprinted with permission of *Public Relations Quarterly*.

David Plotz, "Los Angeles Times Publisher Mark Willes in Praise of the 'Cereal Killer'," Slate.Com an online magazine, October 18, 1997. First published in www.slate.com. Reprinted with permission.

Virginia Postrel, "Technocracy R.I.P.," *Wired*, January 1998, Issue 6.01. Reprinted with permission from *Wired*.

Dan Rather, "Call It Courage," Speech given at the Annual Convention of Radio and Television News Directors Association, September 29, 1993, Miami, Florida. Reprinted with permission from Dan Rather.

John Seabrook, "The Big Sellout: Is Creative Independence a Luxury We Can No Longer Afford?," *The New Yorker*, October 20, 1997. Copyright © 1997 John Seabrook.

Jenna Schnuer, The Color of Money, Part II, *Folio*, November 1996, Vol. 25, No. 16, originally appeared in *Folio: The Magazine for Magazine Management*, November 1996. Reprinted with permission.

Joseph Schwartz, "Tuning Into Generation X," *BTR, Beyond the Ratings Television: A Magazine for the Television Industry*, Spring 1993. Copyright © 1993 The Arbitron Co. Reprinted by permission of Arbitron.

David Shenk, "Antidotes 1–5," from *Data Smog* by David Shenk. Copyright © 1997 by David Shenk. Reprinted by permission of HarperCollins Publishers, Inc.

Index